America's
"Foreign Legion"

ALSO BY DENNIS A. CONNOLE

*The 26th "Yankee" Division on Coast Patrol Duty,
1942–1943* (McFarland, 2008)

*The Indians of the Nipmuck Country
in Southern New England, 1630–1750:
An Historical Geography*
(McFarland, 2001; softcover 2006)

America's "Foreign Legion"
Immigrant Soldiers in the Great War

Dennis A. Connole

McFarland & Company, Inc., Publishers
Jefferson, North Carolina

LIBRARY OF CONGRESS CATALOGUING-IN-PUBLICATION DATA

Names: Connole, Dennis A., 1943– author.
Title: America's "foreign legion" : immigrant soldiers in the Great War / Dennis A. Connole.
Description: Jefferson, North Carolina : McFarland & Company, Inc., Publishers, 2019. | Includes bibliographical references and index.
Identifiers: LCCN 2018053939 | ISBN 9781476675435 (softcover : acid free paper) ∞
Subjects: LCSH: Argonne, Battle of the, France, 1918. | Guerra, Matthew. | United States. Army. Infantry Regiment, 58th—History. | United States. Army—Biography. | Soldiers—United States—Biography.
Classification: LCC D545.A63 C67 2019 | DDC 940.4/36—dc23
LC record available at https://lccn.loc.gov/2018053939

BRITISH LIBRARY CATALOGUING DATA ARE AVAILABLE

ISBN (print) 978-1-4766-7543-5
ISBN (ebook) 978-1-4766-3467-8

© 2019 Dennis A. Connole. All rights reserved

No part of this book may be reproduced or transmitted in any form or by any means, electronic or mechanical, including photocopying or recording, or by any information storage and retrieval system, without permission in writing from the publisher.

The central cover image is of Pvt. Matthew Guerra, Camp Devens, 1918; at top are 4th "Ivy" Division patch and 58th Regiment patch; background illustrates an infantry attack in the woods at the Argonne front, L. Jonas (Library of Congress)

Printed in the United States of America

McFarland & Company, Inc., Publishers
  Box 611, Jefferson, North Carolina 28640
    www.mcfarlandpub.com

To my aunt,
Victoria Palumbo

Table of Contents

Acknowledgments	ix
Preface	1
1. The Quest Begins	9
2. Matthew Guerra in America	21
3. America Enters the War—The World War I Draft Act	26
4. Registration Day	33
5. Selection of the Candidates	38
6. Deferments and Exemptions—The Non-Declarant Alien Dilemma	43
7. Welcome to Camp Upton	52
8. Recruit Processing	61
9. Basic Training—Camp Devens	69
10. Social and Recreational Activities at the Training Camps	84
11. Foreign-Born U.S. Army Recruits—Non-English Speaking Draftees	93
12. Enter Lt. Stanislaw A. Gutowski	100
13. Creation of the "Foreign-Speaking Soldier Sub-Section" (FSS)	109
14. FSS Recruit Training Efforts at Camps Custer and Grant— January–February 1918	116
15. Restructuring Plan Canceled—An Unexpected Reversal of Direction	121

16. The "Camp Gordon Plan"—June 1918	130
17. FSS English Education Program	136
18. Resurrection of the Immigrant Training Program at Other Camps	145
19. The 76th Division Overseas—The St. Mihiel Offensive	150
20. The Meuse-Argonne Offensive—Phase One (September 26–October 3, 1918)	164
21. Meuse-Argonne—Second Phase (October 4, 1918)	174
22. Bois de Fays—"Woods of the Fairies" (October 5, 1918)	188
23. October 5–7, 1918—The Death of a Doughboy	199
Conclusion	208
Chapter Notes	217
Bibliography	233
Index	237

Acknowledgments

First and foremost, I wish to thank author Nancy Gentile Ford. When I first began my research regarding my great-uncle Matthew Guerra and his tragic death in the Great War, I had difficulty locating information about immigrant soldiers in the war. Then, in my quest for details, particulars, and facts about immigrant soldiers, I came across Ford's book *American's All! Foreign-born Soldiers in World War I*. This important work served as my Bible. Without her exhaustive and tedious research sorting through the multitudinous collection of Military Intelligence Division records at the National Archives and elsewhere concerning this particular topic, I would not have had access to these important documents she discovered during her research, as well as the interpretations and opinions she provided.

Other recent authors and historians whom I relied heavily upon include: John S.D. Eisenhower with Joanne T. Eisenhower, Frank Freidel, Christopher M. Sterba, Edward G. Lengel, Christopher Capozzola, Richard S. Faulkner, Keith Gandal, Jennifer D. Keene, David M. Kennedy, Robert Laplander, Edward G. Lengel, David A. Laskin, John J. Newman, David J. Ulbrich, Matthew S. Muehlbauer, Anne Cipriano Venzon, and Paul Miles (see Bibliography).

While conducting previous research pertaining to my father's stint in the military during World War II, I became familiar with the multitude of records available from the National Archives and Records Administration (NARA). President Franklin D. Roosevelt signed legislation on June 19, 1934, creating NARA as an independent agency, to safeguard and protect the vital records of the nation. Opened in 1935, the National Archives has compiled and preserved one of the largest bodies of primary source material relating to the U.S. armed services in existence that is available to researchers and other interested parties. I would like to extend my gratitude to the following individuals at NARA: investigative archivist Mitchell Yockelson; Walter V. Hickey, archives specialist, National Archives, for locating the Bridgeport, Connecticut, "Lists of Men Ordered to Report for Induction" (entrainment lists); a special thanks to genealogist and archivist Jean Nudd, NARA Northeast

Region, manager of the microfilm reading room. All were an immense help in processing my many requests, and I am extremely grateful.

Another important resource in my research was the U.S. Army Heritage and Education Center, Carlisle Barracks, Pennsylvania, the U.S. Army's primary historical research facility. The center is part of the U.S. Army War College and contains Army-related library and archival materials. The current research collection includes military history books, military newspapers, technical and field manuals, periodicals, veterans' surveys, photographs, and oral histories.

Finally, I am also indebted to ancestry.com—the collections are "the world's largest online family history resource." The website is an excellent genealogy resource providing information and records regarding one's relatives and ancestors. Contained within the collection are census and voter lists; birth, marriage and death records; immigration, emigration, and related records. The site contains the U.S. Military Collection as well, including millions of records covering almost 400 years of American participation in wars and conflicts. The website includes "more than 100 million names and 700 titles and databases of military records from … every major U.S. war," draft registration cards, enlistment and service records, and the location of a deceased service member's burial place around the world. Ancestry.com has been invaluable to my research and study.

A special thanks to Martha R. Sell, Freedom of Information Act Representative (FOIA), American Battle Monuments Commission (ABMC), for her assistance in locating Guerra's military records and the cemetery in France where his remains are interred.

I would like to thank genealogist Ellen Rafferty, for locating several important documents pertaining to Guerra at the National Archives and Records Administration (NARA), College Park, Maryland, that were important to my investigation/study.

I received help along the way from a number of individuals, state or government agencies and departments, and others. I wish to thank Brigadier General Leonid E. Kondratiuk (see above), National Commander of the Yankee Division Veterans Association, for all his help and guidance. General Kondratiuk kindly edited several of the chapters and, as mentioned above, suggested the final choice of a title.

Thanks to fellow Knight of Columbus Bob Oetting, who was kind enough to edit two chapters. Bob spent 12 years in the Marine Corps, attaining the rank of captain.

Many thanks to Michael Amir of Michael's Photo Center, West Boylston, Massachusetts, for his fine work in the processing and restoration of the photographs, including those of my great-uncle Matthew, and the other images included in the book.

Acknowledgments

In past years, prior to the advent of computers and the Internet, which provides easy access to information from a variety of sources, in-depth research of this type was an extremely time-consuming endeavor. I would send out letters of inquiry to various sources for specific information or official records and documents. Sometimes, several weeks, or in a number instances, months would pass before I received a response.

Being a librarian has given me a distinct advantage. Members of the profession have been most cordial and a tremendous help in locating and providing me with requested and much-needed information and documents in a most expeditious fashion. Over the years, many have actually gone above and beyond to handle my frequent requests with this and other writing projects. I wish to express my sincere gratitude to the following libraries and staff members: first, my former co-worker and supervisor Wayne Noah, a reference librarian at the Marlborough (Massachusetts) Public Library (retired), for all his help with my research. When I could not find specific information, data, or documentation, or locate appropriate and *relevant* resource material, Wayne was my go-to guy and he never failed me; the staff at the Worcester Public Library, including government documents librarian Paul Pelletier; staff members of the Bridgeport Public Library, including librarian Elizabeth Van Tuyl, Bridgeport History Center; and reference and research librarian Mary Witkowski, who came through on every one of my many requests.

Thanks also to Alix Quan, assistant director/head of reference at the State Library of Massachusetts in Boston, who went out of her way in an attempt to locate needed documents.

* * *

There are several members of my immediate and extended family that I will be forever thankful to for providing information about the past. First, my aunts Victoria and Helen (Connole) Palumbo, and Frances Adinolfi of White Plains, New York, the daughter of my grandmother's sister Lena La Torre. Frances is my mother Mary Connole's and aunt Victoria Palumbo's first cousin. Frances provided the photograph of Matthew Guerra as a young man taken by a professional photographer in Worcester, Massachusetts. In addition, I would also like to thank Susan Anne La Torre, the granddaughter of Lena and Joseph La Torre, who wrote a wonderful narrative about "The Life and Times" of her grandparents based on information provided by her aunt Frances Adinolfi and other members of the family.

Thanks to my aunt Helen's granddaughter (my cousin Matthew's daughter) Gina (Palumbo) Polewaczyk, who discovered two portraits of my great-uncle Matthew Guerra (contained herein; see cover) and several letters of correspondence from the government to the family among her grandmother's effects and turned them over to me.

Acknowledgments

Finally, to my wonderful wife Joyce for her patience and for always being there for me, my son Dennis and daughter-in-law Gail, my daughter Jill and son-in-law Ralph Streete, and especially my grandchildren, Alexis, Anthony, Sydney, and Dominic Connole, Samantha and Nichole Gambaccini, Jordan, Diana, and Melanie Streete. Thank you so much for your love and support. I love you all dearly and consider myself truly blessed.

Preface

The nucleus for this book was a detailed twelve-page handwritten account of my mother's family, maiden name Palumbo, written by my aunt Victoria Palumbo ("Aunt Vi" or "Vicky") at my urging in 1998. She was very reluctant at first, but finally agreed following much persistence on my part. Vicky was my mother Mary's (Michelina) sister, the oldest child and, at the time, the only surviving member of her family. For reasons known only to herself, she never married. The Palumbo family emigrated from Italy beginning with my grandfather Antonio in 1903, followed by his wife Lucia, her sister Libera (Lena) in 1906, and their younger brother Matteo or Matthew Guerra in 1912. Victoria's family history contained a brief note about her uncle Matthew, "an infantry soldier in the U.S. Army who," she added, "was killed in battle during World War One."

When Guerra immigrated to the U.S., he was fifteen or sixteen years old. This fascinating revelation started me on the mission of unlocking my great-uncle's past. This quest developed into a most interesting and rewarding undertaking. I needed to find the answers to the many questions that arose pertaining to this young man's brief life and of his death in battle at the age of 22. My decision to discover all I could about Guerra, and my subsequent findings regarding himself and other immigrant soldiers who served in the Great War, ended up becoming the focal point of this book.

Upon learning of Matthew's participation in the World War, I pressed Victoria for additional details. She mentioned that the military had buried his remains somewhere in France, but said she knew very little else about him. This surprising and unexpected bit of news, plus my longstanding interest in military history (see below), piqued my curiosity. I was, upon the discovery of Guerra's existence and the fact that he died in battle fighting for his adopted country, both excited and intrigued. My aunt's startling revelation with regards to this previously unknown member of the family and his part in World War I was responsible for initiating my search for background information about this man's life and times and the cause of his premature death on the battlefield, which ultimately has allowed me to share his story.

Victoria reported that while he was still living in Italy, Matthew's parents died, his father Michael in 1902, his mother Maria in 1905. His sister Lucia (Victoria's mother and my grandmother), being the oldest child, became head of the household. Prior to their deaths, her parents were in bad health, and Lucia helped look after her younger brother and sisters—Matthew, Libera (Lena), and Raffaela. In a deposition sworn to by Lucia in 1932, she reported that just before her mother passed away she "placed my brother and sisters under my care." When Antonio, Lucia and Lena left Monte Sant Angelo for America in 1906, nine-year-old Matthew remained with Raffaela (approximate age 19), who by then had married. My grandfather Antonio sent money back to Italy on a regular basis for their support.

In 1912, Antonio forwarded a bank draft to Italy to pay for Matthew's passage to America. Lucia's brother lived with the Palumbo family in Worcester, Massachusetts, until sometime in the latter part of 1917, when he moved to Bridgeport, Connecticut, to live with his aunt and uncle, Lena and Joseph La Torre. While living in Bridgeport, Matthew went to work for the Remington/UMC (Union Metallic Cartridge Company and Remington Arms combined in 1912), then in full swing producing munitions for the French and British governments (see later chapter).

Victoria mentioned that the La Torres' daughter, her "Cousin Frances" Adinolfi, then living in White Plains, New York, might be able to provide some additional information about Matthew. I wrote Frances and received a wonderful letter of reply in which she reminisced about my mother's side of the family. Fran said she knew of Matthew and the fact that he had perished in the war, but very little else. My family and the La Torres had visited each other on occasion some years ago, when my mother was alive.

To my complete surprise, Fran's response contained a photograph of Matthew as a young man that she had in her possession. Guerra was at the time about 15 or 16 years old, which would have been about 1914 or 1915. This was in the form of a "photo postcard" of the type that were popular in the early 1900s. Printed on the reverse side was the name of the photographer: "J.A. Cassone Photography Studios, 194 Front St., Worcester, Massachusetts," where Matthew was living at the time the photo was taken. Victoria, sharing my excitement, stared intently at the photo for several seconds, but commented that too many years had passed and she could not recognize him, which was understandable.

Victoria also recounted that upon receiving the news of Matthew's death, she remembers her mother Lucia "being distraught for many weeks." "At times," she said, "my mother would break down and sob uncontrollably." After Lucia's mother and father passed away in Italy, she helped raise her brother Matthew, who was approximately four or five years old at the time, until she immigrated to America. Victoria's mother had revealed to her that "she breast-fed Matthew as a baby in Monte Sant'Angelo in Italy," and stated, "she loved him like a son." This seemed highly unusual to me at the time; however, I later discovered that it is possible for a woman who is not pregnant to induce lactation after suckling. One thought that entered my mind at the time: might Matthew have been my grandmother Lucia's child? Lucia was born in 1877 and Matthew in 1897.

And so, one day in September of 1998, I began my quest to learn more about my great-uncle Matthew, which turned out to be very consequential. Due to circumstances at the time, because I was involved in another writing project, my initial pursuit of information started out as a part-time endeavor. Over the next several years, I continued to gather valuable information by sending out inquiries to various government agencies and scouring Internet sites. Plus, I began reading a number books and articles about the Great War, primarily those containing information with regard to the part played by Guerra's assigned unit throughout the war, the 4th "Ivy" Division. A number of years passed before I decided to put the findings into manuscript form for possible publication.

Delving into Guerra's past has resulted in an awareness that a relatively high percentage of foreign-born immigrants, many recent arrivals to America, as well as a considerable number of the "sons of immigrants," comprised the ranks of the military following the country's entry into the conflict then raging in Europe. Demographers and other social scientists use the term "second generation immigrants" with reference to people with at least one foreign-born parent. Critics state that this definition is an "oxymoron" because of the fact that "second-generation immigrants," born in America, are technically not immigrants (see below).

* * *

On April 2, 1917, President Woodrow Wilson appeared before a special joint session of Congress to seek a declaration of war against the German Empire. On February 3, 1917, the American cargo ship *Housatonic* on a voyage to Liverpool carrying a cargo of grain and flour was sunk by a German U-boat (*U-53*). The entire crew of 25 men managed to board lifeboats and were eventually picked up by a British steamer. During the latter part of that month and March, submarines of the German Navy torpedoed and sank four more (or five, depending on the source) American merchant vessels, as well as a number of passenger ships belonging to other nations with U.S. citizens aboard, incurring a substantial loss of American lives. In the month of February 1917 alone, the German U-boat fleet had sunk 781,000 tons of Allied and neutral shipping. Wilson informed the legislature that it needed to support America's entry into what he promised would be "a war to end all wars," one that the President declared would "make the world safe for democracy."

Four days later, Congress voted to declare war on Germany and the country formally entered World War I. If the decision by the U.S. Congress to enter the war in Europe on the side of France and England was to have an impact on the outcome, government leaders faced the task of significantly increasing the size and strength of the military as rapidly as possible.

War Department officials looked upon the country's foreign-born population as a valuable resource, one that would provide a pool of much-needed manpower for all branches of the armed services. The primary focus of this work is to present a detailed account of the large number of immigrant men, those principally from one of the European nations, who ended up serving in the Great War, both as draftees and as volunteers—"America's Foreign Legion" (see below). Ironically, a sizable percentage of immigrant families fled Europe in the years leading up to the war in Europe in an effort to keep their sons out of the military, as did a number of draft-eligible young men.

Immigrants, classified as "non-citizens" ("'non-declarant' resident aliens"), those individuals who had not declared their intention to become a U.S. citizen, which included my great-uncle Matthew, were under no obligation to serve in the military. Legally, these men could have avoided the draft. Many, however, went willingly (see Chapter 3). An unknown number of non-declarant immigrant men responded to the call of the draft boards or enlisted voluntarily and served honorably, many with distinction. Many native-born Americans reasoned that by not volunteering for military service, these men who were living and working in this country and living fairly comfortably would be shirking their responsibility or obligation to defend their adopted nation, regardless of citizenship status. Many of those young men who did serve thought they were doing what was right and honorable. This may be viewed as being a bit presumptuous on my part to assert that these individuals were anxious to go off to war, but neither did they want to avoid meeting their duty to serve through military service. I would like to think that my great-uncle Matthew was one of these idealistic individuals in the latter category.

* * *

There are several uses of the phrase "Foreign Legion," with reference to American immigrants in the service in publications between 1918 and 1919, that planted the seed for the title of this book. The earliest mention of this term is contained in two unsigned articles published in the U.S. Army *Infantry Journal*, vol. 15, no. 1, September 1918, "'Foreign Legion' Companies" (252–

54), and "The 'Foreign-legion Squad'" (254–55). The third use of the term can be found in Provost Marshal General Enoch H. Crowder's "Second Report" to "The Secretary of War on the Operations of the Selective Service to December 20, 1918" (101), published in early 1919. This government document states that on May 9, 1918, the Congress approved several amendments to the naturalization law designed to facilitate a change in the legal status of aliens in the service, "whether a declarant or non-declarant," to "that of a full citizen." Commenting on the passage of this legislation, Crowder wrote that the measure opened the way for the camp commanders under the direction of the Adjutant-General of the Army to encourage naturalization on a large scale and resulted in the conversion of the "Foreign Legion" of the Army of the United States into a host of loyal American citizen-soldiers.

Brigadier General Leonid E. Kondratiuk (see Acknowledgments), National Commander of the Yankee Division Veterans Association, suggested the final choice of a title for the book—*America's "Foreign Legion": Immigrant Soldiers in the Great War.*

* * *

According to Historian Nancy Gentile Ford in her book *Americans All! Foreign-born Soldiers in World War I*, a definitive study of the subject, immigrants constituted "over 18 percent" of the total number of inductees during the Great War. This percentage equates to "nearly half a million" men, represented by "forty-six different nationalities." The greatest majority of immigrants entering the military lacked the ability to understand orders and commands, which prevented them from participating in existing training procedures. Camp commanders had no choice but to relegate these men to one of the service battalions, consisting of "unattached troops," that made up the Depot Brigade. Considered "not suitable" for regular military service, the majority ended up becoming part of the camp's unskilled labor force. Assigned to work details, these men performed all manner and types of "menial labor duties," primarily a host of dirty and demeaning jobs (see Ford, pp. 3, 127, 137; see also Chapter 11).

The "influx" of inductees from other nations into the armed forces, Ford wrote, "challenged the cultural, linguistic, and religious traditions of the American Army," forcing the military "to reexamine" existing "training procedures" and to formulate a number of "new" policies (see Ford, *Americans All!*, 3). Initially, the dilemma stymied leaders at the top echelon of the military establishment, who were at a loss as to what changes camp officials needed to introduce in order to reverse an unworkable and unmanageable situation, in this instance directly related to the language barrier.

I have spent more than ten years off and on conducting research and gathering pertinent information relative to my study. The initial investigation focused on my great-uncle Matthew Guerra's stint in the military, beginning with his stateside processing and training, movement overseas, and finally, the role of his outfit, the 4th Division, in combat on the battlefields of France. Primarily, my intent was to piece together a detailed account of the two major campaigns the division played a major role in, the St. Mihiel and Meuse-Argonne offensives, as well as the individual engagements in which Guerra's 58th Infantry Regiment participated, from existing military histories, records, and other available sources. In essence, the primary objective of this inquiry was to tell the story from the eyes of the participants—from the perspective of the ordinary ground combat soldier.

Whenever possible, I made a conscious effort, for the most part, to use the words of the combat veterans themselves—officers, noncoms, as well as the ordinary doughboy—who experienced firsthand the brutality and viciousness of war. Researchers can find these first-person accounts and narratives in autobiographies, memoirs, journals, diaries, personal remembrances and correspondence, published by veteran combatants following the war. Other sources cited are unit histories, military records, and relevant documents, including battlefield communications and field messages. These detailed descriptions, vivid narratives of events or situations, enabled me to visualize in my mind what wartime conditions were like during that particular phase of the war. These writings detailed the cruel realities of the various hostile encounters or engagements with an enemy force or forces that these men and their fellow soldiers were subject to in the heat of battle in a war zone on an almost daily basis.

When these veterans wrote about the war, they were aware that many of their experiences lay beyond the ability of outsiders to be able to fully comprehend. No one who has not experienced war can ever come close to imagining the horror, the fear to which these men are subjected for days and weeks at a time at the front, being continually under fire and with artillery shells exploding all around their position. Knowing that death was lurking close by, day in and day out, was a very unnerving experience.

I soon discovered that many of these recollections and reflections were extremely soul-stirring, providing heart-wrenching remembrances of a combatant's experiences. Many contained tales depicting extreme courage, honor, and acts of self-sacrifice by fellow squad members and others in their unit. These sources provide the reader with a gripping and uniquely personal saga of sacrifice, deprivation, and suffering, throughout the duration of their time in combat.

One intended goal was to recreate for myself and the reader, as near as is humanly possible, the appalling conditions faced by the ordinary World War I infantryman on the battlefield. My primary purpose was to gain a thorough knowledge of what Guerra and his fellow soldiers had to endure—to detail the many hardships and horrors suffered by frontline U.S. troops, beginning with their baptism of fire and continuing to war's end. That is, what Guerra and the other members of his regiment and company, right down to his squad mates, encountered while living in the forward trenches day in and day out. Also, I wanted to capture what it was like in both a combat role under attack by opposing forces and during an advance against entrenched German units occupying built-up and heavily fortified and defended positions following years of occupation. The harsh and utterly restricting conditions of life at the front could be an *overwhelming* experience. Men were living outside for days or weeks on end, in most cases with limited shelter from inclement weather. In many instances, they had to stand knee-deep in the muck and mire, made worse by France's fall rainy season, with temperatures often dropping to the low 40s at night.

Combat infantrymen at the front had to endure the unendurable. The physical scars of battle healed, but the psychological and emotional trauma never left them, oftentimes lurking deep in the recesses of their mind to emerge suddenly and without any warning. Following the war, intrusive thoughts of these troubling remembrances often produced persistent flashbacks, nightmares, as well as occasional panic attacks, that would disturb their inner peace and tranquility. The emotional effects of war brought back home by veterans can be extremely distressing (see section on PTSD). These graphic and evocative memories of their experiences in the heat of combat were indelibly etched in the psyche of these young men—many not out of their teens—and haunted them throughout the remainder of their lives. For them to be able to squelch these haunting and disturbing memories was for most an impossibility.

Another objective was to present some of the facts dealing with Guerra's death resulting from wounds received in the Bois de Fays (Woods of the Fairies, see map, p. 200) during the Meuse-Argonne offensive. The successes of the Allies during this offensive beginning on September 26, 1918, the final push of the war, forced German leaders to face the inevitable and initiate negotiations for an Armistice that would finally bring the fighting to a close.

Another intent was to provide details of these extenuating circumstances experienced by combat casualties evacuated from the field of battle and transported to a series of specialized aid stations located at various distances behind the lines, depending upon the nature and severity of their injuries. This process began with first-aid treatment administered by a combat medic in the heat of battle designed to stabilize the wounded man's condition for transport to a rear area (see later chapters). Stretcher-bearers then evacuated casualties to a forward dressing station, to undergo some type of first aid or primary care. From there, ambulance crews transported victims to a casualty clearing station (CCS), a well-equipped medical facility where sorting of wounded men into "light" and "serious" cases took place. Medical personnel would treat slight cases and return these men to their units, while retaining others unfit to travel for further treatment. Finally, personnel transferred the most serious casualties to an evacuation hospital, an advanced medical treatment station located farther to the rear.

Private Matthew Guerra suffered shrapnel wounds on October 5, 1918, and died in an evacuation hospital two days later. He ended up making the supreme sacrifice, as happens to so many young men in wartime. The official figure for total American deaths listed by the U.S. Department of Defense for the period ending December 31, 1918, is 116,516. This number includes 53,402 battle or related deaths and 63,114 non-combat deaths (including disease, accident, and/or death while a prisoner of war). There were 204,002 men wounded in battle (sources vary) and 3,305 men missing in action (MIA). The exact number of fatalities among American soldiers of foreign birth is unknown, as the War Department made no distinction between native Americans and immigrants relating to these statistics.

As my great-uncle's life story unfolded before me, I felt as though I was following along in his footsteps. This was especially true of the last days and hours of his life. I tried to imagine myself in his place and predicament on the battlefield, as revealed by existing accounts and personal narratives of survivors. In closing, I was anxious to discover what Guerra went through leading up to and including his ultimate demise at Evacuation Hospital No. 4. Along the way, my attempt to uncover all the facts relating to Guerra's time in the military and his ultimate fate took many twists and turns. It has been a most exciting as well as rewarding undertaking.

1

The Quest Begins

The first logical step in this research project to find out all I could about Matthew Guerra was to obtain a copy of his military records, and second, to find the location of his burial place somewhere in France. With my prior experience obtaining official documents, reports and transcripts from various government agencies, I reasoned that it should not be too difficult to locate Guerra's military file. That was my initial summation which, as it turned out, was false. I was aware from previous research of the catastrophic fire at the National Personnel Records Center (NPRC) in St. Louis, Missouri, in 1973, that burned for several weeks, and destroyed "about 80 percent" of the World War I and II veterans' files. The NPRC is a repository for the personnel, health, and medical records of discharged or deceased veterans for all branches of the armed services after 1900. I obtained a copy of the Standard Military Records Request Form (SF-180) on the Internet, filled it out and mailed it to the NPRC. I realized, of course, that the chances of Guerra's records surviving the blaze were not very promising. A few weeks later, a negative response from the agency arrived in the mail. Strangely enough, the letter also stated that the staff found no record on file to indicate that a Matteo or Matthew Guerra had ever served in the military. This was, at the time, very puzzling.

Following an Internet search, I discovered that the American Battle Monuments Commission (ABMC), located in Arlington, Virginia, was the federal agency responsible for the management of permanent military cemeteries and memorials overseas. The ABMC, established by Congress in 1923, administers, operates, and maintains 24 military cemeteries honoring those who served and died for their country. There are eight permanent American World War I military cemeteries in Europe: six in France, one in Belgium and another in England. "Nearly 125,000 American war dead are interred at ABMC veterans' memorial cemeteries worldwide, with an additional 94,000 individuals commemorated on Tablets of the Missing" (four large bronze plaques). These rosters bear the names of servicemen missing in action, or those whom graves registration search and recovery operations were unable locate or positively identify. Also included are the names of 974 men buried or lost at sea between 1917 and 1918.[1]

I mailed a letter to ABMC headquarters seeking to ascertain the location of the cemetery where graves registration personnel had interred Guerra's body. A short time later, I received a second negative reply, which was especially disconcerting. There was, the letter reported, "no one named Matteo or Matthew Guerra is buried in any of the national cemeteries in France." Both my aunt and I were baffled.

Late one Friday afternoon about 4:30 p.m., I contacted the ABMC headquarters in Arlington by telephone, expecting to reach a recording. The operator connected me with staff member Martha Sell, Freedom of Information Act (FOIA) assistant (now chief officer). I provided her with what information I had found to date. She checked the agency's files on her computer, which only took a few seconds, but was unable to locate a record for anyone named Matteo or Matthew Guerra. Ms. Sell informed me that during that particular time period, the misspelling of names in military and other government records was a common occurrence. She promised to do some further checking on my behalf and asked me to call her back the following week.

After a search, Ms. Sell discovered that this was indeed the case, as happened to so many immigrants during processing by ship officials at their port of departure in Europe and on other immigration records. This generally occurred when an employee of the steamship company recording the information on the ship's manifest spelled each person's name phonetically, as it was sounded out to them. Ms. Sell eventually came up with the name "Mattes Gerra," who, at the time, was living in Bridgeport, Connecticut, when he entered the army. His residence and the date of death matched. This bit of detective work by Ms. Sell enabled her to ascertain the location of Guerra's gravesite at the Meuse-Argonne American Cemetery and Memorial just east of the village of Romagne-Gesnes, Meuse, France.

Government records and other documents, I learned later, contain various spellings of my great-uncle's first and last names—"Mattes Gerra" (also on his grave marker in France—later corrected), "Matteo Gerra," and "Matthew W. Gerra" (4th Division History). (An Internet search indicates there are no Italian male names that begin with the letter "W.") An acquaintance, a person of Italian heritage, enlightened me that the correct pronunciation of the surname Guerra was actually "Gerra." Hereafter, I use the Americanized version of his name—Matthew Guerra—throughout.

In light of the information provided by Ms. Sell, I immediately dashed off another round of correspondence. I sent a second Form SF-180 to the NPRC, this time under the misspelled surname of Gerra, again requesting a copy of his official military personnel file. The agency's letter of response

1. The Quest Begins 11

Grave location of Matthew at the Meuse-Argonne American Cemetery (copyright American Battle Monuments Commission).

stated that the fire of 1973 had indeed destroyed the records of one "Mattes Gerra," which was at the time, not wholly unexpected, but most disappointing nonetheless.

* * *

Next, I sent a letter to the Historical Section of the Connecticut State Adjutant General's office in Hartford, to see if there was a record of Guerra's military service on file. Within a very brief time span, not more than a couple of weeks, which was surprising considering other experiences obtaining records from various government agencies, a packet arrived containing Guerra's official military service records and, unexpectedly, his birth name. "Guerra" was spelled correctly, which came as a surprise. This was my first major break. Guerra's Connecticut service records contained a wealth of additional information, including his service number (2,673,585) and cause and date of death, "DW [Died of Wounds] Oct. 7/18." His date of induction was listed as April 26, 1918. When he entered the service, his age was "22⅙ yrs."[2]

I later visited Bridgeport's World War I memorial, dedicated on April 19, 1924. The monument is located at Lt. Col. Henry A. Mucci Memorial Plaza on Broad Street. The bronze plaque listed "Matthew Gerra," his last name

World War I Memorial. Bridgeport, Connecticut.

misspelled, among those Connecticut men killed in the war. In World War II, Mucci was a U.S. Army Ranger and a decorated American war hero. On January 30, 1945, the officer led a force of 120 Army Rangers supported by 250 Filipino commandos on a daring nighttime raid 30 miles behind enemy lines against the Cabanatuan Prison Camp in the Philippines. The surprise assault, known thereafter as "The Great Raid," resulted in the rescue of 513 survivors of the fall of Corregidor and the Bataan Death March. At its peak, the camp held an estimated 8,000 American prisoners. During the foray into enemy-held territory past thousands of entrenched Japanese troops, the raiding party stormed the heavily armed camp in a coordinated attack, killing "hundreds" of Japanese troops, and escorted the prisoners to safety. Most were emaciated from the ravages of malnourishment, disease, and torture; many were on the verge of death, a result of atrocious living conditions and brutal treatment at the hands of their captors. Remarkably, only two of the Rangers were killed and twenty Filipino guerrillas wounded. General Douglas MacArthur awarded Mucci the Distinguished Service Cross.

Close up of World War I Memorial (Guerra's name misspelled GERRA) (copyright American Battle Monuments Commission).

Among the Connecticut records was a copy of my great-uncle's "Notice of Death" dated December 30, 1918, addressed to the La Torre family in Bridgeport by the state Adjutant General's Office nearly three months after his demise. The letter had been returned by the Post Office as "undeliverable." At some point during the war the La Torres had relocated to Brooklyn, New York. When this occurred, officials of the agency sent a second notice to the Palumbo family in Worcester. Connecticut officials recorded his last name on the notification as "Gerra," and listed the date of death as October 5, 1918, which was the date he received his wounds. All other papers and documents in the Connecticut file listed his name under the correct spelling of Guerra.

Next was a list of his units and the dates served with each outfit prior to his death. Under "Organization," the document listed "Co. C, 58th Inf." Regiment (4th "Ivy" Division). The "Cause of Death" recorded in the file states: "Killed in action in line of duty and not the result of the soldier's own misconduct," but provided no other details. Under "Emergency Address," the certificate listed "Lena Gerra [her maiden name—then La Torre]. Sister. 58 Crescent Ave., Bridgeport, Conn." This initiated an entirely new phase of my investigation. Armed with this additional information, I began researching the division, regiment, and company he was a member of, adding a few more pieces to the puzzle.[3]

I posted a message on the 36th Division Association Message Board (my father's World War II division), seeking information. A regular contributor noted in his reply that if my great-uncle died in the war, the U.S. Total Army Personnel Command (PERSCOM), 200 Stovall St., Alexandria, Virginia, would have a copy of his "Individual Deceased Personnel File (IDPF)," sometimes referred to as a "Mortuary File" or "Casualty File." The U.S. Army Graves Registration Service Department compiled all records and other supporting papers contained in the file to document the death of a member of the military. Also included in the file was information regarding "the related actions associated with the disposition of the remains." I also learned that the folder "can contain surrogate material for military personnel records lost in the 1973 National Personnel Records Center Fire." News of the file's existence was most welcome. I dashed off a letter to the agency and waited for a reply.[4]

A little more than four months after my initial inquiry, a manila envelope finally arrived from the Veteran Administration's Boston office containing Guerra's IDPF, the contents of which were approximately one and one-quarter inches thick. This U.S. Army Quartermaster Corps report contained therein provided much valuable information about my great-uncle, including some of the particulars surrounding his death. Guerra's medical report, contained in the file, stated that his wounds were the result of "shrapnel," fragments from an exploding artillery shell or grenade, but provided no other details, which was standard procedure. During World War I, and all other wars before and since, military officials did not provide any specifics regarding the exact cause of death, or expound on the nature and extent of wounds, in order to spare the family any undue grief or anguish.

Documents in the file included a number of reports pertaining to the following: identification of his remains and details regarding the initial burial of the body at a temporary cemetery located adjacent to Evacuation Hospital No. 4, where he succumbed as a result of complications related to his wounds, and the exhumation of his body and subsequent reburials to its final resting place at the Meuse-Argonne Cemetery. The records also included correspondence and testimony outlining failed attempts by government officials to contact the family with regards to the return of Guerra's remains to the U.S. Papers in the file also provided a wealth of additional information discussed in later chapters. I spent weeks poring over the contents of the package and the correspondence between government officials and the La Torre and Palumbo families in the months and years following his death.

Among the other documents found in the deceased file were several pieces of correspondence pertaining to the $10,000 insurance policy Guerra had taken out with the Treasury Department's Bureau of War Risk Insurance (BWRI), claims by the family for same, as well as the final disbursement of benefits. Despite the fact that Matthew had specifically named his sister Lucia, my grandmother, as beneficiary (see below), the Palumbo family went through a lengthy process proving Lucia was in fact her brother's legal guardian.

Official BWRI policy did not provide for a lump-sum payment, but dispersed the amount in the form of fixed monthly payments over a period of years. There were two basic classes of benefits: Class A—Widows without children received $25.00 per month; and widows with children, the following: one child—$35.00; two children—$42.50; three children—$47.50; and four children or more—a maximum of $52.50. The second was a Class B Family allowance, for the death of unmarried men, that provided a $30.00 monthly payment to the deceased's parents, and with children (brothers and sisters), not to exceed $50.00.

Among the papers contained in the file was a photocopy of the official Western Union telegram delivered by messenger notifying Guerra's sister Lena La Torre of Matthew's death (separate from the Connecticut notice that had been returned "undeliverable") I reasoned that the Veterans Administration (VA) might have the original copy in its possession. I wrote a letter asking if this could in fact be the case and what I needed to do to obtain the notice. Rather unexpectedly, the VA mailed me the telegram in a manila envelope, which arrived without an accompanying letter or any indication of who might have been responsible for sending the document. Surprisingly, the original telegram, although yellowed with age, was in relatively good condition (see photograph on next page). Papers in the file detailed unsuccessful attempts by the government to return the body to the United States following the war.

* * *

Found in the IDPF were several letters of correspondence between government officials and the Palumbos regarding my grandmother Lucia's efforts in 1930 to obtain "Gold Star Mother" status. American Gold Star Mothers are women who either lost a son, or a widow whose husband is killed in the service of his country. Even though Lucia was only his sister, she had been a surrogate mother to Matthew for the better part of his life in this country after their parents passed away. Her efforts eventually proved successful. Beginning in World War I (June 1917), families having members serving in

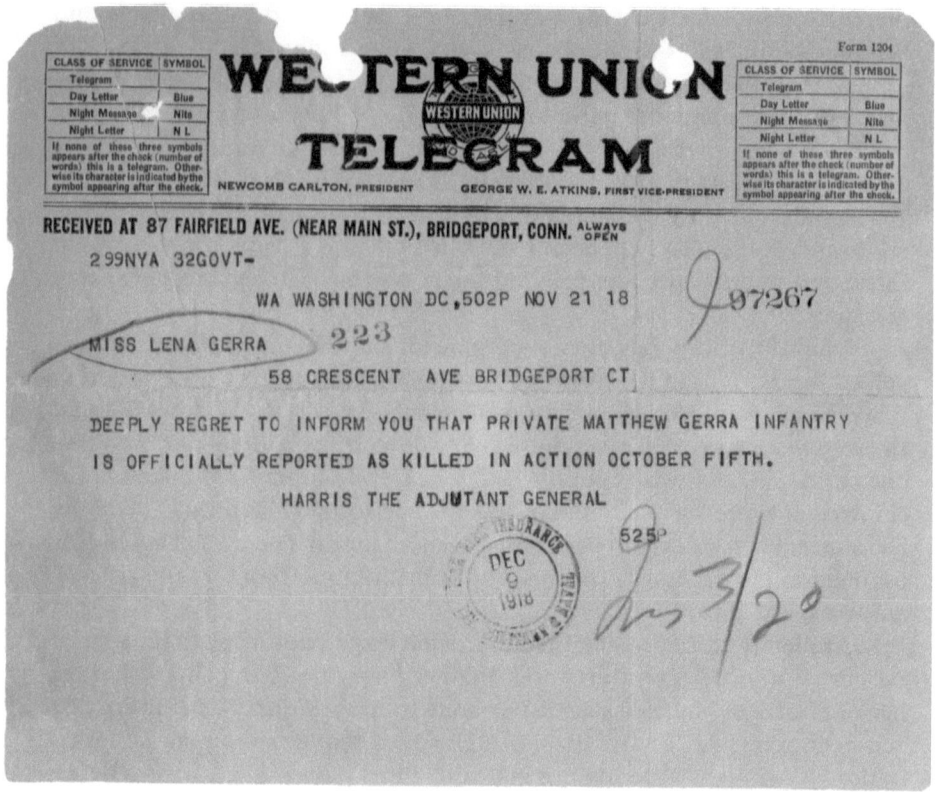

Original Western Union telegram—notification of Guerra's death.

the Armed Forces during any period of the war would display a "service flag" or "service banner" in the window of their homes. The banners, approximately 8 × 15 inches in size, featured "a red border and a blue star on a white background," more commonly referred to as a "Blue Star Flag," that became a national symbol of honor and pride. Families with more than one member in the service displayed an equal number of blue stars. If a member of the service was killed in action or died during service of his country, the family would replace the blue star with a gold star, indicating that a member of this house made the ultimate sacrifice for his country. The gold star was slightly smaller than the blue star so that it had a narrow blue border. In World War II, five Sullivan brothers, sailors serving together on the USS *Juneau* (CL-52), were tragically killed in action on November 13, 1942, when their ship sank after being struck by a torpedo from a Japanese submarine. After Thomas and Alleta Sullivan lost their sons, a flag with five gold stars hung in the window of their home in Waterloo, Iowa.[5]

1. The Quest Begins

In March of 1929, the U.S. Congress enacted a bill establishing a fund that would enable mothers and widows of deceased service personnel lost in the line of duty to make a "Pilgrimage of Remembrance," see their loved one's final resting place. In essence, the purpose of the planned pilgrimages was to allow these women, accounts state, "to find peace in their lives" by saying goodbye to their sons and husbands interred in one of the American military cemeteries in Europe. The Office of the Quartermaster General organized the program and made all travel arrangements and accommodations. All expenses for these "Gold Star Pilgrims" were paid for by the federal government. The bill, unfortunately, excluded fathers and children.[6]

After Matthew arrived in the U.S. at age 11 or 12, he lived with the Palumbo family in Worcester. My grandmother Lucia became his legal guardian or custodian, acting *in loco parentis* ("in the place of a parent"), assuming all parental rights and duties for the boy until he reached the legal age of 18. Following a lengthy investigation, federal officials in charge of administering the program confirmed Lucia's eligibility for Gold Star Mother status, because of her primary role in helping to raise Matthew. As such, Lucia was entitled to visit Matthew's grave in France. Based on these facts, the government had earlier determined that Lucia was qualified to receive Matthew's war risk insurance benefits.

On May 7, 1930, the first group of 231 "Gold Star Pilgrims," mothers and widows, boarded the luxury liner SS *America* in Hoboken, New Jersey, for the voyage to France. Twenty vessels made the trip that summer. Between 1930 and 1933, 6,693 women, who would not otherwise have been able to make the trip, traveled to France to visit their loved ones' graves. Federal officials made travel arrangements and paid all expenses.

My grandmother was in her early fifties at the time and could not speak English. She was very leery and quite fearful, to say the least, of making the trip unaccompanied. So my grandfather Antonio wrote a letter requesting that officials allow the couple's son, my uncle Matthew ("Mitt," my mother's brother and Guerra's namesake) born in 1919, approximately 13 years of age, to accompany his mother Lucia to France. A letter of approval for Matthew to make the trip arrived a few weeks later; however, much to the disappointment of the family, they would be required to cover all expenses incurred by their son. There was the cost of passage aboard ship, as well as travel and hotel accommodations while in country. At the time, the U.S. was in the throes of the Great Depression and the Palumbos' neighborhood grocery business had fallen on hard times. Antonio could not afford the expense, so Lucia would be required to make the voyage alone. Understandably, she later decided against going, a major disappointment, which must have pained her deeply.

* * *

A few years after I began my research of Guerra's life, much to my amazement, something completely unexpected occurred—two additional images of my great-uncle surfaced. These were in the form of a pair of 16 × 20-inch paintings or portraits of Pvt. Guerra in uniform. One image shows him from the waist up, and the second is a full-body portrait of the young man holding an M1903 Springfield bolt-action service rifle (see cover). Shortly after my aunt Helen Palumbo, my father's sister and widow of my uncle Mitt, passed away in 2008, their granddaughter Gina Palumbo Polewaczyk found the two portraits among Helen's effects. Gina was aware that I was researching Guerra's life and turned them over to me for safekeeping. After 90-plus years, what are the odds of this occurring?

Collectors describe these likenesses on Internet sites as "painted photo portraits," "a painted or photographic likeness of a person," "portraitures," and "photographic like images," produced by "portrait painters." The paintings, described as an "artist's representations" of a subject "on linen canvas ... commemorating the young man's departure" to a war zone, were "extremely popular among families." Artists produced "hundreds of thousands" of the images "before the boys left for the war from which millions never returned." They were, one website proclaimed, "a hallmark of World War One soldier portraits."[7]

The artists who created these realistic, photographic-like images set up their studios in storefronts, kiosks, or enclosures on the sidewalk, or in an empty lot in the military towns adjacent to or just outside the camps that soldiers frequented during their time

Portrait of Matthew Guerra during basic training. Produced by artist at Camp Devens.

1. The Quest Begins

off. Departing soldiers presented the paintings to loved ones, in many cases the last time they would ever have contact with the family. Parents had the portraits "placed in rectangular or oval frames" the latter "with convex bubble glass" (a smaller number of frames were octagonal). Some of the rectangular and oval "giltwood gesso frames" were quite ornate, with "faux tiger grain finish" and "gold trim." Sizes varied only slightly.

Lighter shading along the edges of both portraits of Matthew indicated the former presence of rectangular frames. Earlier, Victoria informed me that the family kept the two paintings hanging on the dining room wall of the family home for many years after his death. Victoria related earlier that she had "a vague remembrance" of her uncle when she was a young girl. My aunt was born in 1914, and Matthew left home at some point in 1917, to live in Bridgeport. Quite possibly, the portraits were what she remembered.

The finds were truly astounding. That they had survived after so many years had passed is in itself quite remarkable. At the start of my search, not in my wildest dreams did I ever imagine that an image of Guerra would turn up—in this case not one but three. Prior to that, the man I had been researching these many months was just a name, important to me, but he was a man without a face. After I obtained the portraits, everything about Matthew in my mind changed, and strangely enough the work took on far greater meaning. Thereafter I felt a more intimate connection with the young man who, at the time the artist painted the portrait, was 21 years old.

That evening, after taking possession of the paintings, I sat at the dining room table and stared in awe at the two images. It was truly amazing at how extremely lifelike the artist's renditions seemed to be. Quite amazingly, it actually felt as if I were having a face-to-face confrontation with Matthew. I have held a longtime belief that our spirit lives on after we die. Was young Guerra staring back at me from the great beyond?

While gazing at the portraits, I also experienced a wide array of emotions. Was I actually making a true connection with his spiritual being? It was a powerful feeling, something I cannot quite explain. Was he making his wishes known—that I was his last chance to keep his memory alive—to tell his life's story? I was certain that Guerra would not want all remembrance of his life to fade into total obscurity, as was about to happen had I not intervened.

I felt as if we were looking intently at one another across the boundary between the supernatural world and the physical world. It truly seemed as if the artist had somehow trapped Guerra's spirit inside the image—that was my perception. It is difficult to describe what I was experiencing at that moment. Something about Guerra's facial expression haunted me—his seeming stare was quite intense. I was mesmerized. He had the slightest hint of a smile and there appeared to be a youthful glint in his eyes—could it be the artist had accurately captured not only the image of his subject, but also his inner feelings at the time? From the very start, I truly sensed Guerra's presence emanating from within the images—some type of radiant energy—an aura, if you will. I had an eerie sensation that he was somehow trying to communicate with me across time and space.

Was it also possible that these graphic and lifelike images were also projecting some of Matthew's personality and character? During the course of my research, I discovered that an artist can not only capture a person's physical likeness, but also convey the subject's mental or emotional state at the time as well. It was an uncanny sensation. Someone who painted hundreds of these portraits presumably, with experience, had acquired this very special and gifted ability. I feel as though the portraits of my great-uncle have given me a privileged connection to the past. Had I not learned of his existence, his death, in a sense, would have been final and everlasting, unknown to future generations of the family. It would be as if Guerra never existed.

In all likelihood, Matthew probably delivered the portraits to the Palumbos when he visited the family shortly before his unit shipped out for France. It is also possible that my grandparents visited Camp Devens, located 29 miles from the city on the Worcester-Ayer branch line of the Boston & Maine Railroad, shortly before his departure (see Chapter 19).

In her family history, Victoria mentioned that when her father Antonio was a young man, he "served as a soldier in the Italian Army." I know that Antonio would have been very proud of his brother-in-law and his accomplishment at completing his combat training and going off to defend his adopted country. Among the family's possessions are two photographs of my grandfather in uniform. Palumbo is wearing a distinctive plumed hat, called a "viara," worn by troops who served in the "elite" Bersaglieri Corps, a part of the Royal Italian Army. Units of the Bersaglieri consisted of highly trained "sharpshooters" or "marksmen," armed with carbines. Victoria said her father "was very proud of the photograph and of his time spent in the service of his country."[8]

2

Matthew Guerra in America

In my aunt Victoria Palumbo's family history, one brief entry mentioned an uncle named Matteo Guerra, whom she described as "my mother's baby brother." During World War I, she related, "Guerra was an infantry soldier in the U.S. Army." She continued, "My uncle was killed in action in 1918 during the First World War." Then she added, "He is buried in a military cemetery somewhere in France." This revelation came as a complete surprise, because never before had I heard any other member of the family bring up his name. I was intrigued and pressed Victoria for additional details. She related that he was born in 1897 and came to America from Italy at age 14 or 15 in 1912, shortly after the death of his parents, which occurred within a brief timespan.

Victoria said she had "a vague memory" of her uncle's presence while he lived with the family, and of him in uniform as a little girl. She would have been approximately three to four years old at the time. Later, years after Vicky passed away, two paintings or portraits of Guerra in uniform surfaced. These framed paintings, she had related earlier, hung on the wall of the family dining room for years after his death. It is possible that this is what she remembered.

According to my aunt Victoria's family history, at some point around 1910 or 1911, her father Antonio opened a neighborhood grocery store in Worcester, Massachusetts. It started as a small operation, similar to one of today's ethnic specialty stores, providing specific food products generally not found in local markets for their Italian customers from the Shrewsbury Street neighborhood. The building, located at 4 Plum Street, was a three-family home, called a "three decker" or "triple decker," with an attached storefront. The family lived in the 1st-floor apartment located behind the store. Antonio later purchased the building. A neighbor recalled Antonio tending a huge garden in the back yard that supplied his customers with fresh produce all season long.

Business was good, allowing Antonio to send money to Italy for his brother-in-law Matthew Guerra's support and later for his passage to America. In June of 1912, Matthew left his home town in Monte Sant'Angelo with a few meager belongings and boarded a train bound for the port of Naples. He was likely in the company of other inhabitants from the town on their way to the "Land of Opportunity," who looked out for his well-being. Matthew crossed the Apennine Mountains on his way to Naples, where the group boarded the majestic first-class SS *Canopic*, a White Star Line cruise ship. The *Canopic* could accommodate up to 1,300 passengers—250 1st class, 250 2nd class, and 800 3rd class (steerage). On 26 June, the ship departed Naples Harbor, crossed the beautiful blue Mediterranean Sea, and passed through the Strait of Gibraltar into the vast Atlantic.

After a 14-day journey, Matthew arrived at the port city of Boston, Massachusetts, on the 9th of July. What a grand adventure it must have been for a young lad his age, who had spent his entire life in a small town in the province of Foggia in Italy, and probably never ventured more than a few kilometers from his home. The manifest of the SS *Canopic* listed young Matthew's occupation as "farmhand" or "farmlad" (the poor handwriting is difficult to decipher).[1]

The Palumbos were waiting to greet Matthew when his ship docked in Boston Harbor. The boy processed through the inspection facilities at the U.S. Immigration Service (IS) Station on Long Wharf at the foot of State Street. U.S. Public Health Service doctors conducted a preliminary medical examination and administered a mental test of arriving alien passengers. Immigration agents detained immigrants who failed to pass the initial medical inspection. Inspectors isolated those persons diagnosed with infectious diseases in a detention facility or quarantine station, generally for a 14-day period. Of primary concern were diseases such as tuberculosis, venereal disease, trachoma, and favus (a contagious skin disease). Individuals afflicted with a particular disease or malady had to undergo hospitalization and treatment until deemed cured. Those determined to be "carriers" or presenting symptoms of a particular illness or chronic ailment were kept in isolation or quarantine and received treatment until they recovered. These individuals had to undergo further medical tests before inspectors made a final determination as to their eligibility for admission into the country.

The last time Lucia had seen the boy was in 1906, when he was about eight years old. My aunt Victoria related that her mother "was overjoyed to be reunited with her baby brother." The happy group boarded a Boston & Albany commuter train at Boston's South Station and traveled the 43 miles to Worcester's Union Station, located at the head of Shrewsbury Street only a few short blocks from Plum Street and his new home in America. Shortly after Matthew arrived in Worcester, the boy began helping out in the family grocery store.

2. Matthew Guerra in America

With the inevitability of war looming large in Europe, as well as the distinct possibility that Italy might enter the fighting on the side of the Allies—Britain, France, and Russia (this later occurred on 23 May 1915)—Lucia might have been fearful that the military would draft Matthew into the Italian Army. This may very well have been the reason for wanting to bring him to America at this particular time. In 1870, a prominent member of the Chamber of Deputies, Ercole Lialdi of Lombardy in northern Italy, reported that "several towns" in his district "had already lost half their population through emigration, including many fourteen- and fifteen-year-old males who were shipping abroad in order to avoid military service." In another deposition, Leonardo Tomaiolo, "a friend of the family," testified, "I remember that Mrs. Palumbo told me that she was very anxious to have her younger brother come to this country." This was likely a prime factor in her actions. He stated, "I first remember seeing Matthew Guerra sometime in 1912 or 1913." Ironically, many who fled to avoid conscription in Italy after 1910 ended up serving, and dying, in the U.S. Army during World War I.[2]

On an application "Affidavit of Persons Claiming to Have Stood in the Relation of Parent," filed with the application for Matthew's U.S. Government life insurance benefits, Lucia stated that when her brother first arrived in the United States, he "could not speak English." Matthew, she testified, attended school "in Monte Sant'Angelo for about 4 years" (see below). Lucia stated in her deposition that after coming to America "he went to night school for about one year" to learn English. A pamphlet by Morris H. Cohen, titled *Worcester's Ethnic Groups*, contains a photograph with the caption "Italians, Syrians, and other nationalities at evening school classes, Shrewsbury Street, about 1900."[3]

* * *

According to Victoria, Matthew moved out of the Palumbo family home "about September, 1917," after what she described as "some kind of a falling out with my parents." She understood that the argument "had to do with his wages for working in the store." Most likely, my grandfather Antonio paid him a very menial hourly wage. Her mother, she said, revealed this to her years later. Matthew, at age 20 or 21, probably began thinking about his future and needed to find a job that paid considerably more than he was earning at the market. He moved to Bridgeport, Connecticut, where he found employment at the Union Metallic Cartridge Company (U.M.C.), founded in 1887, originally a manufacturer of cartridge ammunition. Matthew's brother-in-law Joseph LaTorre, who was married to his sister Lena, was employed at the time at Remington as a "machine operator," and likely helped him get a job at the plant. With the war on in Europe, the company needed workers and paid a decent wage.

Matthew Guerra. Age: 15 or 16. Taken in Worcester, Massachusetts, c. 1913 or 1914.

Victoria said she was only about three and a half to four years old in 1917, when her uncle Matthew left her parents' home to go and live with the La Torres. Victoria said she had a vague recollection of Matthew living with the family and working in the family store, but remembers little else about him during that time, which was quite understandable after so many years.

By 1902, U.M.C. had expanded to become the largest cartridge manufacturer in the world. The U.M.C. complex consisted of 168 buildings with a total floor area of 650,000 square feet. Remington Arms Company of Ilion, New York, acquired the company in 1912, and the corporation became Remington U.M.C. When World War I broke out in Europe in 1914, the company received a number of lucrative contracts from the Allies to produce weapons and ammunition. Matthew Guerra's draft registration card lists his occupation as "laborer," and his June 25, 1918, Naturalization Record as "ammunition worker."[4]

On April 6, 1917, the United States declared war on Germany. The country had already begun preparing for war in earnest around the first of the year. Almost immediately, Remington began production of the U.S. Enfield at Bridgeport, a modification of the British .303-inch Enfield (P14). Company officials named the redesigned model the "American Enfield," caliber .30–06 (M1917). The Bridgeport plant also converted to produce the Enfield .30–06 cartridge. In order to meet the needs of the military, the Army Ordnance Department indicated that Remington Arms needed to produce at least 4,000,000 rifles within two years. By September 1918, Remington U.M.C. employed more than 35,000 workers in five factories, 12,000 at Bridgeport. Among this number were approximately 4,000 women, about one-third of the company's work force. By November 1918, the army had equipped approximately 75 percent of the American Expeditionary Force soldiers in France with the M1917.[5]

At some point in 1917, Remington officials also began production of the water-cooled, belt-fed .30-caliber Browning heavy machine gun (M1917), Browning automatic rifle (BAR), .45-caliber Colt automatic pistol (M1911), the Very signal pistol (flare gun), as well as producing 5,000 bayonets and scabbards per day. Company engineers also designed an air-cooled version of the Browning machine gun for use by Allied aircraft.[6]

3

America Enters the War
The World War I Draft Act

On April 6, 1917, the United States Congress formally declared war against the German Empire and entered the conflict in Europe that had been raging since July 1914. Following America's commitment, both the French and British War Commissions were anxious for the U.S. government to deploy an expeditionary force, "no matter how small," to join the fight overseas. The British argued that an American presence would achieve two purposes: first, it would "boost the sagging morale" of the Allied troops, "and second, it would provide the U.S. an opportunity to show the flag and demonstrate its commitment to the cause."[1]

Major General Hugh L. Scott, the U.S. Army Chief of Staff, opposed sending a small force "on the ground that" such a contingency "would belittle our effort; was undignified and would give the wrong impression of our intentions." Scott decided instead to send a full division, in order "to show the quality of our troops" and to "command" respect for the American flag. President Woodrow Wilson was in full agreement that this would be the appropriate plan of action for the initial involvement by U.S. forces.[2]

In early May, Gen. Scott had "alerted" Major General John J. "Black Jack" Pershing, commanding the Army's Southern Department, "about the possibility" of fielding a contingent and sending it to France, later designated the American Expeditionary Force (AEF). He asked Pershing "to select one field artillery and four infantry regiments" for immediate service overseas. Pershing "nominated" the 16th ("Blue Devils"), 18th ("Vanguards"), 26th ("Blue Spaders"), and 28th ("Black Lions") Infantry Regiments, along with the 6th Field Artillery Regiment, as the nucleus of the "First Expeditionary Division," later shortened to the "1st Division." U.S. Army officials organized the force on June 9, 1917 (see note), at Fort Jay on Governors Island located in New York Harbor, where the British liner RMS *Baltic* of the White Star Line waited to carry Pershing and "the first representation of the American army ... to enter the European war." Troops commonly referred to the 1st Division as "The Fighting First." Military leaders officially nicknamed the new division "The Big Red One" after the number on the unit's shoulder patch. Commanded by Major General Robert Lee Bullard, the new division had a strength of approximately 26,500 men.[3]

Pershing chose the 28th Regiment to conduct the first American battle and offensive of World War I—the Battle of Cantigny, 27–31 May 1918. During the engagement, the 28th withstood five German counterattacks and went on to wrest the village of Cantigny from German defenders, capturing 250 prisoners. Following the battle, commanders of the 28th changed the regiment's nickname to the "Black Lions of Cantigny" (or "Lions of Cantigny").

* * *

Immediately following the declaration of war by Congress, Secretary of War Newton D. Baker and General Pershing began taking steps to expand the military at home. In 1917, the standing national army consisted of six divisions. Initially, the War Department decided to form 32 new infantry divisions, 16 National Guard and 16 in the national army. Plans also called for "drafting of the National Guard into federal service and adding another 500,000 men through the selective service system." Between August 22, 1917, and January 5, 1918, the General Staff authorized an additional four divisions, one cavalry and three infantry, for a total of forty-three (this total included the 1st Expeditionary Division). Baker, a forty-five-year-old progressive reformer and proclaimed pacifist, had never served in the military.[4]

When the U.S. entered the war, the federal army consisted of approximately 128,000 men (figures vary), while the National Guard, the organized state militias, numbered approximately 115,000. Facing military planners in the months leading up to the country's entry into the war was the dilemma of mobilizing a mass wartime army of several million as rapidly as possible.

At the time, there existed among government leaders a strong anti-draft sentiment. This included not only President Wilson, Secretary of War Baker, and a majority of Congressmen, but a sizeable segment of the American public as well. Opponents advocated that the government invoke a trial period of the traditional voluntary recruitment system before resorting to conscription. Initially, Wilson proposed to raise a volunteer force to increase the ranks of the army by 1 million men. However, despite four months of intense recruitment efforts by the Regular Army and National Guard nationwide in the three weeks following the declaration of war, only 32,000 men (sources vary) had heeded the country's call for volunteers. Given existing time constraints and logistical considerations, it soon became abundantly clear to the administration that it would be impractical to depend upon volunteer enlistments in meeting the military's manpower needs.[5]

Wilson eventually yielded to arguments by his top advisors, military leaders, and pro-draft supporters that the only efficient and democratic means of raising a sufficient fighting force for deployment overseas, one that would make a serious and significant contribution to the Allied cause, was a stepped-up program of national conscription. Once the president "decided that conscription was 'vital to this grim undertaking,' he was committed," wrote MIT Professor Dr. Christopher Capozzola. By April 1917, Wilson had become the draft's "most vigorous defender." Wilson went so far as to authorize Baker "to print and distribute thirty million draft registration forms before the Selective Service Act had ever passed Congress."[6]

On April 7, 1917, just one day after the Congress declared war on Germany, the president held a press conference and announced to the nation the government's plan for a national draft. Administration officials introduced a bill to Congress titled "An Act to Authorize the President to Increase Temporarily the Military Establishment of the United States," commonly referred to as the "Selective Service Act" or "Selective Draft Act." "By the time Congress passed the Act on May 19," explained Historian John K. Ohl, "the machinery for selecting hundreds of thousands of men for the army was ready to function." Four days later on the 22nd, Baker appointed Maj. General Enoch H. Crowder (a.k.a. E. Herbert, or "Bert"), a lawyer who specialized in military law, to the position of Judge Advocate General of the U.S. Army. He charged Crowder with the responsibility of implementing and administering the Selective Service Act. The primary function of the Judge Advocate General's Office was to supervise the administration of military justice in the U.S. Army. Crowder was appointed the Army's chief legal officer in 1911 and served until he retired in 1923, when President Warren G. Harding appointed him ambassador to Cuba.[7]

On April 13, 1917, President Woodrow Wilson created the Committee on Public Information (CPI) through Executive Order 2594. Members of the committee included George Creel, appointed chairman; Robert Lansing, Secretary of State; Newton D. Baker, Secretary of War; and Josephus Daniels, Secretary of the Navy, to act as ex officio members. The CPI was also known as the "Creel Committee." Prior to the appointment, Creel was an investigative journalist, a freelance writer, a politician, and a government official, among other professions. The committee, wrote historian Nancy Gentile Ford, carried out "a high-pitched, emotionally charged campaign" that "exploited and ignited strong feelings of nativism, xenophobia, jingoism, and superpatriotism." "To 'sell' the war to the public," Ford reported, the committee "hired an impressive group of writers, photographers, historians, and entertainers." Very soon thereafter, she added, the nation was "gripped" by "war hysteria." One of the primary objective of the CPI was "to remind America's ethnic groups of their duty to the United States." To accomplish their goal, the organization "produced thirty different propaganda bulletins ... in various languages." The committee "distributed over 75 million copies." Journalists later criticized Creel and the CPI "for releasing exaggerated accounts of events and for hiding bad or unflattering news about the war by censoring the press."[8]

To ensure an orderly mobilization process, General Crowder faced two primary considerations: first, to create a fair and equitable selection process, and second, to devise one that would cause minimal disruption to the wartime industrial economy. Crowder and his "key aides," Major Hugh S. Johnson and Capt. Cassius M. Powell, were the chief architects of the organizational scheme of the draft and assisted in guiding the bill though the Congress. Following passage, the two men were responsible for implementing the act. Johnson and Powell designed the mechanism of the plan to facilitate the process of induction. Steps included registration, classification, selection, and concluded with the draftee's ultimate arrival at a reception center, usually the camp closest to the inductee's home.[9]

After making numerous modifications and revisions to the proposed conscription legislation, a reluctant Congress adopted a "compromise version of the bill" on May 18, 1917. The vote was 397 to 24 in the House and 81 to 8 in the Senate. The Selective Service Act authorized the federal government to raise a national army through a national draft. Later that day, President Wilson signed the bill into law. Members of the press dubbed the newly enacted military mobilization plan "Selective Service," short for "selective national conscription." The legislation required all able-bodied adult males from 21 through 30 years of age to register for military service. This included all native-born and naturalized citizens as well as all aliens (citizens of a foreign country) then living in America. The bill stipulated that non-citizens register for the draft, but not all were required to serve (see below).[10]

The act made failure to register or agitation against the draft a criminal offense, subject to severe penalties. On June 1, four days before the first draft registration day, newspapers published a list of draft regulations and informed non-citizens about their obligation under the new law.

It was in June of 1918 that Secretary of War Baker issued a "Work or Fight" order, stating that after July 7, every able-bodied American male in the country would be required to contribute to the war effort. The order stipulated that all draft-age males either be engaged in some form of labor in industry deemed vital to the prosecution of the war or through uniformed service. Failure to do so, the War Department threatened, would make them subject to immediate induction. The decree further stipulated that all draft-eligible men employed in "non-essential occupations," that is not directly associated with the manufacture of military supplies, equipment, and arms or armaments, be required to apply for work in the arms industry. Baker charged General Crowder with executing the order.

* * *

In the months following America's entry into the Great War, President Wilson's administration faced the "Herculean task" of mobilizing, equipping, and training a mass wartime army of several million and then dispatching the force to the battlefields of France in the absolute shortest possible time. The first priority would be to establish training areas to accommodate the new divisions. At this particular time, "the Army had only one facility large enough to train a full division"—Camp Funston, a sub-post of Fort Riley, Kansas. On May 16, 1917, Secretary of War Baker ordered the U.S. Army's Quartermaster Corps to construct 16 new National Army cantonments and 16 National Guard camps. Each new training facility would be large enough to accommodate a "Pershing division," approximately 28,000 men, twice the size of an Allied or German division. Army staff instructed territorial commanders to select thirty-two additional sites for consideration.[11]

In an effort to keep construction costs down, in areas of the U.S. having a warmer climate, primarily the Southern states, Baker decided to limit the number of permanent wood-frame buildings and build "tent cities." In these locations, the Army billeted troops in pyramidal tents with wooden floors and constructed buildings of wood for kitchens and mess halls only. Baker ordered the Quartermaster Corps to begin construction by June 1, with a completion date of September 1, 1917, which officials also set as the occupancy date. Initially, the corps designed each site to accommodate a three-brigade ("triangular") division, the standard configuration under the prewar tables of organization. When Maj. Gen. Tasker H. Bliss, Chief of Staff of the U.S. Army, approved the square division ("two brigades of two regiments") in August, contractors had to modify construction of the camps to house the larger units. "Although the changes delayed completion of the training areas," wrote military historian John B. Wilson, "the troops' arrival date, September 1, remained firm."[12]

* * *

The Selective Service Administration established 4,648 local "registration boards," more commonly referred to as "local draft boards" (4,557 located in the conterminous United States); 155 "supervisory district boards," based on Federal Judicial Districts; and 1,319 medical advisory boards. The function of the local boards was to register and select men of military age for conscription. Selective Service officials "established District Boards, primarily to adjudicate claims for exemption and appeals from local boards." Each district board had jurisdiction over approximately thirty local boards. The latter referred questionable cases of physical disability to the medical boards consisting of "leading medical authorities," which "had the power to either unconditionally accept or reject draftees and volunteers."[13]

The creation of local boards, General Crowder claimed, "put the administration of the draft into the hands of friends and neighbors of the men to be affected." This method of selection, he declared, "was the enunciation of the true democratic doctrine of self-government." Members of the board "were supposed to put a familiar face on federal policy, but outside of the smallest of towns," noted Capozzola, "they tended not to do so." Civilian draft boards, Crowder maintained, would act as a "buffers between the individual citizen and the Federal Government." This statement gave the false impression that board members, because they were, in his opinion, members of the same local community—and supposedly "friends and neighbors" of the men they were to evaluate—would act in a fair manner when determining their draft and or exemption status.[14]

As it turned out, this assumption was hardly the case for a majority of the applicants seeking an exemption. In the first place, draft boards, in almost all instances, were composed exclusively of "native-born white men"—"old stock" Americans—"generally" a mix of county clerks, county sheriffs, lawyers, bankers, businessmen, school teachers, and local physicians responsible for conducting physical examinations. Selective Service officials chose these individuals from lists submitted by state governors. If we use above-average income, education, and occupation as the main indicators, all were members of the upper middle class. As historian Jennifer D. Keene explained, the "composition of these boards put the local professional elite firmly in control of deciding the fate of each community's lower and working class."[15]

Board personnel would oversee the induction and/or deferment of registrants based on overall guidelines established by the draft act legislation. The quota system mandated that local boards draft a percentage of the total eligible population in each district. Administrators proposed that these men, "neighbors of the men being evaluated," would staff each local board, but this was not true for most of the candidates. All-white draft boards "proved more liberal in granting deferments to whites," while denying them to blacks. Historian John Whiteclay Chambers II noted that this was "a result of whites' prejudice and blacks' poverty and lack of industrial jobs that might qualify for deferment." Draft boards "drafted one in three black registrants but only one in four whites."[16]

It is also quite likely that many draft boards discriminated against immigrant registrants as well, considering there had been much anti-immigrant sentiment previously displayed by the American public toward foreigners entering the country. Many Americans had a dismaying history of intolerance. Certainly, there was considerable prejudice against German immigrants and German sympathizers that manifested itself during the war years.

* * *

The Selective Service Act divided immigrants into four broad categories:

1. Diplomatic—Diplomats and other foreign embassy officials were exempt from the draft "since they did not technically reside in the U.S."

2. Declarant—individuals who declared their intention to become U.S. citizens. Declarant aliens included immigrants from friendly nations (see 4) "who had filed their first papers of intention to become citizens and were waiting to fulfill their five-year residency before completing the naturalization process." The act made declarant aliens eligible for the draft because the government felt that these individuals "received the benefits of their adopted country and should, therefore, share the nation's burdens."

3. Non-declarant resident aliens—non-declarant status "applied" to those immigrants "who did not file their papers of intention for citizenship." Technically, non-declarant resident aliens were citizens of their country of origin. The government considered this group "transitory" and therefore technically exempt from conscription "due to their temporary resident status."

4. Enemy aliens—immigrants belonging to one of the belligerent nations or Central Powers: Germany, Austria-Hungary, Bulgaria and Turkey, formerly the Ottoman Empire (see Chapter 5).

Historian Nancy Gentile Ford states that by September 12, 1918, the number of foreign-born immigrant draftees and volunteers who served in the military during World War I numbered 487,434, over 18 percent of the total. This included nearly half a million foreign-born immigrant draftees who served. One source, *Ways of War*, by David J. Ulbrich and Matthew S. Muehlbauer, puts the total at 20 percent, or approximately 600,000. Immigrants, however, made up only 14 percent of the total population. Ford puts the total number of non-declarant neutral aliens who served at 191,491, or 39.28 percent of the total, who "willingly waived their right to exemption and accepted conscription into the U.S. Army." My great-uncle Matthew Guerra was among the latter group.[17]

4

Registration Day

Secretary of War Newton D. Baker designated Tuesday, June 5, 1917, as the official date for the first national draft registration day for all men between the ages of 21 and 32. In a letter to President Wilson, Baker wrote, "I am exceedingly anxious to have the registration and selection by draft conducted by such circumstances as to create a strong patriotic feeling." To that end, the secretary explained to the president that he would instruct draft registration boards to make registration day "a festive and patriotic occasion." Numerous articles in the media prior to the registration date urged America's young men to come forward and do their duty for their country. How Americans would react to the draft, historian Christopher M. Sterba says, "was an open question."[1]

In an attempt to inspire patriotic fervor among the local citizenry, many communities declared the June 5 registration day an official holiday. Schools and businesses closed and many industrial plants and manufacturing companies gave workers the day off. In New York City, Mayor John P. Mirchel's Committee on National Defense scheduled "concerts in parks" and provided small American hand flags for each registration place. On the day prior to the draft, the mayor "instructed every school in the city to conduct a half-hour patriotic ceremony." State governors issued a proclamation ordering all establishments such as restaurants, bars, and taverns to refrain from selling alcoholic beverages during the hours of registration and for retail liquor stores to delay opening until the 9:00 p.m. closing of all draft offices. Parades and public gatherings in cities and towns across the country were commonplace.[2]

The opening of all registration offices began at 7:00 a.m. with a chorus of factory whistles, ship's horns, clanging church bells and, in many communities, the ceremonial firing of cannons from past wars on public commons. Many family members accompanied the young men to designated registration sites. Newspapers in New York City, as well as most other urban areas, reported lines of four to five hundred men in several of the immigrant sections hours before registrars arrived for duty. Small numbers of men camped out on sidewalks at the registration places the evening before so they would be the first to register in their precincts. Historian Jennifer D. Keene wrote, "There was much shoving, pushing, and the occasional fistfight ... over who would receive the honor." Most registrants began showing up beginning at about 6:30 a.m.[3]

* * *

Between 1917 and 1918, the Selective Service Agency conducted three primary and one supplemental draft registrations. The second enrollment took place exactly one year after the first on June 5, 1918, for all men who had turned 21 years of age during the interim period. A third and final primary registration took place on September 12, 1918. Selective Service officials referred to the three primary registration dates as the "Class of June 1917, June 1918, and September 1918," respectively. The supplemental registration took place on August 24, 1918, for those turning 21 years old after June 5, 1918. Prior to September 1918, U.S. involvement escalated, and the number of casualties in France had increased dramatically. The need for additional candidates prompted government officials, in early August, one month before the final registration date, to amend the Selective Service Act expanding the age limits to between 18 and 45 years, inclusive.

According to Jean Nudd, archivist at NARA's regional office in Pittsfield, Massachusetts, the agency used three "slightly different" cards, in formats of ten, twelve, and twenty questions. Boards used the twelve-question cards in 1917, the ten-question card exclusively for the June and August registrations of 1918, and the twenty-question card for the final registration in September 1918. All three registration cards asked for the same basic information:

- Full name
- Home address
- Date and place of birth
- Age, race, and country of citizenship
- Occupation and employer
- Physical description (hair and eye color, height, disabilities)
- Additional information included address of nearest relative, dependent relatives, marital status, father's birthplace, and previous exemption from service

Upon completion, the registrant was required to sign the back of the card. Printed across the lower left-hand triangular corner of the ten- and twelve-question cards was the notation: "If a person is of African descent, tear off this corner."[4]

The *Worcester Evening Gazette* reported that upon completion of the process, registrars issued each enrollee for the first "class" (June 1917) "a blue identifying registration certificate." Subsequent registrations used a different color card. If the police or someone else in authority stopped and questioned a draft-age man and that individual failed to produce the document, he was, according to the article, "liable to arrest and imprisonment."[5]

During the first day of registration, problems arose in many precincts because of the unexpectedly high number of registrants that forced many to stand in line for hours patiently awaiting processing. "Long delays," Sterba noted, "were most common in neighborhoods with predominantly foreign-born residents." Many registrars "had underestimated the large immigrant populations living in their district," resulting in long lines for non–English speaking registrants. One *New York Times* reporter noted that "here and there" he heard some of the men in line "complaining," then added that overall "the crowds were generally good-natured." Historian John J. Newman reported that the "average time" for each registrant to fill out the form was 4 to 15 minutes. In the case of many non–English speaking immigrants, it took considerably longer.[6]

In the weeks and days prior to the June 5 registration day, newspapers around the country published press releases issued by the Selective Service Administration to aid registrants in preparing for the process of registering. One release, titled "Facts About Draft Registration," included a detailed set of instructions for eligible male citizens under the sub-heading: "How to answer questions." Publication of this information enabled immigrants encumbered by the language barrier and cultural differences to seek assistance and guidance from bilingual friends and acquaintances, as well as from local ethnic organizations or social clubs and immigrant aid agencies. Consequently, the *Worcester Telegram* reported, "Many of the men had their answers ready before entering the registration stations which expedited the work."[7]

One of the instructions on the press release warned, "Exemption from military service makes no difference, this will be decided later." All men of draft age were required to register, no matter what their status with regard to eligibility. There were many immigrant men, "aliens," who believed that they were automatically exempt and failed to register. The only exception to this rule, the notice stated, was "men who had already enlisted in the military or Naval service of the United States." Also published in newspapers were numerous editorials and columns expounding "the fairness of conscription and the duty of young men to serve the country during wartime."[8]

At one neighborhood precinct in the city of Worcester, local Attorney John C. Mahoney, one of the registrars, told a reporter for the *Morning Telegram*, "that every race on the face of the globe registered there with the exception of the Japanese." Five Chinese men had registered in another precinct "and each one waived all exemption rights and signified his willingness to go over to France and join in the fight for democracy."[9]

In one of the city's predominantly Irish wards, many expressed sentiments similar to those of one Irishman who remarked he "would gladly go to the trenches and fight alongside of the soldiers of France were it not for the fact that England was mixed up in the war." "Irish-Americans harbored long-standing resentments against Great Britain," Keene explained, "which flared anew after the British brutally suppressed the Irish independent movement during the Easter rebellion in 1916."[10]

Nationwide on June 5, 1917, a total of 9,586,508 men registered for the first phase of the national draft. This number included 1,243,801 (12.97 percent) aliens and 737,626 African Americans. Approximately 2.3 million black men registered for the draft (four registration dates) and 367,000, or 15.96 percent of the total, eventually served.[11]

* * *

Edward Boyle, Central Board Chief for the New York metropolitan area, "saw in the city's ethnic diversity a possible obstacle to the success of registration." In an effort to counteract this perceived impediment, Sterba wrote, the Board Chief "made the presence of foreign language speakers [at each registration place] a top priority." The Central Board's office recruited "more than eight hundred interpreters, many of them naturalized citizens," to be on duty at enrollment sites in ethnic neighborhoods, greatly facilitating the process.[12]

The *New York Times* reported that for Jewish, Italian, German, Hungarian, and Bohemian registrants, "and in all quarters where a single nationality predominated," there was no shortage of translators. The *Times* reporter stated that the majority of foreign-born immigrants "found an interpreter for use in case of need, an official who was willing to explain everything to him and listen patiently to his own statements." As a result, "the work progressed smoothly." In New York, as well as many other major cities, there were shortages of interpreters "for immigrants of minority nationalities," such as those from some of the Asian countries. As a result, there was a long delay for many of these individuals while staff members conducted a search of a particular ethnic neighborhood for bilingual volunteers to translate.[13]

Press releases out of Washington, D.C., on June 6, reported that the Selective Service Office had received several "unofficial reports" acknowledging the occurrence of "a few minor disturbances" at various registration places. Officials claimed, however, that there were "no serious disturbances connected with the registration anywhere in the country."[14]

A breakdown of the number and percentages of men who served in the military in World War I, as provided by military historian Gregory J.W. Urwin, is as follows: conscripts totaled 3,091,000, or 77 percent; Regular Army members 527,000, or 13 percent; and National Guard troops 382,000, or approximately 10 percent. Over the course of the war, the government inducted 2.8 million men into the armed forces, while another 2 million volunteered for service with various branches. Sources estimated that as many as "2 to 3 million men" successfully avoided the draft by failing to register and that "338,000 (12 percent of those drafted) failed to report when called or deserted after arrival at training camp."[15]

* * *

On June 5, 1917, Matthew Guerra registered for the draft at Precinct 10 in Bridgeport. According to Guerra's draft card, his address was 56 Crescent Avenue and he worked at (Remington) "U.M.C. Co." as a "laborer." Matthew was 21 years of age, "Date of birth, Feb. 10, 1896." Marital status, "single" with "no dependents," "Race? Caucasian," "Height? medium," "Build? medium," "Color of eyes? Brown," "Color of hair? Brown." He signed his name to verify that the answers provided were "true."[16]

One question arises. Could Guerra have been eligible for a draft deferment because of his employment at Remington Arms Company? Could he have been classified as essential to the war effort? It is quite likely that he was eligible for a deferment. In June 1917, the "local machinists' union" led a strike "in sympathy" with the plant's "metal polishers," who were "demanding an eight-hour workday" and "elimination of the company's piece-rate system." President Wilson "subsequently outlawed the strike, threatening to blacklist the strikers and remove their draft deferments." All evidence points to two possible scenarios: that Guerra allowed his local draft board to induct him, or he enlisted voluntarily. Matthew was ineligible for induction because he had not applied for U.S. citizenship and could also have received an exemption as a non-declarant alien. He was an alien, technically a citizen of Italy. As such, he was therefore under no obligation to serve.[17]

5

Selection of the Candidates

On Tuesday, June 5, 1917, eligible candidates for the draft lottery registered nationwide at designated registration sites, mostly former polling places, for the first phase of the national draft. Upon completing the process, registrars assigned each man a "draft number" in the order of his enrollment. Beginning in the fall, those men holding designated numbers received a red card in the mail that read in part, "From the date herein specified, you will be in the military service of the United States and subject to military law." Draft boards around the country mailed out notification cards ordering the men holding one of the selected numbers to appear in person to substantiate their eligibility status and to undergo an examination by a board physician to determine if they were physically fit for service.[1]

Eight days later, on July 13, officials in Washington issued a press release announcing that the initial call-up ("first levy") by the War Department would be 687,000 men. This total represented the number "needed to fill the war strength of the regular army and National Guard and to constitute the first increment of the national army." "Estimating that it would take two registrants for every soldier accepted," the Selective Service Office needed to call "1,374,000 men ... for examination" in order "to secure that total." Officials based district quotas on population figures provided by the Census Bureau. Each county imposed its own draft quotas.[2]

The drawing of the first Selective Service lottery numbers took place in the hearing room of the U.S. Senate office building in Washington, D.C., on July 20, 1917. From this list, the War Department compiled a national order of selection ("order of call") among the 9,506,508 young men registered for service nationwide. Local draft boards would be in charge of selecting or exempting these individuals from military service. Secretary of War Newton D. Baker presided over the drawing, designed to rank eligible candidates. In attendance were Judge Advocate General Enoch H. Crowder, along with several senators, congressmen, government leaders, and other prominent officials, as well as a gallery of spectators. Blindfolded, Baker reached into a large glass jar filled with 10,500 capsules containing the individual numbers. This total represented the maximum number of registrants in a single district. At the very moment the secretary reached into the bowl, the room was ablaze with the bright lights from newsreel and still cameras recording the historic event.[3]

Baker pulled out the first capsule containing the number 258 to a chorus of loud cheers. The individual in each district holding that number would be the first man called, the next number second, and so on. The lottery continued throughout the day and late into the early morning hours (2:18 a.m.) until all the numbers were drawn. Selective Service officials telegraphed the results to draft boards around the country. Local boards provided local newspapers with a list of the names of all eligible men for publication, making them a matter of public record.[4]

By war's end, the Selective Service administration had effectively registered 23.9 million men and, of that number, drafted 2.8 million men. Approximately 2 million more voluntarily enlisted, "mainly in the Navy." This brought the total number of men who served to over 4.8 million men, nearly 15 percent of the American male population. "Overall," Historian Jennifer D. Keene claims, "20 percent of the draft-eligible male population (aged 18–45) served in the military." More than one million men saw combat or served as supply and support troops in rear areas along the Western Front.[5]

* * *

Responsibility for selection, exemption, or deferment of men holding one of the selected numbers fell to the state governments. Draft boards mailed notification cards ("NOTICE TO APPEAR FOR PHYSICAL EXAMINATION," Form 1009—PMGO) to the candidates holding one of the designated numbers. The notice ordered the selectees to appear at their district draft board office at a specific date and time to undergo an examination by a board-certified physician to determine if they were physically and/or mentally fit for induction. When a non–English-speaking alien received the card in the mail, he would either have a bilingual friend or other person explain the instructions or, possibly, go directly to the board office for assistance.[6]

One of the problems encountered by many boards was that English-speaking registrars filling out the cards, who were unfamiliar with foreign languages or had difficulty understanding someone who spoke with a thick accent, "wrote what he or she heard," noted historian John J. Newman. This resulted, in many instances, in the misspelling of names and addresses. Consequently, a substantial number of immigrants failed to receive their notices in the mail.[7]

The Selective Service System Act of May 18, 1917, consisted of five major draft classifications:

> Class I—all men qualified for immediate service.
> Class II—temporary deferment for married men without children.
> Class III—deferment for skilled workers in industry or agriculture and certain occupations and professions.
> Class IV—married men with children or economic dependents; and key business leaders and non-declarant aliens until they filed for exemptions.
> Class V—those unable to meet physical or mental requirements; and persons convicted of a felony, treason, or other crime of an "infamous" nature, and enemy aliens (as defined in Chapter 3).
> Classes II–V "were known as the deferred classes."[8]

The Notice of Classification card mailed to registrants provided instructions for men filing an appeal for an exemption:

> Appeals may be taken from classification by a Local Board, within five days from the date of this notice, by any person who filed a claim with this Local Board.... To file an appeal it is only necessary to go to the office of the Local Board and write your claim of appeal in the place provided on the registrant's questionnaire.

Deferments for men with dependents were "based on family support needs; if someone else was able to support family members, [or] if a man had children or how recently he had married." Administrators were concerned, with good reason, that some individuals would rush to a Justice of the Peace to prevent induction. After exhausting Class I, boards would call registrants from Class II, III, and IV, in the direct order of their avalibility.[9]

"Enemy aliens," historian Nancy Gentile Ford defined as "both declarant and non-declarant immigrants from enemy nations"—known as the "Central Powers" or the "Quadruple Alliance," consisting of Germany, Austria-Hungary, Turkey, and Bulgaria. These individuals, she explained, "could not be compelled to serve since they would be put in a position of fighting their own countrymen." Board administrators placed enemy aliens, forbidden to fight, in Class V, unless and until they renounced their foreign citizenship. The regulations required all former citizens of one of the enemy nations to register their names with the Justice Department's Enemy Alien Bureau (EAB).[10]

* * *

Foreign-born immigrant soldiers represented over 17.4 percent of the total wartime force in World War I, "even though the foreign-born were only 14.5 percent of the overall American population," noted historian Jennifer D.

Keene. This percentage represented 487,434 immigrants out of 2.5 million men in the military, approximately one in five. The high number of foreign troops, Keene says, reflected "the waves of heavy immigration to the United States in the years immediately leading up to the war." Ford noted that "thousands" of second-generation ethnic Americans, sons of immigrant parents, also served. There are no concrete figures for the latter group.[11]

According to a February 16, 1919, *New York Times* article, a majority of the immigrants who registered "could not speak, read, write, or clearly understand the English language." Many foreign-born soldiers "had mastered only the basics of reading at an elementary school level" and so "were merely 'technically literate.'"[12]

Historian David M. Kennedy wrote, "So polyglot were the American armed forces that some Europeans spoke deprecatingly of the 'American Foreign Legion.'" One French soldier, quoted by Keene, wrote about the composition of the American army in a letter to his family:

> You could not imagine a more extraordinary gathering than this American army. There is a bit of everything, some Greeks, some Italians, some Turks, some Chinese, some Indians [from India], some Spanish, and also a reasonable number of Huns. Truthfully, almost half of the officers have German origins. This doesn't seem to bother them. But doesn't this seem to you a strange outlook?

The Frenchman's final remark, "As for me, I could hardly see myself fighting against my country, even if I had left it a long time ago."[13]

In General Crowder's final report of February 16, 1919, he quoted the observations of a German officer from the man's diary left behind on the battlefield, who also noted the complexity of ethnic diversity among the ranks of the American Army: "Only a few of the troops are of pure American origin; the majority are of German, Dutch, and Italian parentage," he wrote. "But these semi-Americans," the German officer added, "fully feel themselves to be true-born sons of their country." Crowder prefaced the enemy soldier's remarks with the following statement:

> The great and inspiring revelation here has been that men of foreign and of native origin alike responded to the call to arms with a patriotic devotion that confounded the cynical plans of our arch-enemy and surpassed our own highest expectations.... America has fulfilled one of its highest missions in breeding a spirit of common loyalty among all those who have shared the blessings of life on its free soil.

Crowder closed, "No need to speculate how it has come about; the great fact is demonstrated that America makes Americans."[14]

* * *

Matthew Guerra registered for the draft in Bridgeport, Connecticut, on June 5, 1918. Each registrant was technically responsible for filling out his own card. Having lived in America for nearly six years, it is quite likely he had a good command of the English language when speaking. However, his ability to read and write English may have been limited. Evidence exists to show that Guerra, as well as many other immigrants who were unable to read and/or write, did not personally fill in the answers in the spaces provided. Selective Service officials instructed registrars to fill in the answers for illiterate or semi-illiterate persons if the situation warranted. In most of these cases, the registrar enlisted the help of a volunteer interpreter to translate the questions and assist in filling out the cards.

Guerra filled out a twelve-question draft registration card. Question No. 4 regarding citizenship status reads, "Are you (1) a natural born citizen (2) a naturalized citizen (3) have you declared your intention (specify which)?" He answered, "Alien," on the line provided, indicating he had not "declared" his intention to become an American citizen. It is likely the registrar instructed him to do so in this manner. On Question No. 9, he stated that he had no relatives "solely dependent on [him] for support" and acknowledged on No. 10 that he was "single." Question 12 reads, "Do you claim exemption from draft (specify grounds)?" Guerra answered specifically, "No," indicating that he waived his right to an exclusion of any kind.[15]

Guerra signed below the printed statement at the bottom front affirming that the answers given were true. The Registrar, one "Benjamin Factor," signed the back of the card, acknowledging that he witnessed the signature of the registrant and that to his knowledge the above answers provided were true. My amateur analysis of the handwriting indicates that Factor had filled out the answers and that Guerra affixed his signature to the card.[16]

There is a very good likelihood that by this time it was Guerra's intention to make the United States his permanent home and eventually file for citizenship status. He had been residing in the country since July 1912. This decision may have caused him to feel he had obligation or responsibility to fight for his adopted country in time of war. Were there other factors that may have influenced his decision to waive the non-declarant exemption? Had he taken advantage of the exemption and stayed at home, would he have been labeled a "draft dodger" by members of the community?

My thoughts drifted to what a young and idealistic Guerra might have been thinking at this particular time in his life. Did he feel, rather naively, that he was about to embark on some "grand" or "great adventure," like many impressionable young men his age. Almost daily, there were accounts in the press glorifying the daring exploits and acts of courage and heroism by America's soldiers in battle. Guerra was soon to discover otherwise.

6

Deferments and Exemptions
The Non-Declarant Alien Dilemma

All registered persons remained subject to the draft unless their local draft board granted an exemption or excused them on other grounds. Of the 23.9 million men who enrolled, over 65 percent eventually received a deferment from military service. Historian Christopher Capozzola reported that Selective Service inducted "just 12 percent of the men who registered." This low percentage figure was due in part to the signing of the Armistice on November 11, 1918, just two months after the final registration of September 12, 1918, sparing a considerable number of those who had registered on that date from ending up overseas.[1]

When it came to deciding deferments and exemptions, the Selective Service Act gave local boards "broad discretion" and "a great deal of latitude" while providing "relatively little guidance." "This discretion," wrote historian Raymond H. Banks, "led to wide divergence in interpretations." "On the other hand," he added, the concept of "local decision-making" was what initially "helped assure support for the draft system." Secretary of War Newton D. Baker "intended" draft boards "to be responsive to local conditions"; however, as author David M. Kennedy pointed out, "they were also susceptible to local political pressures, and not immune to local prejudices." The results were, he noted, that a number of "inequities inevitably arose from poorly guided discretionary powers of the boards."[2]

Selective Service regulations required that local boards "give every alien a 'full and fair' hearing concerning any draft exemptions." According to Capozzola, many boards conscripted a considerable number of aliens "against both their will and the terms of the Selective Service Act." Presumably, board members often did this in order to meet mandatory monthly quotas, while in many instances sparing men with political or family ties, or other influential connections (see below).[3]

It was the "widespread popular belief" of many local board members, wrote historian Nancy Gentile Ford, that all aliens "should be forced to serve in the army," and "[c]ongressional resolutions and hearings also echoed these opinions." According to historian Jennifer D. Keene, "In their zeal to ensure that all aliens served, local boards ended up over-drafting the immigrant population." Despite these accusations, the number of requests for exclusion from the draft, Christopher M. Sterba says, "was large." The Central Board of New York City reported on June 8, 1917, "that close to half of the 610,000 registered men claimed exemption," and that "the defining factor in this tendency" was "citizenship status."[4]

Each local draft board district set up a volunteer "three-man exemption-determination board," usually with a physician serving as one of the members. The primary function of the panel was "to inquire into the status of any registrant whom they believed eligible for draft exemption." To best accomplish this, many local boards, especially those in cities heavily populated by immigrants, "hired" bilingual interpreters, "'men of foreign race stock,' and social welfare workers," who supposedly had a full understanding of exemption rules and regulations. These individuals, in the opinion of Provost Marshal General Enoch H. Crowder, "took pains to inform the ignorant and protect the helpless." One of Crowder's primary duties was to administer the Selective Service Law. Major dailies and the Sunday editions of newspapers across the country, as well as foreign-language newsprint publications, widely publicized the existence of the exemption and the process of securing one. At the time, this was a very controversial issue presumably widely discussed among the immigrant population, who had to be aware of their rights and obligations under the act.[5]

Despite these provisions and safeguards, Ford contends that "numerous mix-ups did occur," resulting in "the erroneous registration of non-declarants into the Class I status" and their subsequent induction. Ford states that Selective Service officials "blamed administrative errors, overzealous local boards caught up in the 'slacker spirit,' and the ignorance of the aliens themselves for the oversights." Local boards sometimes used the term "slacker" to identify those who failed to register for the draft, and in many cases included non-declarant aliens who were automatically exempt.[6]

Local boards had the power within their respective jurisdictions over the initial disposition of non-declarant aliens. Even though the Conscription Act (May 18, 1917) provided "for their exemption automatically," it required these men to register and to "present their claims to the proper boards in compliance with the rules provided." Those sections of the act pertaining to exemption claims by non-declarants were extremely complicated and difficult for the average person to comprehend, let alone someone with limited English capabilities. Selective Service officials left the burden of proof regarding eligibility status up to the immigrant himself. How the alien would be able "to prove that he had never filed his 'first papers' [application for citizenship] was not made clear," wrote Ford.[7]

One example of a board's discretion, provided by Kennedy, was the liberal interpretation of the provision in the law that exempted men with dependents—wives, children, and extended family. A large number of Americans, as well as many immigrants, claimed an exemption on these grounds. Sterba pointed out, "Since the draft took no one under the age of 21, it was hard to find men who were not already bread winners for their families." The act also provided deferments for men who "were the sole support of needy dependents" and for industrial and agricultural workers "whose skills were deemed essential to the war effort," as well.[8]

Some boards "construed" the marriage provision as giving members the right "to grant deferments to virtually all married men." This was a "practice," Kennedy remarked, "that launched a nuptial boomlet in some communities." Of the total number of applications for deferment on these grounds, noted Keene, local boards awarded 43 percent, "the largest portion," generally, "to married men who were the sole providers of their families."[9]

Technically, a board could rescind a man's dependency exemption if it ruled that the individual arranged the marriage for the specific purpose of evading the draft, based primarily on the date of the ceremony. Another factor that influenced a board's decision was that a husband was not providing adequate support to his wife and dependent children. In "the absence of a uniform national standard, the induction rate of married men," according to Kennedy, "varied throughout the several states from 6 to 38 percent," a considerable divergence. Deferments for married men, non-declarants, and enemy aliens placed an added burden on the ability of local boards to meet strict district quotas. As a result, this draft deferment forced boards, in many instances, to skirt the rules and regulations and draft ineligible registrants, including many not physically fit. Army doctors discovered the discrepancies when these men reached the camps and immediately ordered them home.[10]

* * *

Section 18 of the Selective Service law stated that non-declarant aliens needed to obtain a sworn "affidavit" before a notary public or other person authorized to administer an oath, attesting to the fact that he had not signed his preliminary citizenship papers. No public official would sign off on this stipulation on a man's word alone without proof positive which, under the circumstances, was impossible to obtain. Second, the act required that non-declarants present this document to an exemption panel at their local daft board office within five days of receiving their "NOTICE OF CLASSIFICATION." Every person applying for an exemption or deferment had to fill out a twelve-page "registrant's questionnaire" (Form 1001), as part of the appeal process. "Primarily," the forms, according to Selective Service regulations, "consisted of":

> a number of questions, divided into 12 series of questions (addressed to and to be answered under oath by every registrant), designed for the purpose of ascertaining the status of every registrant in relation to the various matters, things, and circumstances constituting ground for exemption or deferred classification. The Questionnaires shall also contain, as an integral part thereof, certificates and affidavits in support of claims.

The first page of the document contained "a place for the registrant ... to claim exemption or deferred classification and a place for a waiver by the registrant." All answers and affidavits had to be "sworn to in strict accordance" with the "regulations and in strict conformity with the particular rules and instructions relating to the several series of questions."[11]

Keene describes the above mentioned "registrant's questionnaire" as "a daunting" twelve-page document "that was often beyond the capabilities of recent immigrants with imperfect English skills or barely literate workers or farmers." Many, she says, were "unknowledgeable about Selective Service regulations" and "often found themselves caught up in the net of the draft" (see below).[12]

The Selective Service regulations required that draft boards mail the questionnaires to each registrant whose name appeared on the classification list in its respective jurisdiction within twenty days. If a board mailed the questionnaire and for some reason the registrant did not receive the document, possibly due, for example, to a misspelled name, or an incorrect or changed address, that did "not excuse" that person, the regulations stated emphatically, "from responding within the time limit." Neither was it grounds for an extension of time. A number of ethnic groups and organizations in New York City, Sterba reported, opened "facilities for helping immigrant men fill out their exemption request forms." No single ethnic group, he noted, set up as many places for providing assistance as the Jewish community.[13]

Section 95 of the Selective Service Regulations contained a list of requirements titled: "Manner and form of answers to Questionnaires, supporting affidavits, and other proof," that a local or district board required a registrant or person seeking an exemption to provide. The following is a partial list of the instructions contained therein:

    1. "None of the printed portions of any of the questions shall be struck out or erased."

    2. "If registrant can not read, and the questions are read to him and filled out by some other person, all said questions and his answers thereto shall be read over to him by the officer who administers the oath to him

before he signs and swears to the same, and if the registrant cannot write, his cross-mark signature to his answers and to his affidavit must all be witnessed by the same officer."

Every person supplying a supporting affidavit or other written proof "must read every question and every answer to the particular series of questions which he is supporting. All blanks in the supporting affidavits must be filled out in the handwriting of the person making the affidavit."

3. "The persons making a supporting affidavit must insert in the proper blank spaces the number of every answer which he swears to be true, and ... believes to be true."

"All affidavits and other proof (not an integral part of the Questionnaire) filed by the registrant ... in support of any claim for exemption or discharge, ... must be legibly written or typewritten on one side only of white paper of the approximate length, but no longer than a page of the Questionnaire."

It is easy to see why many immigrants with limited or no English skills, even with the help of a translator, could feel threatened and intimidated by this set of extremely complicated and certainly confusing requirements.[14]

The administrative procedure for securing a non-declarant exemption was unduly burdensome and a hindrance to most non–English-speaking foreign-born immigrants or those with limited English skills to respond effectively. This process, without a doubt, stymied individual efforts to comply, resulting in the failure of a considerable number of foreign-born immigrants to file on time or at all, thereby nullifying the possibility of obtaining an exemption they were entitled to under the act. The regulations stated that they were "automatically exempt," yet, on the other hand, the ruling forced them to negotiate a number of bureaucratic hurdles in order to be designated exempt. "Conscription in a multiethnic nation," Ford wrote, "did not come without confusion and debate."[15]

A number of boards around the country routinely drafted ineligible non-declarant aliens. It is doubtful that board members, especially in the inner cities where most immigrants lived, notified every registrant that it was his responsibility to apply for the non-declarant exemption. This fact is borne out by evidence found in the historical record. Nor does it appear that board personnel clearly spelled out a registrant's rights or bothered to take the time, considering existing conditions on registration day, to inform them of the procedure they were required to follow to register a claim. Embassy officials from of a number of foreign governments appeared before Judge Advocate General Crowder in September 1917, to request an investigation into the cases of non-declarant aliens wrongly ordered to report to training camps by their draft board. Crowder immediately issued a cautionary note by telegram to local boards countrywide, insisting that registrars "be very careful and thorough in informing those registrants who appeared to be aliens of their right to file claim for exemption on that ground." Crowder further advised the boards "that in cases where it appeared ... through ignorance, aliens had failed to file claims for exemption the local board should extend the time or reopen the case if necessary."[16]

On this subject, Keene explained that on numerous occasions, "over-eager boards scooped up non-declarant immigrants," to meet the district's compulsory quota. This "practice," she claims, led "to protests from a few thousand men who contested their induction." "Most misunderstandings," Ford reported, "came about because of language barriers." By early 1918, many non-declarants, wrongfully or otherwise mistakenly serving in the U.S. Army at the time, contacted their respective embassies in Washington seeking diplomatic intervention. Embassy officials considered the practice of drafting non-declarants "a violation of international law and existing treaty obligations, which forbade the drafting of aliens from neutral countries regardless of an immigrants' intention to become a citizen." Ford reported that a total of "5,852" non-declarants filed diplomatic protests with the U.S. State Department with regards to their unlawful induction. Many immigrants sought assistance from the American Union Against Militarism (AUAM), predecessor of the American Civil Liberties Union (ACLU).[17]

Between May and October of 1918, more than 6,000 non-declarant aliens applied for discharge with the Selective Service office in Washington. "By the end of the war," Ford noted, "the Army had discharged 1,842 men 'on the grounds of alienage or upon diplomatic request.'" There were, no doubt, many more who would have liked to file a formal complaint with their embassies or the U.S. State Department, but had not done so for a variety of reasons. One of the most prevalent was the fact that these individuals could not read or write English. There was at the time extensive media coverage of the non-declarant conscription problem.[18] Many, despite the publicity, were still unaware or probably thought it was the longest of long shots and would hardly be worth the effort.

President Wilson, concerned over the diplomatic furor caused by the controversy, issued a proclamation dated April 11, 1918, ordering the immediate discharge of all diplomatic request cases from the military. On May 9, 1918, less than one month after the president's edict, the Congress enacted several amendments to existing naturalization laws, which offered citizenship to both declarant and non-declarant aliens, including those from enemy nations ("enemy aliens") then serving in the U.S. armed forces. The process eliminated the filing of a preliminary declaration of intention, the 5-year residency requirement, and the necessity of taking the Oath of Allegiance in an authorized district court serving their home community. It is possible that the War Department wanted to have these men sworn in as citizens before they had a chance to do something about their situation that would obtain their immediate release from service.[19]

War Department officials directed commissioned officers at the camps to assist interested applicants in filling out the necessary paperwork, but cautioned them "not to 'use coercive or persuasive measures' to assure the citizenship of immigrants in their ranks." Beginning on May 8, camp officials across the country held hundreds of naturalization ceremonies where immigrant soldiers took the oath before a visiting District Court judge authorized to administer the Oath of Allegiance to support the Constitution. When the government made this "liberalized naturalization process" available to aliens, according to Sterba, 280,000 (sources vary) foreign-born soldiers took advantage of the opportunity. While a "few thousand" foreign-born draftees "contested their conscription in court or requested aid from their embassies, the vast majority," he noted, "responded positively to the Selective Service call." Of "the 487,434 immigrant draftees, nearly 200,000 were non-declared aliens who waived their right of exemption" and served willingly.[20]

Ford noted "that from May 8, through November 30, 1918, 155,246 immigrant soldiers" in the U.S. opted to participate in the government's revised naturalization program, "along with an indeterminate number overseas" (this likely accounts for the discrepancy between this number and the 200,000). On July 9, 1918, Congress agreed to waive the service requirement of "declarant neutrals" if they agreed to withdraw their intention of becoming a U.S. citizen and to discharge those already inducted. Such a course of action was not without penalty. If a declarant decided to withdraw his intention of becoming a United States citizen, he would "be forever debarred" from reapplying for citizenship status. Only "2,035 neutral declarants," Ford says, "withdrew their intention to become ... citizens." Although not officially included in this congressional stipulation, the War Department "extended this practice to declarant immigrants already inducted," as well.[21]

"Despite this way out," Ford says, "tens of thousands of non-declarant and enemy aliens ... decided to remain in the U.S. Army." Provost Marshal General Crowder was confident that these amendments would result "in the conversion of the 'Foreign Legion' of the Army of the United States into a host of loyal American citizen-soldiers."[22]

It appears that the relaxation of citizenship requirements to expedite the process at this particular time was a strategic move by the government to provide an incentive for those eligible for the discharge to remain in the service rather than opt for an immediate release. The army had already trained and equipped the majority of these men and many units were ready or near ready to ship out as badly needed replacements in France. My great-uncle Matthew Guerra was one of those who appeared to have responded positively to the call to duty. On June 25, 1918, he was among a group of soldiers sworn in as United States citizens by a Massachusetts District Court judge at Camp Devens. Guerra shipped out to France on July 8, 1918, less than two weeks later. Records indicate that he never declared his intent to become a citizen of the United States, which he attested to on his draft registration card, nor did not file for the non-declarant exemption. Several questions remain. Did the registrar inform him of his right to the exemption, and explain all of his options? Could he have not been aware of the exclusion? Living in Bridgeport, a metropolis with an unusually high immigrant population, this is highly unlikely.

*　*　*

The ineligibility status of non-declarant immigrants and enemy aliens, Ford argues, resulted in the conscription of a disproportionate number of native-born Americans and declarant aliens. This was particularly true in the Northeast and Midwest. Washington later "redefined quotas" for those sections of the country "to accommodate areas with high concentrations of immigrant residents." Keene wrote, "Anger that immigrants had migrated to benefit from the economic opportunities available in the United States, yet then refused to serve in the military, bolstered anti-immigrant feelings prevalent in some inner cities."[23]

Expressions of discontent by the public over the situation eventually reached the press, local conscription boards, Congress, and the Selective Service Administration. People began to question why "the draft-exempt 'alien slackers' were able to live comfortably in America while native-born men were risking their lives in France," Sterba wrote. A reporter for the *New York Sun*, quoted by Keene, remarked, "The apparent injustices of stripping the land of American youths to furnish a fighting force in Europe while leaving millions of aliens at home to enjoy the rewards of peaceful industry has undoubtedly got on people's nerves." This statement reflected the rising sentiment against immigrants who were not obligated to serve.[24]

Over the course of the war, Selective Service headquarters received thousands of letters "alleging slackerism or disloyalty on the part of neighbors, colleagues, and even family members," wrote Capozzola. The *New York Times* reported government officials receiving numerous tips from women in many communities, especially those with husbands, fiancés, or relatives, serving at the front. These, he emphasized, had "been particularly helpful in ferreting out young men who failed to register."[25]

As the war progressed, resentment over this delicate issue began to snowball. Congress, "under pressure from the public sector, made several attempts to pass legislation making all aliens, regardless of their status, liable for the draft," wrote Ford. If these individuals were unwilling to serve, many legislators advocated immediate deportation. Efforts by the Congress to enact such a measure ultimately proved unsuccessful, and the issue remained highly contentious throughout the remainder of the war.[26]

Many immigrants had been unaware of the regulations regarding the exemption guidelines, and boards failed to inform them of their rights. To meet each month's quota, a number of district boards drafted many of these men anyway while sparing others with influential friends or family. As the number of deaths in France mounted, anger and resentment over this delicate issue continued to build. "Seeing multitudes of able-bodied men walking the streets of every American city provoked a sense of injustice among the relatives of those serving overseas," Keene wrote. The number of immigrant men in the military who had been wrongfully drafted was substantial. Many were unaware of the regulations, and so did not file for the exemption to which they were entitled.[27]

7

Welcome to Camp Upton

On Friday, April 26, 1918, the 22-year old Matthew Guerra was among a group of 321 draftees who reported to the 10th Precinct Draft Board office in Bridgeport, Connecticut, for induction into the U.S. Army. The inductees represented Bridgeport's quota to the second national draft. Following the registration process and swearing-in ceremony, an officer escorted the group to the Golden Hill Street Railway Station. Here, the group boarded a special New York, New Haven & Hartford Railroad (commonly known as the New Haven R.R.) passenger train bound for New York City, the first leg of their trip to Camp Upton at Yaphank (part of the town of Brookhaven) on Long Island.

When the train to transport the boys to the camp finally arrived "with about 400" of "their future comrades in arms" from points east aboard, the cheering and shouting by the Bridgeport draftees "redoubled in intensity." A detail of "about 40 policemen" were on duty to keep the crowd back until the train pulled in, and "in this way," the reporter commented, "roll calling" was "greatly facilitated."[1]

Hundreds of people—family members, friends, city officials, and a host of onlookers—gathered at the train depot to see the men off and bid them farewell. The gala send-off celebration included speeches by prominent city officials, local politicians, and other dignitaries who were full of praise for the young men, calling them "true patriots." Clifford B. Wilson, Bridgeport's mayor, thanked the group for heeding the call to serve their country in this time of need. A brass band played "Hail, Hail the Gang's All Here," "Keep the Home Fires Burning," "The Star-Spangled Banner," and a selection of other patriotic songs and anthems.[2]

An air of excitement and electricity resonated among members of the crowd.

Among the group of well-wishers was Matthew Guerra's sister Lena and brother-in-law Joe La Torre, who were on hand to say their goodbyes. At the time, Matthew lived with the La Torres in Bridgeport and worked at the Remington Arms Company/U.M.C. Lena, her eyes wet with tears, embraced and kissed her baby brother and whispered for him to take good care of himself. Joe La Torre placed his hand on his brother-in-law's shoulder in a gesture of support and reassurance, firmly shook his hand, hugged him, and said his farewells. It would be the last time the couple would see Matthew alive.

The April 26, 1918, evening edition of the *Bridgeport Post* contained an article describing the entrainment event. The headline, in bold print, read, "5,000 SEE BOYS IN DRAFT LEAVE FOR CAMP UPTON." A scribe for the *Post* (unsigned article) reported that there was "an intense feeling of patriotism" among the departing draftees and the crowd of well-wishers who gathered on the platform at Bridgeport's railway station to see the group off to camp. Among the inductees who entrained for Camp Upton, the article reported, there was a "Snap, ginger, 'pep,' fighting spirit, and that good old 'we'll give 'em hell when we get there' feeling, … to be found in superabundance." According to the reporter, while waiting for the special train to arrive, "Bridgeport's sons showed the real American spirit" as they "laughed and chatted, sang and cheered." The crowd, "carried away by the enthusiasm of the drafted boys responded in kind."[3]

When the conductor announced that the train would be departing the station in ten minutes, the enthusiastic crowd cheered wildly. Family members and friends wished the boys good luck and Godspeed. There were "traces of tears" among "the mothers, sisters, wives and sweethearts assembled on the platform to bid their loved ones goodbye." The reporter continued, "In most of these cases, the cheerful and brave hearted smile was struggling to break through the curtain of grief." The *Post* reported "two cases of hysteria" among family members bidding loved ones adieu.[4]

Fathers stood stoically, trying hard not to reveal their true emotions. With a faint smile of approval, they proudly shook their boys' hands and embraced them briefly. Just before the recruits boarded the Pullman cars, Red Cross workers presented each man with a "comfort bag" containing stationery, a lead pencil, candy, tobacco, comb, toothbrush, small round mirror, pocketknife, and other personal items. After the train departed the station, railroad porters went up and down the aisles distributing "boxed lunches" for the journey.

As the locomotive pulled slowly away from the station, many of the men were hanging precariously out of windows and on the open platforms separating the coaches, waving and cheering enthusiastically to a sea of white handkerchiefs and small American flags. Many of these young men were leaving home for the first time in their lives.

With all the hullabaloo of the gala farewells given to these parting recruits by the people of their home cities and towns, it is little wonder that many began to think of themselves as "somewhat of a hero," wrote author and "amateur war correspondent" Frazier Hunt. The thought "that they were on a great and glorious adventure" had begun to register in their minds. He went on to explain: "They were starting down a new trail to a new life that has the magic thrill of the unknown. They were going forth to adventure, and behind them were the shops and factories and stores and offices and all the life they had known for their twenty-one or thirty-one years." The troop trains that transported them to the camps, Hunt closed, "seemed like nothing so much as football specials on their way to the great game of the season."[5]

Once the recruits settled in, many lit up cigarettes, cigars, and pipes, filling the coaches with a thick pall of acrid, pungent smoke. In each car a number of small cliques formed with the men sharing talk and cigarettes. Some of the recruits took bottles and flasks of whiskey or other alcoholic beverage from inside coat pockets, downed a hearty swig, and passed them around. Here and there, a card game broke out and soon the betting began in earnest. All along the line, the train made stops at every station to pick up each municipality's quota of young draftees.

It must have been quite a sight for many of the recruits when the train made its approach to New York City from the north across the East River. The inbound train traveled over the elevated tracks through the city's crowded, bustling neighborhoods lined with shops and other commercial establishments before entering the Park Avenue tunnel to the magnificent new Grand Central Terminal in Midtown Manhattan, which opened on February 2, 1913. By the time the train arrived, the coaches were crowded with wildly cheering would-be heroes, many of them inebriated. For the majority of the recruits, it was their first look at the incredible expanse of the New York metropolitan area, the skyscrapers of the Manhattan skyline, and the other sights and sounds of the great city.

At Grand Central Station the group disembarked and boarded the eastbound subway line for the trip through the Belmont (Steinway) Tunnel under the East River to Long Island City, the westernmost neighborhood of the New York City borough of Queens. At the Long Island City Terminal, the group climbed aboard a Long Island Railroad passenger train for Camp Upton, sixty miles distant. Upton was the home of the 77th "Statue of Liberty" or "Metropolitan" Division, consisting of recruits from the New York metro area, including New York City's five boroughs, Long Island, and several Hudson River counties. The Long Island cantonment, besides being a training facility for inductees from metro New York, served also as a reception and processing center for the overflow of draftees from other regions of the northeast.

* * *

7. Welcome to Camp Upton

Upon arrival at the Camp Upton Railroad Station, the draftees piled out onto the platform. A contingent of officers and noncoms (noncommissioned officers with a grade of corporal or sergeant) were on hand to meet the train and greet the group as they disembarked. A sergeant lined the men up into some semblance of a military formation for a roster check.

The recruits came from every walk of life—professionals, nonprofessionals, laborers, the unemployed, college students, and many young men just out of high school, among others—as well as from every class of society. Adjutant General of the Army John H. Gregory instructed camp commanders to conduct a census of religions and nationalities at each of the cantonments. According to the final report, the inductees represented more than forty nationalities and "sixty-seven different religious groups." The most prominent religions, based on the Camp Gordon report, included 41.9 percent Catholic, 14.2 percent Methodist, 11.1 percent Baptist, 7.3 percent Jewish, and 18.2 percent "other." The Gordon report also listed "twenty-four soldiers as atheists, and six as pagans." A survey at Camp Upton listed "forty-three different nationalities" among the troops of the 77th Division.[6]

A considerable number of the new recruits were foreign immigrants who spoke very little or no English. "Interpreters," historian Norval Dwyer wrote, "had to be culled from the crowd [of new arrivals] immediately." These men assisted with the roll call and translation of verbal orders and instructions. Posted throughout the camp, however, were notices "that all commands were to be given in English" (see below).[7]

The majority of the new recruits had arrived in old tattered clothing and hats, as per notification by their local draft boards. "Some of the more naïve appeared destined for some sort of elegant spa," wrote author Alan D. Gaff. "Everyone carried valises, grips, suitcases, or hastily folded bundles of necessities." "Despite an admonition" by the draft boards "to come attired in old clothes," a number of the men arrived all decked out in "dinner jackets, Palm Beach suits, and ... Sunday-go-to-meeting outfits," wearing shirts with "starched collars," while others had on "silk stockings," he declared in amazement. These men wore a wide variety of hats including, Gaff exclaimed, "Panamas, smashed derbies, and top hats that looked as if they had been stolen from corpses." One "Victor Catarino," he noted, "a Harlem barber, came directly from an all-night wedding reception, garishly attired in a red shirt, pink bow tie, borrowed patent leather shoes, and a stunning green Alpine hat."[8]

Some of these men, referred to by Gaff as "rubes," "could be identified by their umbrellas" and "tennis rackets," and the more bizarre outfits they wore, which included "bathrobes ... and bathing suits." A number of the arrivals "proudly sported remnants of uniforms from bygone days in the

Mustering recruits, Camp Upton, Long Island, New York.

National Guard or at military school." Gaff remarked, "Crusty old sergeants could only look at such sights and shake their heads."[9]

* * *

Officers lined the men up, formed a column of twos, and moved the group down the "dusty road" to registration booths located just inside the entrance of the cantonment. Here they began their initial phase of processing. At Camp Devens, each of the booths had a sign bearing the name of one of the New England states and one for the state of New York. A noncom checked the "name tags" presented to each man at the local draft board office for "identification purposes." Board personnel had instructed the men to attach the tag to a shirt button. Processing included confirming names and verifying identification against accompanying draft board records. The cards bore the draftees' home district number, which would determine a man's assignment to a particular unit, the recruit's (draft) identification number, as well as his medical status as determined by the board physician. Author Roger Batchelder explained, if a man "forgets his district," or for some reason "is unable coherently to express himself," as in the case of many non–English-speaking immigrants, camp officers would have access to this information.[10]

Next, the officers "shunted" the group off to one of several field ambulances parked a short distance from the registration booths. At this station a team of Medical Corps doctors conducted a superficial examination to determine the general physical condition of each recruit. Medics checked for evidence of contagious diseases—pinkeye, diphtheria, scarlet fever, measles, or some other malady. Medical personnel pulled anyone out of line with a suspicious body rash—most common were hives, shingles, and eczema—or anyone having unusual growths or moles. The medical staff checked for obvious physical impairments or mental disorders and other disabilities. During cold or intermittent weather, the exams took place in a medical building or infirmary. Doctors quarantined infected men or sent "those whose condition might be remedied by treatment" to the base hospital until fit for duty.[11]

"Theoretically," individuals examined and passed by local draft board physicians were supposed to be in "good physical condition." Medical personnel at the camps, however, found numerous and "flagrant violations" of federal regulations, which "stated specifically that none but the physically fit" be accepted for military service. Doctors at the camps sent rejected men home immediately.[12]

"Medical Authorities," Batchelder reported, "were greatly surprised and annoyed, when, on superficial examination … they found men who were obviously unfit for service." He noted that while the "great majority of the district boards did their work well," many others "refused to comply with regulations." They did so, he says, "in order to fill the [allotted enlistment] quota from their districts." Some boards selected and approved individuals for the draft with obvious and serious physical and or medical defects. A number of men, according to Batchelder, "came to the camp who could see nothing without glasses," and that "some had missing fingers or toes." He reported seeing "one man whose right leg was three inches shorter than the left." *Boston Globe* staff reporter and correspondent William J. Robinson observed others with similar disabilities, as well as debilitating chronic diseases and conditions, such as heart problems, asthma, arthritis, syphilis and tuberculosis. "From some of the Boston draft boards," he wrote, "came men who were actually cripples—one man had only one hand," while another "had only one eye." "One chap was so near death from heart disease that the doctors ordered that he be rushed back to his home as quickly as possible."[13]

Officials at Camp Devens in Ayer, Massachusetts, sent an official letter of reprimand to one Boston draft board, a frequent offender, demanding an immediate explanation why it had sent men "from their jobs and homes" who were clearly unfit for service, wrote Robinson. The subsequent reply was that board members "thought" the government "wanted an army and surely something could be found for these men to do." Devens officials responded with complete indignation. They chastised the board sternly for its irresponsible actions, stating that the military "wanted an army, but it must be an army of fighting men, not of invalids." The correspondence ordered members to send replacements immediately for those "found unfit for service."[14]

* * *

After undergoing their initial processing upon arrival at Camp Upton, the recruits received a temporary assignment to the 77th Division's Depot Brigade. Depot brigades consisted mainly of a number of holding companies to which a division or department assigned men until needed for distribution or transfer to other units. The brigade supplied men to the 77th at Upton and to other divisions around the country. In some cases, men with a special talent or expertise in a particular field or profession would go directly to the American Expeditionary Forces (AEF) in France.

A sergeant assembled the group, took roll call, and assigned each man to a company or other unit. "Lists of draftees forwarded by the local draft boards," Gaff commented, "never, ever matched up with the squads of men who actually reached camp." "Roll calls commenced in a vain effort to sort out the discrepancies," explained Gaff, "but there were just too many men who could not speak English." One Italian immigrant, Gaff pointed out, "knew only three words of English—two were 'Merry Christmas' and the other was fuck." From there, personnel from each unit escorted the various groups to their respective company areas and the barracks that would serve as their temporary living quarters until they completed their initial processing. At Upton, Matthew Guerra became a member of the 21st Company, 152nd Depot Brigade. My great-uncle remained at the camp for three weeks before he received an assignment to Camp Devens in Ayer, Massachusetts.[15]

* * *

Each of the individual barracks buildings at the camp was a long, two-story structure. These were typical of barracks at camps around the country (see postcard of Camp Devens barracks). The lower floor consisted of three main sections—two large rooms—one a kitchen and a mess hall furnished "with two long tables and benches and a serving counter at the far end." Located at the opposite end was a smaller room that served as the company "orderly room," the administrative office of the company commander and his staff. The sleeping quarters filled the entire open second floor, with the exception of four smaller rooms at one end that served as quarters for the noncommissioned officers. Lined up the length of the room in long rows on each side were "iron cots with a spring." The men folded mattresses and blankets at the head of the bed frame with the pillow on top. Each barracks could accommodate 200 to 250 men, approximately one company.[16]

Attached to the rear of each barracks building was a lavatory, or "latrine," containing a row of toilets on one side and sinks on the opposite wall. At the far end was an adjacent "shower room" equipped with "eight nozzles," referred to as "shower baths." In the center of the latrine was a large boiler that provided heat for the building as well as sufficient hot water for the entire company. A high percentage of these men came from remote rural locations of the Northeast, without electricity or indoor plumbing and had never before experienced such, in their minds, "luxurious accommodations."[17]

As the recruits filed into the barracks, an officer told the group to move to the second-floor sleeping quarters where a noncom would assign each man a bunk for the duration of his stay. Next, the supply sergeant issued each man a six-piece mess kit and two standard olive drab wool army blankets. Following that, the sergeant instructed the group on how to make up their bunks, "in accordance with the military regulations." Cadre provided no pillows. The men could purchase this item later at the Post Exchange (PX) or, if they so desired, have one sent from home. Noncoms instructed the men to arrange all clothing and personal items neatly beneath the bed and to hang coats on wall pegs. When the bunks were not in use, the recruits were required to fold and stack "all blankets and bed clothing in a pile at the head of the bed." The sergeant informed the men that under no circumstances were they to switch bunks with anyone, as the assignment of bunks was the only way to determine if someone was missing.[18]

Later that afternoon, a sergeant gave the group a tour of the camp so they would be familiar with the layout of the grounds and its physical characteristics. During the walk, the noncom pointed out all major landmarks—the water tower, the camp (division) headquarters, the post office, telegraph office, theater, hospital, and other prominent buildings, as well as the names of the main streets that a lost soldier could use for orientation purposes. Upon returning to the barracks from the orientation tour, the recruits proceeded to the first-floor mess hall for the evening meal scheduled for 5:30 p.m.[19]

Following supper, the officer in charge (OIC) ordered the men to write a letter home informing their wives or parents that they had arrived safely at the camp and to tell them all about their first day in the Army. Between the supper meal and lights out, the men were required to shower, shave, and if need be, do their personal laundry, usually in one of the washroom sinks.

* * *

Later that evening the men spent time relaxing and becoming acquainted with each other, learning about what part of the Northeast or upstate New York they were from, and forming friendships with men from the same area or similar background. Men of different ethnic backgrounds who spoke no English or had only minimal English skills were naturally drawn together for mutual support, which provided them with a sense of comfort and security.

The evening passed quickly and soon it was time for bed. It had been a long day. Taps sounded at 10:00 p.m. and then it was lights out. For most recruits, historian Christopher M. Sterba wrote, "Sleep did not come easily." Recruit J. Irving Crump, stationed at Upton, related: "That most of us worried until far into the night is certain. I know I did, and the Italian on my left cried himself to sleep, and didn't try to hide his unhappiness either." In 1918, Crump wrote a book about his stint in the military, *Conscript 2989: Experience of a Drafted Man*. After the war, he became a writer and editor with *Boys' Life* and went on to publish a number of popular children's books.[20]

To read most period writers' accounts of the first evening in the barracks, one would think the recruits were a bunch of well-behaved, fine, upstanding young men. Gaff provides a completely different view of what transpired. "One draftee," he said, "was appalled to find himself 'in the midst of an awful crowd who continually cursed and urinated out the windows of the barracks.'" At 9:00 p.m. (2100 hours) a sergeant poked his head in the door and bellowed "lights out." "The novelty of the situation," however, "kept sleep at bay" for the majority of the men. Once the lights went out, the building erupted in "a cacophony of belches, animal sounds, real and mock farts, conversation, shouts, and just plain odd noises." A number of the men, tired from the journey and the long day, fell fast asleep. There were among the group a number of "practical jokers," Gaff reported, "who pounced upon those who nodded off early and either folded them inside collapsible cots or encased them in their mattress and threw the entire bundle down [the] stairs." "Gradually," Gaff said, "even the most-rowdy dozed off to sleep."[21]

8

Recruit Processing

The following morning, reveille sounded sharply at 5:45 a.m., jolting sleeping men awake. A detail of noncoms, sergeants and corporals, came "swaggering" through the door and went up and down the center aisle banging on the metal bed frames with their batons. At the top of their lungs, they shouted, "Everyone get dressed and be out on the parade ground for roll in ten minutes." One could hear groans and muttered curses throughout the barracks as the men dragged themselves out of the bunk and hurriedly dressed. Each man "made up his own bed," wrote author Alan D. Gaff, "a novelty since" in most homes at the time, "that had always been considered women's work." Men staggered out of the barracks and assembled on the street in front of the building. The platoon sergeant called "Ten-HUT!" and the bedraggled group stood in a faint semblance of a military formation.[1]

Sure enough, a late arrival came stumbling out of the barracks while trying frantically to button up his clothes. A buck sergeant, wanting to set an example, started yelling and screaming in the recruit's face to drop and give him twenty pushups. To do all twenty without stopping was a difficult task for most, and near impossible for some overweight and out-of-shape recruits. For some of the "screw-ups" in the company, the number of required pushups would eventually increase over the next three weeks of the procession and induction period to as many as fifty or more. At 6:30 a.m., following roll call, the group marched to the mess hall for "a hearty breakfast." Processing began immediately thereafter. Hand clippers.

Immediately after breakfast, noncoms escorted the recruits to the processing center barber shop to have their hair shaved off in a "buzz cut," sometimes referred to at the time as an "induction cut," with hair length about ⅛ of an inch or so. This process, part of the initiation into the service, even before the entrance of electric clippers, usually took all of 40 to 50 seconds at most. Reportedly, the standard military haircut dates to the Revolutionary War. At that time, General George Washington ordered his men to keep their hair clean and short, known then as a "warrior's cut," for hygiene and sanitary purposes, primarily for the prevention of lice breeding on the scalp.

Next, the company marched to the camp's administration building to begin what historian Christopher M. Sterba referred to as the process of "matriculation." On the first floor of the building was a large room partitioned off into a number of stations. At the initial stop, a clerk fingerprinted each man. Following that, the recruits had to fill out and sign an "interminable" number of required forms and other documents. At the next station, an officer recorded each of man's "personal history" on "qualification cards" for later reference, described by Sterba as the "most important part" of the draftee's basic training admission process. This information included family background, educational history, trade or profession, "employment experiences," and prior military service, that might be used determine a man's placement following basic training.[2]

A few of the older recruits had served previously with various branches of the armed forces of the United States or with state National Guard units. A number of foreign-born inductees also had prior experience as a member of the military in their home countries. One inductee, 25-year-old Flag Allen Drewry of Greenfield, Tennessee, had already completed a tour of duty with the U.S. Army from 1912 to 1914. While stationed at Camp Gordon, Georgia, he had been involved in the training of infantry recruits where he rose to the rank of 1st sergeant. Even though Drewry had prior service, "he had to start over as private." Upon discovery of his previous experience, military officials at the camp quickly promoted him to 1st sergeant as of Nov. 1, 1917, ready to assist in the training of the raw recruits almost immediately. He became a member of 7th Co., 2nd Training Battalion, 157th Depot Brigade. Drewry later rose to the rank of 2nd lieutenant (June 1, 1918) and later to 1st lieutenant. He eventually attained the rank of captain, retiring on April 30, 1933.[3]

Men with typing skills were in high demand. One very important question asked by the officer was whether an individual was bilingual. Many were second-generation immigrants and were equally proficient in two or more languages. Headquarters personnel immediately recruited a number of these individuals to serve as translators and interpreters. The army was especially interested in anyone who could speak fluent French, for obvious reasons.

Next, the group marched to the regimental medical building where doctors conducted what author William J. Robinson described as a "thorough physical examination, inside and out." Medical Corps personnel recorded height, weight, body measurements, and noted their general fitness overall. Doctors checked eyes, ears, nose, throat, condition of teeth, and for signs of a hernia. The physician used a stethoscope to check for heart murmurs, signs or symptoms of a thoracic aortic aneurysm or aortic dissection, two closely related conditions, generally caused by a ballooning or tear that develops in the inner layer of the aorta, thus weakening the vessel. Someone with this condition has a potential for rupture (bursting) or dissection (separation of the layers of the thoracic aortic wall), which may cause life-threatening hemorrhage (uncontrolled bleeding) and possibly death. Next was a screening test for high blood pressure, irregular pulse, or signs of hardening of the arteries. An ophthalmologist administered the visual acuity and refraction test, used to evaluate the recruit's eyesight, followed by a vision test to screen for colorblindness.[4]

Each man received the first of five immunization shots for tetanus, diphtheria, smallpox, typhoid and paratyphoid. Recruit J. Irving Crump provided a vivid, rather exaggerated description of the process. "A physician," he explained, took "a sponge covered with iodine" and dabbed a section under the left shoulder blade and upper arm. Each man then "moved on to two more physicians.... One dug a hunk out of our arm and inserted [typhoid] vaccine in place of the skin removed." The second doctor "jabbed at the iodine mark" below the shoulder blade with a needle he described as "a villainously long hypodermic," injecting a dose of serum. Crump remarked that before he "really knew what it amounted to," he "would rather have faced typhoid than face that 'needle.'" "Initially" Crump said he experienced "a little wooziness in the head, and a sore shoulder." That night he had trouble getting to sleep, and the next morning, he complained, "my arm and back were as sore as can be."[5]

Another recruit, Grover A. Moran, wrote to his family from Camp Lee, Virginia, on October 14, 1917, to tell the folks at home about this unpleasant experience:

> The boys are all feeling better now as they are about well of both the small-pox and typhoid vaccination. They gave us both 'shots' at once. It served some of the boys pretty rough. Five of them fainted in ranks one day and had to be carried in. I was some way able to stand the strain and I think it is only a matter of a few days until we will all feel better. Imagine a big hard scab on your left arm just above the elbow about the size of a half dollar and you will see about how my arm looks at present.

A week after receiving the typhoid vaccine, Moran wrote home "that the shoulder and arm pain had finally subsided."[6]

The second inoculation, described by Irish immigrant Walter H. Lockard, another inductee at Camp Lee, was for "para-typhoid." Paratyphoid fever is a contagious disease caused by a *Salmonella paratyphi* infection. Doctors group paratyphoid and typhoid fever together under the collective term of "enteric fever." Ingestion of contaminated water or food is the principal means of transmission. Paratyphoid is generally a milder disease than typhoid fever. Lockard described the process to his dad: "They sink the needle in about three inches into the arm and give you twice as much [serum] as the first one," obviously exaggerating the experience. "I have alternately had chills and fever every hour since." Lockard complained that after receiving the injection, he "had to walk guard just the same." He added, "My arm is black and blue clear down to the wrist and I can't raise it at all." That evening Lockard visited the YMCA hut. "Every time you move," he said, "some rookie cusses you out for bumping his arm. I can't raise mine at all." His adverse reaction to the second shot lasted throughout the night and for several days thereafter.[7]

About a week later, Lockard received his third vaccination, and related to his family that it was "fully as bad as the second, and gave me sharp pains around my heart that frightened me for a while." He added a humorous anecdote: "There is an Irish fellow here who wrote his Dad telling him he had been 'shot twice' since he had been here, (meaning in the arm), and his Dad wrote back saying he always thought him a liar but now knew it."[8]

Interestingly enough, when Lockard joined the army he was fully aware that he had "a heart problem." In 1917, 23-year-old Walter traveled to Chicago from his home in Scottdale, a small town 49 miles southeast of Pittsburgh, Pennsylvania, to enlist in the Army Air Corps. During his physical examination, "doctors determined that Walter had a heart murmur, probably caused by a bout of typhoid at age 17." Doctors "rejected" him "as unfit for active military service." Prior to receiving his draft notice, he devised "a scheme to hide" his "heart condition from the medical examiners." At Camp Upton, as Walter stood in the long line waiting for his physical, he asked the men coming out of the examination room whether the doctors had issued each of the men a medical record as to the results of the exam. When they answered in the negative, "he crossed over to their line, and sidestepped the medical examination which would have kept him out of the war."[9]

* * *

Next, the recruits had to undergo a battery of psychological tests. In 1917, a team of Army psychologists, working under the direction of American psychologist Robert M. Yerkes, designed the World War I U.S. Army intelligence-testing program to measure the general mental ability and aptitude of recruits. Prior to entering the army, Yerkes served as president of the American Psychological Association (APA). A group of psychologists administered the intelligence quotient (I.Q.) tests to classify incoming recruits. This was a concerted effort by the U.S. Army to determine which men were well suited to specific positions and/or leadership roles. Army psychologists developed three types of psychological or intelligence measurement tests:

> Alpha Test—A written, multiple-choice test for literate recruits. The Army Alpha was a group-administered test containing eight parts that measured verbal ability, numerical ability, ability to follow directions, and knowledge of information.

Beta Test—The Army Beta was a non-verbal counterpart to the Army Alpha test. This seven-part test presented questions in the form of pictures and graphics, including picture completion tasks, number work, and running a maze. Army psychologists used the Beta to evaluate the aptitude of illiterate, unschooled, or non–English speaking draftees and volunteers, or men who failed the Alpha test.

Individual Oral Examination—A spoken test for men who failed the Beta.

Psychologists could administer the Alpha and Beta tests to large groups, which generally took less than an hour to complete. During the war, more than 1.5 million recruits took the tests.[10]

Based on the results, the Army graded each recruit from A to E, with suggestions as to suitable placement. Individuals who scored below a C were ineligible for officer training.

Ranking Points:
- A   Very Superior 135–212
- B   Superior 105–134
- C+ High Average 75–104
- C   Average 45–75
- C- Low Average 25–44
- D   Inferior 15–24
- D- Very Inferior 0–14
- E   Reserved for those considered unfit for duty because of mental inferiority and discharged (approximately .5 percent).

Psychological Operations personnel generally assigned low scorers to "labor battalions" in the Depot Brigade.[11]

William J. Robinson related that the recruits referred to the staff of psychologists and their assistants as "nut pickers" and the intelligence examinations as "nut tests." There were two versions of the Alpha test, he reported, one for officers and another for enlisted men. Test scores were strictly confidential, even to the individual test takers. When the general staff considered a man for promotion, it factored the test scores into the final decision. When psychologists later compared tests with the individual's "practical results," Robinson noted, the tests "showed that the men and officers both did just about what ... might be expected of them."[12]

* * *

Later in the day, officers escorted the men to a Quartermaster Corps supply depot. Here, they entered a large room with a long line of tables where personnel stood waiting to measure the men for their uniforms. The recruits passed from one station to the next, where an NCO with tape measure in hand had them stand with arms outstretched and legs apart as they recorded their measurements and sizes for a particular garment or accessory item.

Following the measurement process, Quartermaster Corps personnel lined the men up to receive their clothing allowance and equipment. Clerks issued each man an O.D. (olive drab) tunic, shirt, trousers, overcoat, raincoat, dress shoes (two pairs), and one pair of "trench boots." J. Irving Crump referred to the boots as "trench brogans" (Model 1917 "Pershing" boots), with half-inch-thick hobnail soles and steel heel plates. In a letter to his mother, Walter Lockard claimed that they weighed "ten pounds apiece" (actually seven and one-half pounds for both). In Lockard's case, the boots turned out to be "two sizes too big." Also issued "were towels and soap."[13]

Because of temporary shortages, not everyone received the full issue of clothing and accessory items. The latter included a campaign hat, necktie, belt, underwear, handkerchiefs, socks, and "two tightly rolled bundles of wool called spiral puttees," approximately "four inches wide and three yards long." These were wound from the ankle to just below the knee to form what some accounts referred to as "thick woolen leggings." This particular item of clothing was what gave everyone the most trouble. Pvt. Andrew Johnson, an African American veteran interviewed by a WPA worker in 1938, described the dilemma faced by the men, which was, he said, "how to get what looked like a roll of O.D. bandage wrapped around one's leg!" "This last," his final comment stated facetiously, "almost made me quit the Army."[14]

Johnson, a native of Swarthmore, Pennsylvania, was a member of Company G, 368th Infantry, 92nd "Buffalo Soldiers" Division, stationed at Camp Meade, Maryland. As an interesting aside, the soldiers of the 92nd, more than 350,000 African Americans, served under and alongside units of the French Army. Both the AEF and the British Army refused to have "negro" soldiers serve under them in combat. The men of the 92nd, referred to as a "black unit," served with distinction.[15]

After picking up their clothing allowance at the Quartermaster supply depot, the men marched back to the barracks with uniforms and other articles of clothing stacked high on outstretched arms. Next, off came the "civvies" followed by a trip to the "shower baths," after which the men donned the new uniforms, transforming them into newly made soldiers. They rushed to the latrine and crowded around the mirrors trying to get a glimpse of themselves looking fit and dapper in their brand-new army duds. Smartly attired young men stood at attention with a broad grin and a sense of newfound pride. Robinson described the change:

> With the donning of the uniform there seemed to come something more than a physical transformation. Was there a straightening of those already straight shoulders? Was there a new brightness in the eye, a squaring of the jaw? There was. And that was the mental, or, if you prefer it, the spiritual transformation. For these men the war had begun, and they were in it; in it up to their eyes and with all the ardor of their high young spirits and the strength of their vigorous young bodies.

In spite of the measuring process, there were many individuals, much to their dismay, who experienced numerous problems with ill-fitting clothing and accessory items.[16]

Pvt. Johnson explained what happened while the men of his outfit were "engaged in taping, lacing, and buttoning these strange garments which go to make up a U.S. Army uniform." Without any warning whatsoever, and before the vast majority of the recruits had completed the task of getting into the new uniforms, an orderly stuck his head through the doorway and bellowed that everyone had sixty seconds to fall in at the parade grounds. Men panicked! Everyone made a hurried attempt to finish dressing and be in formation before the sergeant ordered them to attention. Johnson provided a vivid description of the scene: "Imagine a thousand men," he wrote, "unused to Army life, gathered together on a parade ground and told to stand at attention when coat-collars were threatening to choke half of them into insensibility and the other half were entangled in spiral puttees improperly wrapped."[17]

Over the next several days, a lot of exchanging of individual clothing items took place. Johnson wrote that there were "about 250 men" in his barracks, "and each one of them was struggling with tunics with too-tight collars, or complaining about too-large shoes; hardly anyone had been lucky enough to get a perfect fit." A number of the men who happened to be overweight, or exceptionally short or tall, had to have tailored uniforms custom-made for them. In some cases, it took several weeks before all the oversize men received their full-issue of clothing.[18]

"To get out of camp," Crump explained, each man "must be able to pass inspection with [a] perfect and well-fitting uniform." There were many men who were missing items of clothing because of shortages in their particular size. "Since many did not have a full uniform," Crump complained, "we had to hustle around and borrow articles ... that would fit and look satisfactory." There was "much bartering, exchanging, and renting" of various items of clothing from men not leaving the camp. He related how "overcoats were going for a dollar a day and breeches and jackets for fifty cents each."[19]

At approximately 3:15 p.m. every day, the company gathered in the assembly hall, where the officers began a series of lectures, instructional classes, or informal talks on various topics that the men would receive over the next three weeks. The first was a one-hour classroom period on the rudiments of military discipline and courtesy. The latter included instruction on how to salute properly, a gesture of respect toward an officer, the flag, or our country, and the regulations governing its use—generally when the U.S. National Anthem is being played and during reveille or retreat ceremonies. Classroom training also included "Infantry Drill Regulations, United States Army, 1911." Over the next several days, instructors covered such topics as "school of the soldier," "instruction without arms," "setting-up exercises" (calisthenics), and "steps and marches," among others.[20]

* * *

Upon completion of the testing phase, Army psychologists relegated all foreign-born immigrants who could not speak or understand English to one of the camp's labor battalions. Those deemed to have sufficient English skills to be able to understand verbal orders and commands received an assignment to a basic training company. By 1918, Matthew Guerra had been living in America for nearly seven years and likely had attained a level of English proficiency that permitted him to participate in the training regimen.

Following their initial processing, the New York metropolitan area recruits understood they would remain at Camp Upton for basic training. Matthew Guerra and the other men from New England and parts of upstate New York received orders to report to Camp Devens, in Ayer, Massachusetts, the training cantonment for recruits from the New England states and those from outside the metro New York area (northern and eastern New York).

9

Basic Training
Camp Devens

In 1917, the U.S. government was ill prepared for war on a massive scale. Combined Army and National Guard forces consisted of only about 370,000 men. Secretary of War Newton D. Baker and his advisors determined that the War Department would need to field an army of two million men between April and December of 1917, a lofty goal. This, however, did not happen as originally planned. During this period, the military managed to train an estimated 200,000 troops ready for overseas duty. General John J. Pershing's insistence that American soldiers receive adequate training before going to Europe was the prime reason so few troops arrived in France before 1918.

The overall training regimen, "insisted upon by General Pershing's staff," and endorsed by Secretary Baker, required "a three-stage course of instruction for most American soldiers." Part one of the prescribed program, considered "ideal" by military planners, according to Christopher M. Sterba in his book *Good Americans: Italian and Jewish Immigrants During the First World War*, "consisted of six months of basic and intermediary training in the United States" before deployment overseas. Upon arrival in France, units were required to undergo the second phase of their training, which included "three months of trench preparation." Following that, prior to ever experiencing combat, the plan called for units to spend an additional "three months occupying a quiet sector on the western front." This would, of course, have been the ideal situation. To implement part two, War Department officials directed Pershing to set up the necessary overseas training facilities staffed by battle-hardened and tactically astute veteran British and French officers and non-coms.[1]

The inductees who came to Camp Devens from the depot brigade at Upton, having completed the initial processing, were ready to begin their basic training period almost immediately. The morning following their arrival, the bugler sounded reveille at 4:30 a.m., about one hour before sunrise.

Examining new arrivals, Camp Devens, Ayer, Massachusetts.

After the recruits washed and dressed, the first sergeant blew his whistle for the companies to assemble outside the barracks to answer roll call and to submit to an in-ranks inspection. That included the individual's uniform as well as personal appearance, and later cleanliness of his equipment and service weapon.

Immediately following roll call and inspection, the company marched to the mess hall at 6:30 for a hearty breakfast. Following the morning meal, the trainees returned to the dormitories "to police up their quarters" and "to arrange their effects neatly and in a uniform manner" in preparation for the arrival of the in-quarters inspection party. Each morning, the officer in charge (OIC) conducted a formal inspection of the barracks and equipment. Men had to align the bunks, fold bedding at the foot of the bed in the prescribed fashion, store specific items, and hang all clothing in wall lockers. Specific items of equipment had to be displayed in an orderly manner on top of their bunk according to regulations. Mess kits—knives, forks, and spoons—had to "shine." Everyone had to organize footlockers—specific items of clothing (underwear and socks) and equipment, along with personal possessions and toiletries, had to be arranged in a uniform manner. "Cleanliness was the watchword," wrote historian Roger Batchelder, author of *Camp Devens, Described and Photographed*, published in 1918.[2]

Trainee Grover A. Moran explained in a letter home what the consequences were like for failing any part of the inspection: "We must be shaved and in full dress and have all our belongings on our bunks and stand at the foot of same at attention, while the officers go from one to the other and if things are not just right?????" He left the dire consequences up to the individual reader's imagination. Any soldier who did not make his bunk properly, or neatly arrange his belongings as instructed, "received extra fatigue duty." "Or worse yet," Moran reported, "kitchen police" (KP). Fatigue duty referred to an assignment to a detail involving manual labor, sometimes strenuous physical labor and usually unpleasant, such as, for example, road building, digging ditches, or collecting garbage. Next, it was a walk outside to start "policing the grounds"—"tidying up the area around their barracks."[3]

Per order of the sanitation officer, the men kept windows opened six inches during the night and all the way for "one to two hours per day" to air out the quarters. In addition, the recruits had to "thoroughly air" their mattress and blankets each morning. They accomplished this by hanging the bedding out the window, weather permitting, during the drill period. The "sanitary staff" of the division surgeon's office, consisting of two medical officers and four enlisted technicians, were accountable for ensuring the health and welfare of military personnel as well as the general sanitation of camps and living quarters. Inspectors made regular daily inspections of billets and barracks and were responsible for overseeing compliance of necessary sanitation and hygiene measures designed to prevent the spread of communicable diseases. Sanitary detachments were also responsible for all matters concerning the water supply, which included the testing of drinking water for the presence of bacteria or other pathogens, as well as for any problems regarding any other contaminants.[4]

* * *

Next, the men marched to the Company Arms Room to draw their personal weapon from the unit armorer. The sergeant in charge issued each man an M1917 U.S. Springfield, caliber .30, bolt action breech-loading rifle. The piece held six rounds, five shells in the magazine and one in the chamber. Initially, the schedule set aside one hour each day for preliminary indoctrination and training "in the proper care and use of the rifle," to familiarize the recruits with the M1917. The purpose of these preliminary measures was to prepare these rookies for firing live ammunition at the ranges. First on the list was a lecture on safety and the dangers involved in careless handling. Next, the soldiers received instructions on proper methods used in the care and maintenance of the weapon. Following that, instructors demonstrated how to disassemble and reassemble the weapon. In the days to follow, each recruit did this repeatedly until he could complete the operation while blindfolded.

The first phase of "marksmanship training" with the M1917 began with

Arrival of the drafted men, Camp Devens, Ayer, Massachusetts.

"sighting or aiming practice" to familiarize the recruits with standard sight alignment procedures. Instructors explained the function of the sights "and their effect on the position of the hit," as well as making adjustments for elevation (distance) and windage—the point or degree at which the sight of a rifle must be set to compensate for the effect of wind on the course of the projectile. Following that, the trainees participated in dry-fire tasks until they became proficient in operating the weapon.[5]

In the week prior to line firing, instructors conducted classes designed to instruct the men in the fundamentals of shooting—breathing control, trigger control, how to sight the weapon, and how to take accurate aim. Staff taught recruits to use proper rear and front sight alignment and natural point of aim. The men practiced setting the rear sight for different distances and adjusting for windage. Trainees also spent time learning the essential fundamentals of the four basic positions—standing, sitting, kneeling, and prone— and how to employ and adjust the sling for purposes of firing.

During week four, training companies marched to the rifle ranges located between the towns of Ayer and Shirley for practice firing. A considerable number of the men, most from the cities, author Alan D. Gaff noted, had never held a firearm before, but they proved to be "quick learners." Members of the training staff at the camp remarked "that scores made by the troops have been remarkable in view of the fact that very few of them had ever fired an army rifle of any kind before." "One lieutenant," quoted by Gaff,

Clean up after mess. Camp Devens, Massachusetts.

claimed "that of the fifty-eight men in his platoon only three had ever fired a rifle." Quite a few of the new trainees were country boys, brought up to hunt beginning at a young age, and could handle themselves quite well with a rifle. A certain percentage of the recruits, despite the lack of familiarity with weapons of any kind, Gaff reported, "could shoot naturally."[6]

With each passing day, the men became more and more proficient with their personal weapons. Once they mastered the basics, recruits spent a minimum of three hours each day taking target practice at the ranges. Roger Batchelder, author of *Camp Upton, Described and Photographed*, wrote that after just a few weeks, the troops became so adept with the Springfield they could "bring down a German at five hundred yards." When not at the range firing the weapons, the troops marched to one of the trench systems "constructed in various corners of the camp" for practicing going over the top (see below). Daily hikes of five to eight miles during the afternoon were the norm.[7]

* * *

During week one, company drill sergeants "started the men on a regular course of physical training and instruction that had been mapped out in detail by the general staff." Cadre allotted one hour each day for calisthenics, usually in the morning, to prepare the troops for the more strenuous activities to follow. Every morning at approximately 7:00 a.m., "the men of the company began the day's schedule of drill and classes." A noncom marched the company to the training field for instruction and practice in the rudiments of military march and drill three hours per day, beginning first by squads and later by platoons, eventually graduating to battalion formations and movements.

Training and instruction took place seven hours a day, five days a week, not including night maneuvers conducted later in the training cycle (see below). On Saturday mornings, officers conducted a full field inspection. The "week's work" was usually over by noon on Saturday, unless an officer or noncom assigned a company additional drill if needed, or as punishment.

One recruit, quoted by author Willis J. Abbot, described what the first day of drill was like:

> Back and forth, back and forth, we marched.... I had never walked so much in my life, and sweat rolled from every pore. My back ached dully; my feet burned. But the Second Lieutenant (a youth with a pale, thin fringe above his lip) continued to command sharply "One, Two, Three, Four; One, Two, Three, Four."

At one point, the drill instructor "wheeled about and came up to me briskly," the recruit related. "'Get in step!' he shouted, 'glaring at me. 'You are not dead yet.'" After that, "I fell in step and ... kept up with the count."[8]

Recruit J. Irving Crump described the typical day's training regimen: "All morning long we ambled across the landscape, doing squad and company movements. It was just drill, drill, drill, for fifty minutes of every sixty minutes, the ten minutes being allowed as rest periods." After lunch, it was rifle drill. "We mastered all the movements of the [M1917] Springfield rifle," Crump wrote, and "snapped our pieces up to position with real vigour." The sergeant shouted:

> Let me hear them hands slap them pieces.... Ri—shoulder—harms! One-two-three-four! Pep, that's it, pep an' snap. Slap 'em ard. Ordah—harms! One-two-three! Don drop em—don slam 'em—don slam 'em down. Nex' man slams 'em gits kitchen p'lice.

Crump complained, "We drilled until our arms ached, and rifles that weighed eight pounds at the beginning of the drill seemed to have increased to fifty pounds, and felt as long as telephone poles." At the end of the day, dog-tired men filed into the barracks and flopped down on their bunks.[9]

The workday for the trainees, however, was far from over. After the hard day's training, before they marched to the mess hall for the supper meal, recruits scrubbed the barracks throughout—they mopped and polished floors, washed windows, and cleaned the latrine until it was spotless.

In the following days, instructors also began a series of one-half-hour classes on such topics as guard duty, care of the rifle, and infantry drill regulations. In the evening, the recruits studied the *Infantry Drill Regulations Manual* (United States Army, 1904). Some of the many topics covered in this publication included: school of the soldier, how to march to drill commands, steps and marches, and the manual of arms. Recruits also studied the *Field Service Regulations Manual* (United States Army, 1905), which included details of organization, issue and transmission of orders, the service of security, outposts, marches, combat, the plan of attack, and night operations.

* * *

Combat veteran French and Canadian officers assigned to train the men of the 76th Division at Devens conducted a Staff and Field Officers School beginning on May 17, 1918, with every officer participating, from the commanding general on down. The course lasted three weeks. The officers received practical training in tactics and strategies, mastered in the classroom, under simulated conditions of war. The various maneuvers began with smaller units and progressed to larger and larger units. Historian William J. Robinson noted that "every arm of the service," including infantry, machine gun battalions, field artillery (heavy and light) battalions, trench mortar battalions, signal battalions, engineers, and supply and sanitary trains, "got a chance to put what they had learned into practice."[10]

Bayonet training classes by British instructors, veterans of combat in France, also began the second week. The men, Batchelder says, were "trained according to certain principles which the English have found most successful and efficacious." Initial instruction began with charging and stabbing dummies made of burlap sacks filled with straw. Instructors demonstrated the basic offensive and defensive positions, preliminary movements, and attack procedure. Robinson provided a vivid description of one such demonstration:

> Taking the rifle and bayonet and throwing his British cap to one side the cockney backed off, eyeing the dummy nearest him malevolently. His eyes gleamed brighter and brighter and fiercer and fiercer and his lips began to curl back over his teeth in a fiendish snarl. Suddenly he crouched, ripping off a string of curses that would make the blood of a thug run cold. Then, with a screech of fury that fairly raised the hair on the heads of his pupils, he leapt at the dummy and sank the cold steel into its wishbone, assuming that it had one.

The "British theory," as explained by Robinson, was "that when you charge a German you can win half your victory by scaring him."[11]

Taking the initiative from their enthusiastic instructors, the boys, "with teeth gritted in a perfect frenzy of rage," charged the dummies while screaming and whooping "like young Sioux braves." The "yells of the youngsters," encouraged by those exhibited by their instructors, "were hair-raising and sometimes their language in addressing the dummies was not the kind to be found in a Sunday school quarterly." Many a visitor to the camp who happened to stop and observe one of the bayonet classes in action, Robinson related, "got the start of his or her life."[12]

Bayonet drill at Camp Devens, Ayer, Massachusetts.

The men "were going at it in earnest," Robinson commented. "Many a man," he wrote, "was 'bunged up' in those battles," and not a few of the men ended up "with black eyes, bloody noses," and an assortment "bruises." During one of the practice sessions, one of the young soldiers, Corporal Timothy J. Daley of Waterbury, Connecticut, a member of Company H, 304th Infantry, "was accidentally impaled on the bayonet of another soldier," receiving a fatal wound to the abdomen. He died on February 26, 1918, before doctors could perform an operation to save his life. Daley graduated from Holy Cross College in Worcester, Massachusetts, Class of June 1917. Robinson says he "was a most popular lad," and "his death in such an unfortunate manner cast a gloom over the entire camp."[13]

* * *

During week four, veteran French and British officers began a series of exercises to familiarize the trainees with their knowledge of the very latest methods of trench warfare. The instructors, familiar with German tactics and strategies, were there to impart to the troops the most recent developments on both sides and to keep the men apprised of the ever-changing conditions of the battlefields in France. They also provided detailed diagrams showing the typical layout of the trench systems and other defenses then in use by the enemy.

Designers set up the camp's assault course to simulate battlefield con-

9. Basic Training

Camp Devens, 1917. Barracks and boys on hillside writing letters.

ditions as close to the real thing as was physically possible—trench systems, barbed wire entanglements, hurdles, and shell holes. At the beginning of the course, the class, divided into teams of eight, one officer and seven enlisted men, entered a trench facing the forward area. In this exercise, the team would continue through "no man's land," a crater-pocked area about twenty yards long, and proceed to the enemy trenches beyond.

The lieutenant shouted "fixed bayonets" and ordered the men to be at the ready. He blew his whistle and went "Jack-in-the-boxing out of the trench" followed by his squad of seven. "With a yell and a snarl and a growl (these chaps had learned the trick from the Britishers)—all rolled into one utterance—

they leaped into the air" and charged down the forward slope "to the ground eight feet below." At the top of the trench, trainers positioned sandbag "dummies" representing enemy soldiers. Shouting all the while, soldiers running full tilt "buried" their bayonets into the bags and "almost in the same movement ... jerked [them] out again." The squad quickly regrouped and sprinted another ten yards to the second defense line. Each bayonet again found its mark in the row of sandbags that were the enemy. Once more, the squad pressed on to a third line of dummy defenders positioned in a trench about twenty yards beyond, capturing the enemy position and taking up a defensive posture. The only thing wrong with this scenario was that enemy riflemen and machine gunners were not firing back.[14]

* * *

Devens was the first cantonment in the U.S. to establish a "bombing field" for hand grenade practice. The men armed the grenades, then stepped out from behind a protective concrete barrier and lobbed the "hand bombs" toward the forward area, described by Robinson as "a sea of shell holes and torn ground." Batchelder provides the following description of the grenades used by the troops at Camp Devens:

> The grenade is made of cast iron and is about the size and shape of a lemon. The outside of the casing is corrugated, so that when it explodes, it bursts into fragments. The grenadier holds it in his right hand, removes the safety pin with his left, and hurls the grenade in the direction of the enemy trenches. Five seconds after the grenade leaves the hand, it explodes, scattering some fifty bits of iron in all directions, with such force that they are dangerous at a distance of a hundred yards [actually a radius of eighty feet].

Referred to as a "pineapple grenade," the device weighed twenty-two ounces (1.375 pounds).[15]

Initially, the recruits had some difficulty trying to master the art of throwing the grenades. They were "tempted," Batchelder said, "to throw it like a baseball" which, because of the weight, limited the distance. For "maximum distance," the author explained, the most effective method was for the soldiers to hurl the grenade "with a circular overhead movement, by swinging the arm as the pitcher does in the English game of cricket."[16]

* * *

Gas training began the following week. Every man in the cantonment, no matter what his military occupation, was required to attend and pass "Gas Defense School," conducted by a training staff of noncommissioned officers. Prior to taking the course, "gas officers drilled their men until they could put the mask on in a matter of seconds." The staff considered anyone "who could not get the mask on and properly adjusted in twelve seconds ... a dead man."

The gas training school, located "opposite the Base Hospital," consisted of two "little buildings" and a series of "trenches and dugouts."[17]

The training staff used one of the buildings to introduce the men to the debilitating effects of "lachrymating or tear gas." Troops, without any type of protection, filed into the building and the door closed behind them. The gas, "about one twentieth as strong as that they were told to expect from the Germans," seeped slowly into the room. Tears flowed copiously from irritated eyes until the men were unable to see. They gagged and retched. At this point, some of the trainees began to panic and screamed for the staff to let them out of the chamber. A number of the men found some measure of relief by breathing through articles of clothing. The primary purpose of this aspect of the schooling was to familiarize them with the peculiar smell of the gas, which, in the future, would alert them of the need to don their protective masks as quickly as possible.[18]

Staff members used a second building to teach troops the necessity of the gas masks, as well their effectiveness in saving lives. Small groups of soldiers entered the room with gas masks on and stood in a circle. In this exercise, trainers released chlorine or other potentially lethal gases used against the Allies by the German Army. The sergeant instructed the men on what to expect and, most importantly, to do exactly as ordered. He told the men to remain calm and cautioned them not to panic or the results might prove disastrous. The leader then gave the signal to release the potentially deadly fumes. After a predetermined time had elapsed, the sergeant ordered the men to exit the building. The primary purpose of the exercise was to build confidence in the use of the protective devices.

The next phase was the use of gas against the men in the trenches. Noncoms divided the classes into smaller groups and distributed the men along the line, as they would be in battle opposite the German lines. Staff placed canisters of chlorine, mustard, or some other deadly gas used by the Germans in front of the trenches, and without warning released what Robinson described as the "silent death." A slight breeze carried the "yellow poison" (mustard gas) toward the line. Lookouts in the trenches sounded the alarm and the troops donned and adjusted their masks, just as the gas swept over the area.[19]

* * *

Later in the training cycle, personnel moved the battalions of infantry to the combat and artillery ranges at Still River, a tributary of the Nashua, where they camped for days on end "fighting mock battles" under all kinds of scenarios and conditions, both day and night. During this phase of training, units practiced advancing "close in under ... their own barrages," as artillery fire thundered overhead. The big guns of the artillery battalions sent "streams of shells" over the waves of troops, "tearing ... the rugged landscape ... to pieces," Robinson wrote. The countryside resounded with what seemed like the never-ending echo of exploding artillery shells.[20]

During week five, the companies began scheduled night training, including "night marches" and "night trench work ... in the various trench systems ... built throughout the cantonment." Troops spent all day and night in the fields and forests" of Massachusetts taking part in exercises and maneuvers. Robinson described the "night sky" as "aflame with star shells and rockets and colored fire." In the darkness, "the New England lads were in the trenches or crawling silently across some 'No Man's Land,' while machine guns sent a deadly hail over their backs at some invisible 'enemy.'"[21]

In a simulated exercise, an officer would send out a party or detachment on a scouting mission into "enemy" territory to gain vital intelligence. They crawled forward imperceptibly, moving on hands and knees, many nights across rain-soaked, muddy terrain. Each man carried only a bayonet for a weapon, as the flash from a rifle would give the squad's position away. Under battle conditions, night patrols, observing with "night eyes," went out to gain information about enemy defenses, searched no-man's land for survivors of previous attacks, and raided German trenches in the hope of capturing enemy soldiers for interrogation or finding valuable documents for intelligence purposes.

* * *

The final exercise of basic training consisted of a "real trench attack and a sham battle." This was the men's "first actual experience against living, breathing, yelling, eager flesh-and-blood antagonists, even though they were their own 'buddies.'" Instructors informed members of the attacking force that "the enemy was holding a series of trenches" and that the objective of the exercise was to force them to abandon their positions and retreat. Officers sent word up and down the line for units to prepare for the impending attack. Troops armed with rifles minus ammunition, and fixed bayonets with scabbards attached for safety purposes, poised for the assault. With one hand gripping the rifle, the other on the rung of the trench ladders, the lead men waited anxiously for the signal to go up and over the top.[22]

At the appointed time, a loud shrill blast from the officers' signal whistles sounded up and down the line. The troops scrambled out of the trenches and charged across the open ground "like madmen." Officers, serving as umpires, would judge the exercises and decide which side was the winner. One unit would attack another and then they would regroup and reverse roles. "And so it went.... Few remember now which company was adjudged the winner," Robinson commented about the games, "and few care ... but whichever one it was, the other company was the winner the next time." "What everybody remembers," Robinson emphasized, "is that the spirit exhibited by the men

Judge Morton of Boston moved court to Camp Devens. Thousands of Devens men thus became citizens of our country for which they were prepared to die. Source: *Forging the Sword: The Story of Camp Devens New England's Army Cantonment.*

on that auspicious occasion augured well for what was to be expected of them when the real thing came."[23]

To complete the program, the staff had "planned ... a tremendous, thrilling finish" to the training program, "in which the entire division would take part." "At the last moment," however, the command staff "had to abandon the finale" because of several days of heavy rain, "which," Robinson reported, "fell in torrents."[24]

The basic training period officially ended on Saturday, June 15. On Sunday, June 16, Cardinal William Henry O'Connell of the Boston Diocese held a ceremony to officially bestow his blessing on the troops of the 76th Division before their deployment overseas. An estimated 5,000 soldiers "knelt reverently ... and heard the cardinal's parting message." Division held a "grand review" on Wednesday, June 19, attended by Maj. Gen. Thomas Q. Donaldson and two assistants from the Department of the Inspector General in Washington. This was the last public appearance of the division before shipping out to France.[25]

* * *

The naturalization of all aliens at Camp Devens began on Monday, June 24, 1918. The War Department wanted the members of all divisions about to

leave for France to "go as full-fledged American citizens." The first naturalization ceremony, held in the YMCA auditorium, Robinson reported, "was an impressive one." It was the first time in the history of the Federal District Court of Massachusetts that a justice sat outside his conventional chamber. Presiding over the proceedings was the Honorable James H. Morton, Jr., of Boston, a district judge. Eight hundred men "seeking citizenship" stood in uniform before the makeshift bench, "a kitchen table," ready for the magistrate to swear them in as citizens.[26]

The group, according to Robinson, included "Italians, Russians, Turks, Portuguese, Norwegians, Greeks, Swiss, Belgians, Swedes, Romanians, Dutch, Persians, Austrians, and subjects of Great Britain." Judge Morton began the ceremony with "an inspiring speech." A court officer ordered the men to raise their right hand and repeat the oath administered by Judge Morton, "pledging their allegiance and their lives to the United States." Pvt. Matthew Guerra was among a second group naturalized on June 25, the following day.[27]

* * *

While undergoing his basic training at Fort Devens in Ayer, Massachusetts, from May 21 until July 8, 1918, Matthew likely visited his sister

A large naturalization ceremony during World War I at Fort Ethan Allen, Vermont, on June 25, 1918.

and her family on a weekend pass or possibly on leave just before shipping out to France. Worcester was only 29 miles away and on the main passenger rail line from the camp to the city. He must have looked very impressive in the uniform of the U.S. Army. My grandfather Antonio, a former soldier in the Italian Army, was without a doubt very proud of his brother-in-law, I'm sure.

10

Social and Recreational Activities at the Training Camps

Within the training camps across the country, various community organizations sponsored a number of recreational facilities and programs providing a variety of activities and services for the trainees. At Devens, the Young Men's Christian Association (YMCA) constructed an administration building, a main auditorium with a capacity of 3,000, and a total of "nine recreation huts." The huts were situated at convenient locations within the cantonment. In addition to a staff of administrators, the association employed more than fifty individuals known as "Red Triangle workers," ready to assist the trainees in any way they possibly could. Author Roger Batchelder called the YMCA "the greatest non-military organization which has ever become attached to the army." He described a YMCA hut as "a fraternity, church, a theater," and "a common meeting place" as well. Every worker, he added, is a soldier's "friend and is doing his best to make them comfortable and happy."[1]

Trainees referred to the huts as "Y.M.C.A. shacks." Veteran J. Irving Crump wrote that the buildings were "the centers of amusement and entertainment for us all ... we have some corking concerts and other forms of entertainment." Pvt. Crump had nothing but praise for the YMCA and its dedicated staff members. "It's bully," he stated. "We all wander over there sometimes during every evening, if it's only to listen to a new record on the phonograph." The soldiers "feel at home and have a real time, and can smoke and put their feet up on the tables." Crump called the YMCA "social work humanized." One of the fellows in his unit expressed it this way: "It is the thing that puts the soul in soldier."[2]

Attendants were on duty at the huts day and night. Located along the side walls of the buildings were "writing benches," stocked with an ample supply of free pens, paper, envelopes, and U.S. postage stamps. There were

10. Social and Recreational Activities at the Training Camps 85

adjacent stacks filled with current magazines, periodicals, newspapers, brochures, and pamphlets on a wide variety of relevant topics, again many also available in different languages for soldiers with limited English skills. In the center of the floor were rows of bookcases filled with every type of literature—fiction, historical, scientific, poetry, operas, comedies, tragedies, and plays. "For men of foreign birth," Batchelder wrote, there were "numerous volumes in foreign languages." If the demand required, there were multiple copies of popular works on the shelves. The American Library Association (ALA) also established a well-stocked library at each of the camps with all manner of reading material, "including many religious publications." There was a wide assortment of daily newspapers as well, and like the YMCA, available in a variety of different languages.[3]

Located at the far end of each building was the stage with an upright piano. If necessary, the staff could set up rows of benches out front for members of an audience. Located adjacent to the dance floor, there was a player piano and a Victrola. Every night of the week, YMCA staff members presented a number of different events—it might be a lecture by a well-known guest celebrity or public figure on a host of popular subjects, a movie, band concert, sing-along, or a show or performance by a talent from one of the companies. On Sundays, members of the clergy held "three services" (affiliations not indicated) at the YMCA, "which are," Batchelder noted, "the only religious activities on the weekly calendar." During the remainder of the week, he noted, the YMCA staff seeks "to entertain, amuse and gain the confidence of their protégés, and thereby exert a beneficial influence over them."[4]

The Knights of Columbus (K of C) organization built three large huts, similar in construction and style to those operated by the YMCA, and with a nearly identical calendar of events. The facilities served primarily as "Recreational Buildings" and were equipped with "almost every kind of recreational [and sporting] apparatus known to man." Staffers organized an elimination basketball league and invited every unit to form a team to compete for the championship of the division. The Knights' staff scheduled entertainment and/or sports activities practically every night of the week, including basketball games, volleyball, boxing, and pool and billiards tournaments. Officials of the organization appointed athletic officers whose prime responsibility it was to organize and train teams in every sport and arrange schedules.[5]

Everything was free of charge. Although the K of C is primarily a Catholic organization, the buildings were open to "any man in uniform, regardless of sect, creed, or religious belief." A large sign above the door read, "EVERYONE WELCOME." Each Sunday a Catholic chaplin celebrated mass at the main K of C hall. Weather permitting, the cleric held a "field Mass" outside "Building Number 1" (?) at Devens. On one occasion, Batchelder reported that 18,000 men attended the service, very likely shortly before the units of the 76th Division shipped out for Europe. Internet sources indicate that Jewish chaplains held services at 6:30 p.m. on Fridays in the "K of C Building" or "in chapel."6

* * *

Another organization, the War Camp Community Service Division (WCCS), a civilian social welfare association established in May 1917, was "in charge of ensuring that training camps and the areas surrounding the cantonments would be filled with well-organized social, recreational, and athletic activities." Supervisors hoped these would "provide positive alternatives to prostitution, alcohol, gambling and other vices" (see below). Staff members sponsored "community dinners, dances, banquets, pageants, festivals, and parades." The "most significant program" established by the association, and one that was very popular with members of the local communities around the camps, "opened civilian homes to soldiers—referred to as the 'Take a Soldier or Sailor Home to Dinner' Campaign." Other functions sponsored by the WCCS "included special holiday events as well as receptions, dances, lawn parties, automobile rides, picnics, musicals, concerts, organ recitals, and other civilian-soldier programs."7

Author William J. Robinson related two incidents involving the invite-a-soldier-to-dinner program at Camp Devens that occurred in the fall of 1917. One is very touching, in contrast to the other, which, while being typical of the times, is also quite humorous. The latter illustrates the prevalent attitude of many Americans at the time toward people of different ethnic and religious backgrounds. The first incident involved a very caring and companionate woman from Nashua, New Hampshire, who sent a letter to the camp commander, Brig. Gen. Harry F. Hodges, "asking to have a 'lonely solder' sent to her house for Thanksgiving dinner." She wrote, "I don't care who you send me. No matter if they can't speak English even. If they're good enough to fight for my home, they're good enough to eat at my table."8

Another New Hampshire woman, obviously quite well-to-do, also wrote the camp commander requesting that forty soldiers be allowed to attend Sunday dinner at her home. "In her letter," Robinson reported, "she specified that she did not want any men of 'Hebrew or Irish extraction.'" Gen. Hodges ordered a member of his staff to select the men, being mindful of the woman's wishes, and to arrange for the necessary transportation. The officer, quite likely an Irishman or a Jew with an active sense of humor, selected "forty lads from the sunny southland—colored soldiers from Florida." Robinson quipped, "No acknowledgement of his favor has been received to date," and, he related, "the men had a good time despite the 'sudden illness' of the hostess."9

* * *

In April 1917, just eleven days after the declaration of war, Secretary of War Newton D. Baker established a new arm of the military, the Commission

10. Social and Recreational Activities at the Training Camps 87

on Training Camp Activities (CTCA). Baker appointed Raymond B. Fosdick, his assistant at the time, to head up the new agency. The assignment was "largely based" on Fosdick's prior "experience as a special representative of the War Department investigating troop conditions on the Mexican Border during the Mexican Punitive Expedition in 1916." During that assignment, historian Joseph W. Ryan wrote, Fosdick had witnessed firsthand "the effects of alcohol, prostitution, and venereal disease on U.S. troops, and recognized the need to preserve combat power by limiting vice." Creation of the CTCA, which "became popularly known as the 'Fosdick Commission,'" was part of endeavors by the secretary to prevent the spread of venereal diseases and other sexually transmitted infections to personnel within the military.[10]

The increase and frequency of VD infection among the troops was staggering, raising deep concerns among military officials. If allowed to continue at the current rate, the number of disabilities could have a serious impact on the U.S. Army's capability of supplying replacements in adequate numbers for overseas duty. This, of course, would weaken America's fighting ability. Baker charged administrators of the program with setting stringent guidelines to ensure that cantonments around the country remain "as free from vice and drunkenness as is humanly possible." The principal aim of the commission, and one Fosdick believed would reduce the rate and number of personnel infected, was to provide wholesome alternatives to drinking and prostitution for the young men in uniform.[11]

As the months wore on, concerns over the loss of men to the ravages of venereal disease, which required a recovery period of two months in the hospital, continued to mount. Second Lt. John G. Buchanan, U.S. Army Sanitary Corps, wrote, "Of all the diseases," venereal disease is "the greatest cause of disabilities in wars, even, I regret to say, in the present one." In an attempt to prevent the incapacitation of soldiers by the ravages of VD, Secretary of War Baker ordered the Surgeon General's Office to establish a special section for combating sexually transmitted diseases, the Division of Venereal Disease Control (very little information pertaining to this agency can be found). Baker ordered the agency to begin a campaign against prostitution.[12]

The division staffed the new section with personnel from the Sanitary Corps of the Army's Medical Department. Secretary Baker directed members of the division to establish a number of enforcement measures to help combat the problem and, second, to conduct an extensive study into the medical aspects of the problem. Lt. George J. Anderson, director of the Section on Vice and Liquor Control, an arm of the CTCA, claimed that once military officials instituted the new enforcement measures, the venereal disease rate for the army decreased by more than 50 percent.[13]

* * *

Every evening thousands of soldiers went into the nearby town of Ayer for a night of entertainment and socializing. The "little New England hamlet," with "a population before the war of about 2,500," according to Robinson, "suddenly found itself besieged" by "40,000 men" from around New England "sent to Camp Devens in the first draft." Soon after the camp opened, the population of the town of Ayer "almost doubled." The vast majority of the town's resident population welcomed the servicemen warmly. "To their everlasting credit," Robinson wrote, the citizens of the town "did their utmost for the soldiers." Many of the officers and men at the camp "made lifelong friendships among the people of Ayer."[14]

There were a number of soldier-friendly "hang outs" in the downtown area, similar to those "found in any college town," wrote Robinson, where the men congregated after a hard day's training or on the weekends. The War Camp Community Service (WCCS) organization opened a "Soldier's Club" on West Street, where the men could find all types of recreational activities to pass the time—card or board games, puzzles, and arts and crafts, for example—or they could just sit around smoking, chatting, joking, or sharing the latest gossip. The club had "a fine cafeteria" where the men could buy a snack or a meal "at reasonable prices."[15]

Shortly after Camp Devens opened, the Massachusetts governor ordered the state police to establish an office in the town of Ayer and station a contingent of officers, members of a "vice squad," in the once sleepy little hamlet. Heading up the office was Edward P. O'Hallorhan, an "inspector" with the Newton (Massachusetts) police force. Officials were expecting a multitude of "camp followers" to "materialize" in and around the camps as they had in previous wars. There were many among this group consisting primarily of criminals, drug addicts, shysters, and other shady characters, as well as many prostitutes, that gravitated to the town of Ayer. The prime intention of these individuals, generally considered low-life creatures who skulked around the downtown area, was "to prey on the New England fighting men." The role of the detail of troopers was to keep the now bustling town free of vice and corruption. "And they did," Robinson commented. Members of the Military Police, wearing the dark blue brassard with the letters M.P. in white, also patrolled the streets and were "constantly on guard" to prevent or address any kind of wrongdoing.[16]

State officials sent Officer Mary A. Sughrue to Ayer to serve as a "police matron." One of her duties was to assist the police in dealing with female offenders in cases deemed inappropriate for male officers to handle. She is described by Robinson as a "motherly big-hearted woman" who gave "another chance" to "many a foolish young girl, that might have been sent to an institution." These young female offenders were "sent back home with a warning" they "could hardly forget." Sughrue was also active in a program of rehabilitating individuals incarcerated in the Ayer Police Department jail. Robinson says, "she was loved by the whole town and by every soldier who knew her." The state police, the matron, and Police Chief Patrick J. Beatty of Ayer worked closely to incorporate measures to suppress all forms of vice and criminal activity.[17]

In a 1919 article titled "War Legislation against Alcoholic Liquor and Prostitution," written by 2nd Lt. John G. Buchanan, U.S. Army Sanitary Corps, outlined a section of the Selective Draft Act (of May 18, 1917). This portion of the act was designed to combat the "three principal vices" affecting the troops—prostitution, drinking, and gambling. Of greatest concern to military officials were the first two offenses, primarily because of their effect upon the health and efficiency of "their victims." Congress embodied a section devoted to each—Sections 12 and 13, respectively.[18]

Section 12 contained regulations governing the prohibition and sale of alcoholic beverages in or near military camps. A violation of this section "made it a misdemeanor to sell intoxicating liquor to any officer or member of the military forces while in uniform." This provision made the offense punishable by a fine of not more than $1,000 or imprisonment for not more than twelve months or both. Section 13, "a companion weapon to Section 12," dealing with prostitution, directed the Secretary of War "to do everything by him deemed necessary to suppress and prevent the keeping or setting up of houses of ill fame, brothels, bawdy houses within such distances as he may deem needful of any military camp." Lt. Buchanan stated that "medical examinations show that eighty to ninety percent of the prostitutes arrested during the war have one or more venereal diseases." The penalties for violation of this section of the act were the same as those imposed for the sale of alcoholic beverages.[19]

The regulations prescribed the designation of "vice districts within an effective radius of the camps." Military authorities established a prohibited zone of "5-miles" around "a military camp, where "the sale, service, gift, and transportation of alcoholic liquor were forbidden, except to civilians in private homes." Any soldier in possession of alcohol or found under the influence was subject to discipline by the army, and if found to be in violation of section 12, would also be subject to trial by court-martial.[20]

Another aspect of the commission was to restructure the atmosphere of the training camps by offering a number of intellectual and athletic activities that stimulated the mind. That measure would, theoretically, reduce sexual urges and desires among servicemen. There was a concerted effort to make sure the World War I training camps and the surrounding or adjacent civilian areas were healthy environments, free of sexual temptation, thereby preventing the rampant spread of venereal infections within the ranks. To help organize a plan and assist in helping to meet the Army's recreational goals and objectives, the CTCA enlisted a number of private agencies, including the Young Men's Christian Association, Knights of Columbus, Jewish Welfare Board, American Library Association, Salvation Army, and the War Camp Community Service.

* * *

At each of the camps, CTCA officials authorized the appointment of an athletic director to organize and schedule sports programs and other recreational activities and events for the troops. General Hodges appointed his aide de camp, Lieutenant W.W. Cowgill, to the position of division athletic director at Devens. These were highly qualified individuals with much prior experience in various sports endeavors and activities in civilian life. Directors sponsored football, baseball, track, tennis, boxing, wrestling, volleyball, and a host of other popular sports activities at their respective camps.

The CTCA provided a full supply of athletic training equipment for every sport, including exercise and physical fitness apparatus. Camp athletic officers formed interregimental leagues consisting of teams from each company. Teams participated in elimination tournaments for the championship of the regiment, battalion, and eventually for the division. Competitive sports, commission members believed, "brought out the fighting instincts in the troops." Staff members left "Wednesday and Saturday afternoons and most evenings, free for recreation." Athletic officers scheduled sporting events during the evening hours as well. Organized league teams played games before capacity crowds as the troops came out to cheer on the men from their units. The "spirit spread among the various regiments," wrote Batchelder, "until footballs and baseballs were flying every spare minute."[21]

During the design stage of the various cantonments, planners laid out baseball diamonds, football fields, tennis courts, running tracks, and facilities for swimming. At Devens, the 301st Engineers converted Hell Pond, a natural body of water, into a swimming pool. Officials at the camp made it a requirement that every man be able to swim seventy-five yards. Local golf clubs allowed soldiers from the camps to play free of charge. Out of all the sports made available to the troops, baseball was by far the most popular. Professional teams from the major and minor leagues played charity exhibition games, drawing capacity crowds and taking in considerable gate receipts.[22]

Boxing was the second most popular activity among the troops and the most challenging. Athletic directors promoted the sport, "due" primarily "to its 'war-like' quality." Squaring off in the ring required a unique blend of speed, strength, and endurance to stand up to the punishment inflicted by an opponent. To succeed, a fighter must have the mental fortitude to be able to withstand a combination of pain and fatigue. Aside from being an off-duty form of recreation or pastime, drill instructors integrated boxing into

10. Social and Recreational Activities at the Training Camps 91

the camp's regularly scheduled training regime, setting aside a forty-five-minute block of time each day. Willis J. Abbot reported, "The wide-spread draft had caught in its net several hundred practicing pugilists who were assigned to instructor's duty." Pvt. Walter Lockard noted that the instructors were "some of the best ring men in the country."[23]

The boxing instructor at Camp Upton on Long Island was lightweight champion Benny Leonard (Benjamin Leiner), a native of New York City, known for his "speed and boxing technique." Benny was raised in the Jewish neighborhood on the lower east side of Manhattan, where he learned to fight in the streets to protect himself. His nickname was the "Ghetto Wizard." Credited with 213 career matches, Leonard compiled a record of 157 wins, 67 by KOs, 11 loses, 5 draws, and several no-decisions. He held the lightweight championship for a division record 7 years and 6½ months. The fighter's record indicates that "he did not lose a fight over a twenty-year span from May 1912 until October 1932, except for a single disqualification in 1922." Leonard put on frequent exhibitions for the troops at Camp Upton.[24]

Abbot wrote that during the training exercises, "as many as a thousand men would be engaged in taking fistic lessons." A boxing instructor "perched on a lofty platform" directed the exercises, shouting instructions and commands through a megaphone. Several rounds of boxing took place every weeknight under the supervision of experts. On Friday evenings, the Knights of Columbus scheduled a big boxing night with a full card. "The biggest athletic event of the season" was the camp boxing championship for the various weight classes. Many of the top boxers were "real prize fighters," or "former pugilists," noted Crump.[25]

* * *

The Commission on Training and Camp Activities (CTCA) sent trained voice teachers to each camp to teach the soldiers how to sing. Army leaders considered singing to be a great morale-boosting activity. One day at Camp Devens, American tenor Vernon Stiles, a well-known concert singer, showed up at 76th Division Headquarters and announced that Washington had assigned him to Devens to provide singing lessons for the troops. Stiles, a performer with the Metropolitan Opera in New York and the Royal Opera in Vienna, had "a mezzo voice." News of the army's intentions raised a few eyebrows among the ranking officers at headquarters, and some among their number uttered not just a few disparaging remarks. "After the first few weeks," Robinson wrote, "some of the skeptics had shivers running up and down their backs when they heard thousands of doughboys roaring out the most inspiring war music any nation ever heard." The doughboys also sang as they marched. Reportedly, this activity helped the men keep cadence and played a part in boosting confidence and morale as well as relieving homesickness.[26]

At Camp Upton, Pvt. J. Irving Crump was a member of a chorus "5,000 strong," sitting on the side of a slope one evening performing in concert for the troops. The choral group sang a number of popular selections that included "Columbia the Gem of the Ocean," "America," "Dixie," and "Maryland." "We sang until our voices were husky," Crump recalled after the war. "That chorus was wonderful; that crowd was wonderful; everything about it was wonderful." He described the moving experience:

> I have never heard a more stirring chorus and as we raised our voices loud and clear shivery thrills raced up and down our spines, and we were stirred to the highest pitch of patriotic fervor. Indeed, there were some among us who could find no better way of expressing the emotion that swelled within save by tears. I was one of them.

After the concert, the entire camp was still singing. On the walk back to the barracks, "Over There" and "The Yanks Are Coming" "swelled forth" down every street. Crump lay awake in his bunk "for a long, long time," thinking about the "whole wonderful occasion," before finally falling off into to a deep slumber. On Monday morning following the weekend concert, Crump left Camp Upton "on the first leg of that longed-for journey to France."[27]

11

Foreign-Born U.S. Army Recruits
Non–English Speaking Draftees

One of the most pressing problems facing military officials during the early months of World War I was how to deal with the large numbers of non–English-speaking draftees flooding U.S. Army cantonments across the country. Language deficiencies prevented the majority of the new recruits from participating in the normal training regime. For the first eight months of the war, commanders at the various cantonments had no choice but to relegate thousands of these inductees to the holding companies of the Depot Brigades, where they essentially ended up becoming a part of the camp's labor force.

Beginning in the summer of 1917, the first of the foreign-born inductees began reporting to their assigned U.S. Army training camps. Historian Nancy Gentile Ford reported that the foreign-born immigrant recruits consisted "of forty-six different nationalities." Their numbers grew as the war progressed, eventually reaching "nearly half a million, ... over 18 percent of the total," and therein lay the crux of the problem facing leaders of the military. Out of the 516,212 eligible immigrant men who registered for the June 1917 national draft, local boards certified 76,545 for military service.[1]

The majority of the new recruits were primarily from Eastern and Western Europe and the Scandinavian countries. Fred H. Rindge, Jr., Secretary of the International Committee of the Young Men's Christian Association (YMCA), provided a detailed breakdown: "18,131 Russians and other Slavs, 15,348 Italians, 13,233 Austrians, 5,794 Mexicans, 3,675 Greeks, 1,600 Turks, 1,355 Swedes, 1,000 Norwegians, over 900 Portuguese, more than 500 Japanese, 280 Chinese, [and] 150 Dutch," for a total of 61,966 or 81 percent of the drafted immigrants. The remainder consisted of smaller numbers of "Belgians, French, Rumanians, Serbians, Swiss Bulgarians, and other nationalities." Nearly half had only recently arrived in America from Europe and elsewhere.[2]

Subsequent drafts brought the number of soldiers of foreign origin to 487,434, comprising an estimated 17.66 percent (11 percent resident aliens and 6.66 percent naturalized citizens) of the 2,758,542 men inducted into the armed forces over the course of the war. This equates to approximately one draftee in five.

Sometime in the spring of 1918, Secretary Rindge visited a number of the U.S. Army cantonments around the country. The purpose of his tour was to check on the progress of the organization's troop education program, responsible for instructing immigrant soldiers in the English language, civics, and citizenship (see following chapters). Rindge determined that the several camps he traveled to had an average population of between "30,000 to 40,000" trainees, and of that number he estimated there were "4,000 to 5,000" immigrant recruits "who understand little English and speak still less." A 1918 article in the U.S. Army *Infantry Journal* reported that the lack of sufficient English language skills was a major "handicap" that "cut" the foreign-born "off from all chance of improvement." Rindge commented that the officers at the camps all agreed that training these men was, at the time, one of the "greatest problems" facing the military.[3]

For the first several weeks of the war, the army "mixed" non–English-speaking immigrant recruits with native-born Americans in "polyglot companies," or, as described by Ford, "conglomerate masses," during basic training cycles. Commanding the training companies during this period were English-speaking officers and noncommissioned officers.[4]

Among the immigrants arriving at the camps, Capt. Edward R. Padgett of the War Department's general staff estimated that "not more than one in a hundred knew the English language well enough" to be able to understand orders and commands "given by the drillmasters." This, of course, greatly hindered the ability of cadre to administer the standard basic training soldier-making process then in place specifically designed to prepare the recruits for a combat role. It did not take military officials long to discover that, because of the language differences, this type of arrangement made for an unmanageable situation. This failure of the U.S. Army's recruit training program eventually reached crisis proportions. Under the circumstances, standard training protocol was clearly not getting the job done. This intolerable situation forced "the military to re-examine its training procedures."[5]

Capt. Padgett noted that at several of the camps there "were few" bilingual foreign-born or second-generation officers and NCOs among the ranks who were able to translate orders and commands which, Ford wrote, "greatly exacerbated" communication and morale problems. Their numbers were hardly enough to affect the enormous task of making combat-ready soldiers out of the thousands of immigrant recruits pouring into the cantonments on a daily basis. These individuals worked diligently "to bring some sort order out of the chaos," but the "sheer force" of the vast numbers among the recruit trainees at the camps "neutralized their valiant efforts."[6]

It became evident to camp administrators early on that cadre could not properly train these men in the same companies with English-speaking men commanded by native-born officers and noncoms. The problem seemed at the time so complex, War Department officials were in a quandary as to the proper course of action to pursue in dealing with the situation and no solution seemed to be forthcoming. Conditions forced the camp's general staff to classify all non–English-speaking recruits "unfit for service" and exclude them from the ranks of the training companies. Camp commanders had no other choice than to relegate these men to the companies of the camp's depot brigade, where they languished. Morale among foreign-born inductees in this predicament was understandably low.[7]

A memorandum issued by Military Intelligence Section (MIS) officials near the end of July 1918 "estimated" that for "each such wasted man" assigned to the depot companies, the cost to the army was approximately $1,000 in "pay, clothing, food and time expended upon them in training." For every 1,000 men trained, the U.S. government is "financially bettered [by] $1,000,000." By the time the army finally came up with a solution to the immigrant training problem, it had ended up costing the government untold millions.[8]

Generally, depot or "replacement" brigades, first established in World War I, functioned as "holding units" for men awaiting transfer. The brigades consisted of a number of companies formed for billeting new draftees while they underwent processing through the "receiving station" prior to beginning their basic training cycle; as a temporary holding area for men awaiting orders for a permanent assignment; to be companies from which the military could withdraw enlisted men as well as officers as replacements, referred to as "fillers," in other outfits as needed; and for units shipping out to France. Medical personnel also temporarily assigned physically disabled or mentally unfit individuals to a designated depot company until they recovered or their cases could be resolved.

The depot brigades were also a place for detaining "enemy aliens," immigrants from the Central Powers—Germany and the Austrian-Hungarian Empire—and "allied enemy aliens," those from the territories under their control—Turks, Syrians, and Bulgarians. At Camp Devens, the 151st Depot Brigade housed a "detachment of one hundred general prisoners sent ... to finish out their terms for various offenses" and "to perform whatever labor was required of them." Also billeted in several of the barracks "were nearly 2,000 colored troops," assigned to the New England cantonment "to form labor battalions." In addition, there was "a special company" made up of "conscientious objectors" that local boards "drafted into the service," many against their will.[9]

According to a Provost Marshal General's report, the government could not compel enemy aliens to serve, "since they would be put in a position of fighting against their own countrymen." There were, however, "[a]pproximately 9,000 enemy aliens from the Austro-Hungarian Empire" (consisting of Austria, Hungary, Bohemia, Moravia, Slovakia, Romania, Slovenia, Croatia, Italy, and parts of Poland), Ford added, who had "waived their exempt status … and expressed their desire to fight with the United States military." "Although technically the 'enemy,' this … group considered themselves from the '"oppressed races' of the Austro-Hungarian Empire and expressed their desire to fight with the U.S. military to free their homeland from the Central Powers." They viewed this as a chance "to fight not only the battles of their adopted country but likewise opportunity to avenge some of the wrongs perpetrated upon their own countrymen in the past by the unholy Hun, the treacherous Austrian and the 'unspeakable Turk,'" wrote Padgett.[10]

A number of prominent military leaders were of the opinion that the "bulk" of the foreign-born soldiers were "disloyal and hopeless." In their frustration, many officers and noncoms erroneously deemed the immigrant recruits "ignorant and illiterate," which was essentially a mistaken and an unfair assumption. The consensus among the training personnel at the camps was that the majority were "indifferent" and that "they had no sense of discipline." Cadre generally believed, wrongfully so, that the men who were refusing to obey orders or follow directions were being uncooperative and insolent, when in fact, they simply could not always comprehend whatever commands or orders training personnel were asking them to execute or perform.[11]

Among those immigrant men relegated to the depot brigades, there were many foreign-born inductees who were sincere about wanting to serve their adopted country. They "had answered the call to the colors with enthusiasm" and showed up at the camps ready to train and fight, "not to lie around and grow discontented and lazy as part of a badly disciplined rabble," explained Capt. George B. Perkins, chief of the War Department's Military Morale Section (MMS). Some were "already trained soldiers," having had previous military service in their country of origin. Because of their limited English skills, these men experienced increased levels of anger and frustration by their exclusion from the training process. A number of other immigrant soldiers "had been successful professionals in their civilian life." Examples provided by Ford included "lawyers, doctors, businessmen, and newspaper editors."[12]

Capt. Padgett described "most" of the immigrant recruits as "splendid physical specimens." Again, the lack of English language skills, however, placed them at a distinct disadvantage and put a damper on any hopes they had about actively contributing to the cause.[13]

"There were also men who did not want to fight," Padgett added. Many individuals, because of their pacifist or other beliefs, "refused to don a uniform" or "pick up a rifle and learn to drill." There were some who "actually did not understand why they had been put into a military camp." Many inductees had not filed for citizenship ("nondeclarants") and were therefore technically exempt, but found themselves selected anyway "due" primarily "to drafting errors" and "numerous mix-ups." Historian David Laskin related how the "soldiers [recruits] of German and Austrian ancestry passed around stories that their families in the old country would be found and killed once word got back that [their sons] were serving in the American Army." "Supposedly," Laskin added, "German agents had initiated the rumor as a way of undermining morale."[14]

"By September, 1918," Ford states, a total of "191,419 nondeclarant draftees asked to waive their right of exemption." They did not contest their ineligibility and accepted their draft status allowing their local draft boards to induct them. Some among them went down to their draft registration office and enlisted. Apparently, Matthew Guerra, a non-declarant immigrant, did either one or the other. There is no way of knowing for sure. Nothing in his draft records give any indication that he made any attempt to prevent his induction.[15]

At camps around the country, officials "mixed" the immigrant inductees "indiscriminately" in depot brigades containing men who were physically disabled, mentally unfit, and "those crippled and diseased." Likewise assigned to the depot brigades were all recruits regarded as "undesirables," which included a number of aliens considered disaffected or disloyal persons. Placing non–English-speaking recruits in integrated multilingual units within the depot brigade companies created what turned out to be a very volatile situation.[16]

This tension and friction generated by existing conditions led, in many instances, to numerous confrontations and clashes between members of the various ethnic groups. The men of different nationalities began to "quarrel and bicker" with one another, creating an atmosphere of prejudice and antagonism. "Old scores from the pages of history," Padgett wrote, "were dug up and reopened." These factors added to the turmoil and discord that existed in many of the depot companies.[17]

There was also much consternation and strife between the different factions within the same ethnic groups. Arguments arose amongst themselves "based upon politics or religion or upon ... one of [the] many points of difference." These altercations "began to spring up," frequently disrupting "the scant harmony that did exist," thus creating a host of discipline and other problems that the officers and noncoms were forced to deal with on an almost daily basis. There were also frequent encounters between blacks and whites. The situation severely undermined morale among the non–English-speaking recruits who found themselves in this predicament. "Week after week," the men assigned to the depot companies "drifted along," and over time "grew discontented, restless, resentful, [and] sullen." Morale plummeted.[18]

As the immigrant population at the camps continued to increase, the depot brigades became exceedingly overloaded, creating a nuisance situation for everyone involved. The sheer number of incoming trainees from subsequent inductions overwhelmed staff, resulting in the need for additional officers and enlisted men to provide constant supervision and care. In a number of instances, this tied up a considerable number of officers and noncoms, causing staff shortages in other areas as well, preventing their deployment to France.[19]

Commanders were at a loss as how to deal with the castoffs. A considerable number of the non–English-speaking recruits who were wasting away in the depot brigades had been in the army since the fall of 1917. In an attempt to keep the majority of the men in the depot companies "active" or "occupied," officers regularly assigned them to work details performing menial labor, generally referred to as "fatigue jobs" or "fatigue duty." Generally, these included unskilled menial tasks and assignments such as cleanup details, maintenance, kitchen police (KP), loading and unloading trucks carrying supplies, and garbage details (picking up and transporting waste from the mess halls to the refuse station). A certain percentage were confined to construction gangs, performing the most strenuous types of manual labor—mostly pick and shovel work—building roads, digging ditches, and constructing bridges, in all types of weather. These were jobs the immigrants absolutely "detested." Incidents of physical and verbal abuse by officers and noncoms acting as supervisory personnel were commonplace.[20]

In August 1918, a "group of immigrant recruits" at Camp Devens decided to do something about their situation. A contingent acting as representative for the group informed the morale officer, Capt. Ernest J. Hall, that some noncommissioned officers "regularly" assigned them to work details involving "hard labor" and a host of dirty jobs. As one recruit described the situation, "Details of us non–English speaking soldiers" have performed some of "the hardest and dirtiest work." The disgruntled soldier bemoaned his predicament, "We are a laboring party, instead of soldiers." Putting these men to work as laborers performing unrewarding, menial tasks that required little skill or thought was also very demeaning. One African American soldier at Camp Gordon wrote directly to the War Department to complain "that black soldiers were worked seven days a week and were never given passes." This type of abuse may very well have been true of the foreign-born recruits at some of the other camps as well.[21]

Officials of the Military Intelligence Section were well aware of "the dispiriting effect that this prolonged duty" had on the morale of the immigrant soldiers. Yet the MIS did not address this problem until just prior to the conclusion of the war when, on October 22, 1918, intelligence chief Brig. Gen. Marlborough Churchill issued a general order prohibiting officers from assigning the members of foreign-speaking companies to details as "menial 'fatigue' laborers."[22]

The War Department "finally came to the conclusion that having about 100,000 [foreign-born] men in the army for six months, clothing them and feeding them, with no benefit, no result in any form" was "a serious waste or misuse of manpower." As mentioned above, many of the foreign-born had previously seen military service in their country of origin. Technically, these individuals could provide valuable assistance with the training process or contribute toward the war effort in a position related to their particular specialty.[23]

The inability of the immigrant recruits to participate in the training process prevented their availability for overseas duty. What was even more disturbing to a number of military officials was the fact that the vast majority of the troops shipping out for France were American boys, while the foreign-born men, deemed "un-trainable," remained stateside.

12

Enter Lt. Stanislaw A. Gutowski

Near the end of November 1917, seven months after the start of the war, the U.S. Army's Military Intelligence Section (MIS) had yet to resolve the existing morale and training issues affecting incoming immigrant soldiers. In their desperation, War Department officials "tapped" a young officer in his late twenties named Stanislaw A. Gutowski, "born in Russian Poland," to assess the situation and develop a practical and effective means of resolving the Army's dilemma. Lt. Gutowski, having worked as a social worker in Boston before the war, was a man familiar with society's immigrant issues and problems. His current assignment was to recommend needed modifications and/or improvements to existing training policies and procedures that up to that point in time had proven ineffective. It is likely that Gutowski came to the attention of army officials because of an earlier relationship with D. Chauncy Brewer, chief of the Foreign-Speaking Soldier Sub-section (FSS), while a resident of Boston (see later chapters).

A 1918 article in the *U.S Army Infantry Journal* described Gutowski as "tall, fair-haired, [and] boyish, despite his close-cropped mustache, slender, alert of eye and mien." The officer, who immigrated to America in 1907, was fluent in Russian, Polish, and Ukrainian, as well as "many" other languages, "and specialized on the problem of the foreigner" (see below). Gutowski became a naturalized American citizen on September 24, 1917.[1]

In late November of 1917, the War Department charged Lt. Gutowski with the task of assessing the current state of affairs at the camps with regard to the immigrant morale and training problems, which had become a critical concern of military officials. Gutowski proceeded to identify the circumstances surrounding the root causes of the heretofore unmanageable and unworkable methods of training non–English-speaking recruits. The majority of these men were languishing in depot brigades at camps across the country. Upon completion of his evaluation, superiors instructed Gutowski to submit a report outlining the major issues adversely affecting troop morale, along with a list of recommended changes for the express purpose of reversing this intolerable situation in the fastest possible time.[2]

Military authorities ordered Gutowski to proceed to Camp Devens in Ayer, Massachusetts, to conduct an investigation into reported morale problems that were seriously affecting the Slavic soldiers stationed there, primarily the Russians and Poles, with Company F, 303rd Infantry Regiment, 76th "Liberty Bell" Division. Apparently, the Slavs had registered numerous complaints with military officials alleging verbal and physical abuse by the officers and noncoms at the cantonment. Gutowski later reported that the "overwhelming majority" of the foreign-born soldiers stationed at Devens spoke little or no English.[3]

During the course of his investigation, Lt. Gutowski's initial game plan for dealing with English-language-deficient recruits at Devens was to recommend a number of changes to existing policies and procedures with regards to the disposition of these men. What he "proposed" to the Camp Commander and his staff was "that each racial group [nationality] should be dealt with separately." The basic premise of his plan of action involved the creation of "ethnic-specific units" commanded by bi- and multilingual officers and noncoms, what camp officials began to commonly refer to shortly thereafter as "'Foreign Legion' Companies." In essence, what Gutowski was advocating was the segregation of immigrant trainees into ethnic specific "auxiliary units," to facilitate the training process. Upon completion of Gutowski's initial investigation into the morale and language issues at Camp Devens, he submitted his model for the restructuring of existing training policies and procedures to FSS Chief Brewer in late December of 1917, who decided to adopt and implement the proposed recommendations.[4]

Speaking before an audience of "Intelligence Officers" from several of the training camps shortly after completing his work at Devens, Lt. Gutowski made the following appeal: "If every one of you will give to [the] Government 1,000 [properly trained foreign-speaking] men, then [the] Government will get 50,000 men who will fight at the front." Thereby, he emphasized, "more American lives will be saved." "If you do not," he stated emphatically, "American boys will have to go to the front, fight and die." MIS chief Brig. Gen. Marlborough Churchill calculated that for each 1,000 fully trained immigrant soldiers ready for duty overseas, "the Government is financially bettered $1,000,000."[5]

* * *

Lt. Stanislaw Gutowski's formal education in Poland, "subjected to many interruptions," he explained in an article written for *Scribner's Magazine* published after the war that contained a brief autobiography, "was equivalent only, more or less, to two years of American high school." Gutowski described himself as an "avid reader." Following his immigration to America he lived with his mother, father, and two sisters in a section of Newark, N.J., he described as "a large multi-ethnic working-class industrial neighborhood of many forges and foundries." For several years, Gutowski toiled at a number of very low-paying jobs in the area's factories and sweatshops with frequent long periods of unemployment in between. And so he had become all too familiar with the predicament as well as the plight of America's working-class immigrant population.[6]

Prior to joining the U.S. Army, Gutowski attended American International College (AIC) in Springfield, Massachusetts, beginning in 1913, where he earned a bachelor's degree. Following his graduation in 1916, Gutowski relocated to Boston. He lived at 78 Myrtle Street, located on the "northern slope" of Beacon Hill, a neighborhood populated by "free blacks," Irish, Italian, and Jewish immigrants from eastern and southern Europe. Gutowski described this area of Boston as a place of "old houses, ... absolutely neglected," with "narrow and zigzag streets ... full of dirt and garbage." "A section of the city," he added, "profaned with filth and entirely inhabited by foreigners." Many families lived in one room of a shared house or apartment under deplorable and unhealthy living conditions. By comparison, the southern slope of Beacon Hill, with the Massachusetts State House (built in 1798) overlooking the Boston Common, became the seat of the city's wealthy and powerful.[7]

With the help of one of his "former college professors" at AIC, Gutowski secured a position as a social worker in one of Boston's "well-known settlement houses, ... situated in the city's North End." During the course of his duties as a staff member with the social service agency, Gutowski had become all too familiar with many of the issues and problems plaguing society's poor urban immigrants. "The purpose of the settlement house," Gutowski wrote, "was to educate the foreigners so as to elevate them to the standards of American life and ideals." In essence, these efforts were part of a nationwide "movement" to promote and advance the general well-being of immigrants. This was part of an "Americanization movement" launched in the 1910s, a nationwide effort organized and coordinated by civic, religious, and settlement workers to transform immigrants into patriotic American citizens.[8]

While a resident of the city, Gutowski enrolled in the Boston University School of Law, where he obtained his postgraduate degree. During his first semester at BU, he participated in the Harvard University Reserve Officer Training Corps (ROTC) program. In the late summer of 1917, Gutowski attended the National Army's Officer Candidate School (OCS), near Plattsburgh, New York, part of a three-month volunteer pre-enlistment program "of intensive training" for college graduates. Participants were required to

12. Enter Lt. Stanislaw A. Gutowski 103

pay their own expenses. Upon completion of the course (second class of 1917, conducted in August, September, October, and November), officer candidate Gutowski received a commission as a 2nd lieutenant. He was a member of Company H, 17th Provisional Training Regiment, composed of men from the New England states. By June of 1918, the school had produced more than 57,000 graduates who went on to serve in the new national army. Stanislaw Gutowski spent five years in the U.S. Army, eventually attaining the rank of captain.[9]

* * *

As mentioned above, Gutowski's first assignment with the MIS was to conduct an investigation into reported morale problems that were seriously affecting the Slavic soldiers (primarily Russians and Poles) with the 76th Division at Camp Devens. Capt. Ernest J. Hall, the "Morale and Intelligence Officer" at Devens, reported "to Chief Brig. Gen. Churchill seven months later on July 22, 1918, that 4,735 of the 17,932 troops were of foreign extraction (26 percent), the majority Italians and Slavs. What Hall learned during the course of his duties was "that his foreign-born soldiers 'were very willing to serve and are loyal, but [do] not understand what they were fighting for and why.'" Hall arranged for weekly meeting with the troops of various nationalities for in-depth discussions on this as well as other related topics and issues of concern.[10]

The young lieutenant began his investigation at Camp Devens by interviewing individual immigrant soldiers to determine the root causes for the frustration and unrest. He personally conversed with the Slavs in Russian and Polish. For assistance with some of the other Slavic languages, with which he had only a basic familiarity, Gutowski enlisted the help of a Camp Devens officer, one "Major Rantlett" (possibly Leon W. or Leon L. Rantlett—see Draft Cards). The major, he related, "could manage practically all the Slavonic languages," a group of closely related native tongues and dialects spoken by the Slavic peoples. Collectively, they are a subgroup of the Indo-European language family (approximately 439 specific languages and dialects). These languages were common to most of Eastern Europe, much of the Balkans (southeastern Europe), parts of central Europe, and the northern part of Asia. No other information is available about Rantlett or his background.[11]

The Slavic recruits informed Gutowski and Rantlett that the officers and noncoms at the camp "could understand neither their language nor their psychology." The two officers listened to their many complaints and concerns, which previously they had been unable to convey to those in charge because of the language barrier. Gutowski witnessed what he described as "a very pathetic scene." "With tears in their eyes," the lieutenant related sadly, the Poles "began to ask different questions and explain their hard position in the

Army." Since they were put in the rank," they "have had no chance to speak, to tell their troubles."[12]

In his report to War Department officials dated December 28, 1917, Gutowski outlined his "Observations" regarding conditions at Camp Devens. "After three months' training," he emphasized, "most" of the Slav recruits "had learned absolutely nothing," a complete waste of the men's "time and energy."[13]

Some of the Slavs, Lt. Gutowski related, also complained that their "religious needs were not being met." The two main religious denominations within the countries with Slavic populations are Orthodoxy and Roman Catholicism. Gutowski "pressured the military" to affect a number of changes aimed at improving conditions, thus increasing troop morale. He conferred with members of the camp's "Chaplain Corps," commissioned officers who were ordained clergy—priests, ministers, pastors, and rabbis, nearly all of whom spoke primarily English, and asked for their cooperation in being more respectful and attentive to the cultural diversity and spiritual needs of the foreign-born men of different faiths. Gutowski also informed camp officials of the urgent need to secure a number of bilingual clergymen.[14]

A lack of bilingual chaplains prevented many of the Slavs from going to confession and doing the assigned penance for forgiveness of their sins (absolution) before receiving Holy Communion. "The prospect of being shipped overseas and dying in a state of sin weighed heavily on their souls," historian David A. Laskin wrote. There were "those who believed they must go to confession, and if they did not, [H]ell would instantly follow in case they were killed." With assistance from the Knights of Columbus (K. of C.), Lt. Gutowski was able to secure "a number of Polish priests" from nearby communities "to hear and conduct mass in the Polish language."[15]

Gutowski "successfully convinced" military officials to allow for the observance of major religious holy days and holidays, and finally, to grant the foreign-born servicemen "special leave," if at all possible, to spend time with their families during days of religious or cultural significance. Many of the soldiers at Devens lived within a relatively short distance of the training camp with easy access to rail transportation. Ayer was a major rail junction for both east-west and north-south rail lines, a prime consideration when choosing a suitable location for the training facility. In addition, the lieutenant made arrangements for Catholic priests at the camp to conduct a special "Slavic Christmas service" for the men during the approaching holiday season.[16]

Lt. Gutowski also arranged for the Commission on Training Camp Activities (CTCA), headed by Raymond Fosdick, to work closely with a number of civic organizations such as the K. of C., YMCA, and the Jewish Welfare Board (JWB), to assist in providing "for the specific spiritual needs of the immigrant servicemen." In September 1917, a number of prominent Jewish leaders "from twenty-two different national Jewish organizations" formed the JWB "for the purpose of serving the religious and morale needs of Jewish service personnel in the Armed Forces." More than 200,000 Jews served in the American armed forces during the war, and a considerable number of these men were immigrants. The K. of C. arranged for bilingual Catholic clergymen to be available in their buildings on a regular basis and provided a place to conduct religious services, usually on the stage, complete with an altar, sacristy, and confessionals.[17]

Another immediate change made by YMCA officials was to hire a number of bilingual secretaries to be on duty in all the organization's hostess huts. Generally, the YMCA would sponsor events for Protestant soldiers and the K. of C. would be in charge of hosting those for members of the Catholic faith, the latter estimated to be about 35 percent of American servicemen. Activities and programs sponsored by both organizations were open and available to all soldiers regardless of creed.

During the course of the interviews conducted by Gutowski and Rantlett, the pair discovered that many immigrant soldiers had very little or no knowledge of the government benefits available to all servicemen. Apparently, officials at the camps had neglected to inform immigrant soldiers of the existence of these assistance programs or the process for filing the necessary paperwork to obtain benefits. Many in the military were unaware of the existence of government life insurance policies available through the Bureau of War Risk Insurance (BWRI) that would provide compensation to the families of armed services personnel in the event they lost their lives while in the armed services. The BWRI also paid benefits to soldiers permanently or partially disabled in the line of duty, up to a maximum of $200 per month. Insurance policies also included a provision for the specialized treatment and rehabilitation of disabled veterans as well.[18]

"Up to June of 1918," William J. Robinson reported, "51,000 men had taken out $449,000,000 worth of Government insurance." The War Department "considered it the duty" of every soldier to buy the government insurance to safeguard his family if he died in the service of his country. The optional insurance was "expensive," six to seven dollars per month. Over 93 percent of those eligible, the Department of Veterans Affairs reported, had applied for the coverage, and most of those took the maximum amount of $10,000.[19]

The United States government's "involvement in the insurance business began with the outbreak of war in Europe in 1914." At that time, America was "a major supplier of food and war materials to the European allies." As the war progressed, German U-Boats began sinking U.S. commercial vessels in the north Atlantic in greater and greater numbers. According to the Department of Veterans Affairs, "Private insurance carriers were either unwilling to provide insurance, or would do so only at a cost that was much too expensive from the merchants' and ship owners' perspective." Congress passed the War Risk Insurance Act of 1914 to provide owners and merchants with much-needed affordable marine insurance to protect their vessels and their valuable cargoes. Shortly after enacting the legislation, the government added an amendment to the act extending coverage to the captains and crewmembers of these ships. When the U.S. entered the war in 1917, the legislature further amended the act to include "a provision for voluntary life insurance on the lives of servicemen." Approved June 12, 1917, the amendment provided insurance against loss of life or disability and established a compensation schedule as well as allotments and survivors' benefits for family support. During World War I, the government issued over 4 million policies.[20]

Congress passed the War Risk Insurance Act (WRIA) in 1914, which established the BWRI as a separate agency within the Treasury Department to provide insurance policies originally for U.S. Merchant Marine crews of civilian and federally owned vessels engaged in the Atlantic trade during the war. In October 1917, Congress amended the program to include members of all branches of the service. War Department officials "considered it the duty of every soldier" to purchase government insurance "to safeguard his family" in the event of a serviceman's death or injury. Before Matthew Guerra left for France, he took out a $10,000 policy naming his sister Lucia (my grandmother) as beneficiary, which the government paid out over a number of years (expounded upon in another chapter).[21]

Members of the military could subscribe to the relatively inexpensive "optional renewable one-year life insurance policy" that guaranteed between $1,000 and $10,000, based upon premium costs, to a deceased soldier's beneficiary. Rates for insurance varied depending on age, with a monthly premium of "between .63 and $1.08 per $1,000 of coverage." War Department officials "considered it the duty of every soldier to buy inexpensive government insurance to safeguard his family" in the event he did not survive the war.[22]

The War Risk Insurance Act also provided for the welfare of a soldier's dependent family members—parents or a spouse and children—while serving in the military. An amendment to the act, dated October 1917, mandated that members of the military be required to contribute toward the financial support for loved ones at home. Congress created a system of payments, officially referred to as "Allotments and Allowances," allocated under the WRIA, for the distribution of federal aid to beneficiaries. Recipients estimated at 2.1 million received more than $570 million in monthly allotments and allowances both during and after the war.[23]

The army automatically deducted the payments from the soldiers' paychecks and the government added an equal amount that would go directly to dependents. Congress mandated that enlisted men send a minimum of "$15 of their army pay home to care for any relative, ... who relied on them for support," and that the Army would send an additional $15 to supplement the allotment. A soldier's wife received a minimum of $30, plus $10 for the first child, $7.50 for the second and $5 for each additional child up to six.[24]

Agents of the Military Intelligence Section (MIS) worked "to educate" soldiers about the cost and availability of War Risk Insurance and allotment checks. Thereafter, at Gutowski's insistence, camp officials instructed bilingual officers to carefully explain to non–English-speaking immigrants how the government would take care of their families while they were in the service. Capt. G.B. Perkins arranged for MIS personnel to produce and distribute pamphlets that provided a translation of the allotment and insurance information in various languages. During the interviews, Gutowski and his team discovered that many immigrant families previously approved as being eligible for benefits faced a number of problems with lost or undeliverable allotment checks because of "long, strange and difficult names and [misspelled] addresses."[25]

* * *

Following Gutowski's stint with the U.S. Army, he "served abroad" in the Polish military during the "Polish-Russian War" (February 1919–March 1921), an armed conflict that threatened the existence of Poland as a separate nation. Historians describe the dispute as the "Great Polish Uprising," a military insurrection of Poles to reestablish Poland as a self-governing sovereign state. The struggle pitted the Soviet Ukraine and Russia against the Second Polish Republic and the Ukrainian People's Republic over the control of an area equivalent to what today is Ukraine and parts of modern-day Belarus. The Peace Treaty of Riga, signed by representatives of Poland and Soviet Russia on March 18, 1921, divided the disputed territory between the two nations. No other information is available regarding this aspect of Gutowski's military career.[26]

Following his service with the Polish Army, Stanislaw Gutowski returned to Newark, New Jersey, where he worked for many years as an attorney. Shortly after returning to the U.S., Gutowski met and married Hedwig R. (maiden name not known). A check of census records indicate the couple had no children.

In 1944, Gutowski was president of the Casimir Pulaski Foundation, "an independent, non-partisan institution" based in Warsaw, Poland, "with a mission to promote freedom, equality and democracy as well as to support actions of strengthening civil society." In August of that year, he became national secretary of the Polish American Congress, with 2,600 delegates from Polish-American communities around the country, representing an estimated 6 million American citizens of Polish descent. Gutowski passed away in 1954 at age 66. His grave is located in the Holy Cross (Roman Catholic) Cemetery, North Arlington, Bergen County, New Jersey. Hedwig, born in 1909, died in 1992.[27]

13

Creation of the "Foreign-Speaking Soldier Sub-Section" (FSS)

In early January 1918, Secretary of War Newton D. Baker created the Foreign-speaking Soldier Sub-section (FSS). Initially, Baker attached the FSS to the War Department's Military Intelligence Section (MIS) headed by Maj. Ralph Van Deman. Historians Bruce W. Bidwell (U.S. Army Ret.) and Thomas F. Troy stated that "the primary responsibility" of the new department was to bring about an "improvement in the treatment of alien personnel within the army." Van Deman appointed D. Chauncy Brewer, a distinguished Boston attorney, to head the sub-section. Prior to his installation as chief of the FSS, Brewer was director of the North American Civic League for Immigrants (NACL), an immigrant-aid society established in 1908. The NACL, headquartered in Boston, did much to direct the attention of civic and other charitable organizations to the plight of the country's ever-increasing immigrant population. Brewer reported directly to MIS chief Col. Ralph Van Deman (see below).[1]

War Department officials established the FSS shortly after Lt. Stanislaw A. Gutowski filed a report to superiors on December 28, 1917, providing a summary of his investigation into the morale and training problems affecting the immigrant soldiers at Camp Devens, complete with an outline of the changes he incorporated there designed to alleviate the situation.

In the first two years of its existence, the NACL conducted an investigation into the "deplorable" living conditions plaguing immigrants, and placed a strong emphasis on the role of immigrant education. Officials of the War Department, Ford wrote, "considered the Civic League a 'patriotic and philanthropic' organization" whose primary mission was to help "assimilate and Americanize the nation's immigrants with a 'sympathetic personal approach and education in American ideals.'" She added that the agency also "provided [financial?] aid to new immigrants."[2]

The War Department charged the FSS with conducting an investigation into the many difficulties plaguing training efforts of the foreign-born recruits at the camps. Second, the agency was to provide a plan outlining a list of the necessary recommendations and changes to existing training policies and procedures, designed to turn around what many native-born officers considered an almost impossible situation. Lt. Gutowski had a great deal to do with providing valuable input in formulating the objectives of the agency going forward.[3]

Part of the proposed plan called for FSS officials "to work closely with ethnic leaders and Progressive reformers" to "increase the morale" of the immigrant soldiers and "instill" a strong spirit of "American patriotism and loyalty." This included teaching inductees "the principals [sic] of American citizenship," a major component of the overall process aimed at turning them into loyal Americans. In doing so, graduates of the restructured training procedures would eventually become "an important part of America's overseas forces."[4]

Chief Brewer appointed Lt. Gutowski to the position of team leader for the training reorganization staff. Brewer and Gutowski discussed at length immediate solutions to the immigrant training situation as well as the changes army officials needed to make going forward. First and foremost, Brewer also realized that in order for the proposed revisions to be successful, the FSS needed to establish a viable English education program as part of the reorganization plan. This was a philosophy that Brewer brought with him to the FSS (see below).

The NACL, with Brewer as director, "saw its role as helping to transform 'unskilled, inefficient immigrants' into 'skilled workers and efficient citizens.'" Bringing the same "ideology" with him to the FSS, Ford explained, Brewer sought to "turn 'unskilled' immigrants into skilled and efficient soldiers." To facilitate the training process, which up to that point had basically been ineffectual, early efforts by the FSS focused on the reorganization of the non–English speaking troops into ethnic specific units under bilingual officers and noncoms. At Camp Devens, Gutowski proved the workability of the concept and demonstrated its viability. The first step taken by Brewer and Gutowski was to put together a "select staff" of foreign-born and second-generation officers to assist with the proposed restructured training efforts similar to the changes made at the Massachusetts camp.[5]

* * *

A considerable number of immigrants from the Central Powers (Germany and Austria), or one of the territories under their control, entered the army following the June 1917 draft, many "mistakenly." The draft act, passed by the Congress in May 1917, "had been designed to tap as much of the

13. Creation of the "Foreign-Speaking Soldier Sub-Section" (FSS)

national manpower pool as possible." "Granting few exemptions," author John Patrick Finnegan wrote, "the act impartially swept up American citizens and resident foreign nationals, including citizens of enemy countries." The U.S. government considered many non-citizens "temporary residents." A sizeable number of these individuals traveled back to Europe to spend the winter months, where the climate is considerably milder. Much of the European continent is classified as a temperate oceanic climate, strongly conditioned by the Gulf Stream, keeping mild air over the region during the winter months. Immigrants who returned to their home country in the winter were referred to as "swallows."

A large number of German and Austrian immigrants had also joined the U.S. Army prior to the war. Shortly after the U.S. entered the conflict, War Department officials ordered commanding generals at each of the camps to have subordinates "interview" non-citizen soldiers who fell within this category in an attempt, first, to determine if they "wanted to remain in the service," and second, "to evaluate their loyalty." Those "deemed loyal" by investigators received clearance to retain their military status.[6]

A number of high-ranking army officials, including MIS chief Col. Ralph Van Deman, were highly suspicious of these individuals and had serious doubts concerning their loyalty to the United States. The MIS "was concerned particularly with the problem of possible subversion within the vast new citizen forces being raised by the draft." Van Deman regarded "this heterogeneous force as posing a serious threat to national security." He also "believed," Finnegan wrote, "that the newly forming National Guard and National Army divisions" at the start of the war "were infested with German agents and sympathizers."[7]

In October 1917, Col. Van Deman "ordered the divisional intelligence officers just assigned to these units to come to Washington, D.C. "under tight security." Van Deman "was obsessed with possible plots hatched by subversive immigrants and German spy rings" and ordered the officers "to set up surveillance networks [within their divisions] to spy on immigrant recruits." This was a concerted effort to determine the inclination of certain individuals and exactly where their sympathies lay. Van Deman's staff drew up a "confidential pamphlet," titled "Provisional Counter-Espionage Instructions," for the guidance of camp officials in planning and implementing just such a covert operation. The intelligence chief "envisaged the creation of a clandestine agent network extending throughout the Army down to company level ... managed by an assistant to the divisional intelligence officer." There would be at least two "operatives ... recruited from each company" to "submit intelligence reports on their fellow soldiers" upon discovery of any dissention. Division intelligence would relay all reports to the MIS staff in Washington for immediate investigation. Much to the colonel's "surprise," as mentioned previously, intelligence officers found that the vast majority of America's foreign-born soldiers were "overwhelmingly loyal," wrote Laskin.[8]

* * *

In May of 1918, after the War Department became aware of the importance of morale building on the psychological well-being and performance of the troops, the General Staff created the Military Morale Section (MMS). The MMS reported directly to the Military Intelligence Section (MIS). MIS officials "charged" the new agency "with the 'psychological stimulation of troops to promote fighting efficiency.'" Van Deman appointed Capt. George B. Perkins to serve as chief of the section. The MMS, Ford wrote, "closely studied morale issues and implemented innovative policies designed to increase morale and instill an esprit de corps within the troops."[9]

One of the first acts by the MMS administration was to create the permanent position of "morale officer" at each of the thirty-eight U.S. Army training camps, open to personnel with "the rank of major or captain." Camp commanders would appoint qualified individuals, which included bilingual individuals, both "native-born men" and "foreign-speaking [immigrant] soldiers," to the post. Morale officers would have "no duties other than those relating to the stimulation of military morale." They would do so by conducting "loyalty meetings" and giving "talks ... on pertinent subjects" to the troops "in their own language." These men were required "to keep camp commanders informed of the 'state of morale in each unit.'" Officials of the War Department determined that the "upbuilding of morale should begin with the first arrival of a new draftee.... Anything that can be done to make the new man feel reasonably at home and glad to be in the Army ... will be of the first importance," wrote Ford, quoting from an article in the U.S. Army *Infantry Journal* titled "Treatment of New Men."[10]

The morale officer also handled complaints of any mistreatment or abuse lodged by immigrant soldiers against native-born junior officers and noncoms." Another responsibility of the MMS was "to educate all camp officers on the importance and 'value of morale work' and to report any circumstances that 'tend to depress morale.'" Members of the morale officer's immediate staff "included a sergeant to act as an office assistant and two non-commissioned officers within each company." Thereafter, the "bolstering of morale became a regular part of military training."[11]

On May 15, 1918, shortly after the inception of the MMS, officials of the agency held an informational conference on the "Control of Morale." The primary purpose of the symposium was to discuss morale issues and the implementation of innovative policies designed to boost the confidence, enthusiasm, and self-esteem of the troops. One of the major points of discussion by attendees was the flagrant use of "racist language" by commissioned

13. Creation of the "Foreign-Speaking Soldier Sub-Section" (FSS) 113

and noncommissioned officers. Of major "concern" was "the damage done to the 'morale' of ethnic ... troops." MMS officials hosting the conference brought up "the need" for camp officials "to eliminate racial [and ethnic] slurs from the working vocabularies of officers." The section published a report of its findings on May 15, which stated in part, "Depression of morale," in this instance relative to Italian Americans, resulting primarily from the use of racial epithets and other insults, the panel determined, was "largely due to lack of skill and tact among ignorant non-commissioned officers." The report further stated that "many of [the] latter seem to have no comprehension of the problem."[12]

Participants of the May 1918 conference noted also that a "similar ... but even more serious" problem existed among "the colored troops," who "at present," were "much disturbed and depressed." "Bulletin No. 34 prepared [sometime prior to May 1918] for the purpose of minimizing friction between white and colored troops," stated, "Owing to some unfortunate phraseology the colored population was infuriated. Their resentment was deep, widespread and still continues." The report noted, "In the handling of colored troops, education of the officers—both non-com. and commissioned—is of central importance."[13]

Two months later, on July 17, 1918, MIS officials circulated Confidential Bulletin No. 17, which "formally prohibited" the use of derogatory ethnic names and racial slurs by officers and NCOs, "since they created discontent among immigrant soldiers and hurt their 'national feelings.'" Bulletin No. 17 reads in part:

> All officers should exercise great care that no discrimination shall be allowed among non-commissioned officers and soldiers generally, against [foreign-speaking] soldiers in the training companies. Prompt steps shall be taken to prevent the use of such epithets as "Guineas," "bohunks" or "wop."

Likewise, the order "prohibited calling Negro soldiers 'niggers' and 'coons'" (see next paragraph). MIS chief Churchill ordered intelligence officers at the camps to see that any reported violations "be 'brought promptly' to the attention of the 'proper authorities.'" Officials "followed through on the policy," Ford wrote, by directing commanding officers at the camps to reprimand officers and enlisted men found guilty of violating the order. "The directive," she pointed out, "received high praise from the immigrant soldiers."[14]

At Camp Devens, immigrant soldiers registered numerous complaints with the Military Morale branch and its agents regarding the contempt and prejudice exhibited by Anglo-Saxon junior officers (see Faulkner below). Recruits reported a high incidence of verbal abuse, which was having a detrimental effect on their state of mind. Apparently, camp commanders had been ignoring violations, despite orders from the MMS to cease and desist, as outlined in Bulletin 17, thus allowing this misconduct to continue.

Soldiers surveyed by the morale officer at Camp Devens reported "that OTC officers" (90-day wonders) "tended to abuse their authority and take an unnecessary strict and unbending approach to discipline." What is more, the report continued, "the groups who tended to be on the receiving end of much of the abuse were non–English-speaking immigrants and African Americans." One Devens soldier wrote, "We must have discipline in the Army, but not like some of these 90-day lieutenants think." Another soldier quoted by military historian Richard S. Faulkner stated, "There is such a thing as carrying [discipline] to extremes, which I have noticed most of the National Army officers, who have never had a man under them before in their lives, practiced."[15]

On July 20, 1918, Captain Ernest Wood, the Camp Devens intelligence and morale officer, submitted a report to his superiors on the camp's general staff regarding the "negative attitudes" of the officers and NCOs toward the foreign-speaking recruits. In his opinion, they were "not treating all those of foreign-birth with consideration" and that they were "constantly calling them" derogatory names such as "'Guineas,' 'wops,' 'dagoes' … 'squareheads,' etc.," and other stereotypical terms, which in effect, he stressed, "was turning a 'patriotic and loyal soldier' into a disciplinary problem." Capt. Wood's "pleas" to his superiors to put an end the abuse, it seems, "had little effect." Wood also noted in his second report that the officers at Devens frequently resorted to "physical abuse" when disciplining the immigrant troops as well.[16]

A second report by Wood dated August 10, 1918, less than one month later, indicated that recruits at the Massachusetts cantonment again complained of being "continually humiliated … and often assaulted and kicked" by "some" of the "noncommissioned officers." Wood's third report, submitted on September 9, 1918, stated that when the immigrant soldiers at the camp failed "to perform promptly commands which they do not understand," there was "a tendency" on the part of officers to resort to the use of "personal violence." Once again, he stressed that the "negative attitudes toward 'non–English-speaking selectives'" by camp officials had not abated. My great-uncle Matthew Guerra had been in the U.S. for more than six years and had likely learned enough English so as not to be subjected to this abuse during his training period.[17]

Numerous reports submitted by morale officers from a number of the camps around the country indicated that physical and verbal abuse incidents were not limited to Camp Devens. One FSS agent, an officer named Budrewicz, assigned to Camp Lee, Virginia, "reported that the immigrants were not getting a 'square deal' by some of the commissioned officers who treated them as an 'inferior class of people.'" Brig. Gen. Marlborough Churchill, the new MIS chief (see below), forwarded a copy of the report (dated June 8, 1918) to Camp Lee's intelligence officer and ordered him to see

13. Creation of the "Foreign-Speaking Soldier Sub-Section" (FSS)

"that the situation ... 'be 'brought promptly' to the attention of the proper authorities." Confidential Bulletin #17, issued to all camp commanders, forbade the use of ethnic slurs and specifically directed them to "follow through on the policy by reprimanding officers and enlisted men who violated the order."[18]

14

FSS Recruit Training Efforts at Camps Custer and Grant
January–February 1918

Lt. Stanislaw Gutowski's first assignment as a member of the Foreign-speaking Soldier Sub-section (FSS) was to report to Camp Custer near Battle Creek, Michigan, in early January of 1918. Custer was the home of the 85th "Custer" Division consisting of three brigades—the 160th Depot, 160th Artillery, and 169th Infantry. Heretofore, "the language and morale problems," which severely hindered the training of foreign-born soldiers at Custer and other camps around the country, "had gone unchecked." At the Michigan camp, Gutowski would oversee the implementation of his innovative model for the reform of the existing training methods designed to accommodate non–English-speaking recruits. Secretary of War Newton D. Baker "put his full support behind the immigrant soldier reorganization project." The restructuring effort, if successful, would become a model for the other cantonments around the country.[1]

Upon arrival at Custer, Lt. Gutowski reported directly to Major Lawrence C. Crawford, Camp Custer's intelligence officer. Crawford was "in charge of all foreign-born recruits in the division." Gutowski and Crawford spent several hours getting acquainted and discussing the current situation. The two men exchanged viewpoints regarding a master plan and possible solutions going forward. Crawford recommended that Gutowski appoint Lt. Francis X. Swietlik, an attorney in civilian life, to the position of "assistant intelligence officer." In addition to Polish, Lt. Swietlik spoke Ukrainian and French, as well as "some German and Spanish." In a report to Major Ralph Van Deman, chief of the Military Intelligence Division (MID), Major Crawford "assured" that Lt. Swietlik "was admirably suited to continue and perfect the reorganization and training of the foreign-born recruits." Gutowski later expressed the view that he "considered" Swietlik "a 'first class man' in personality and intelligence."[2]

14. FSS Recruit Training Efforts at Camps Custer and Grant   117

Lieutenant Swietlik was born in Milwaukee, Wisconsin, in 1889 to parents who had recently emigrated from Poland. He earned his bachelor's, master's, and law degrees at Marquette University. In 1915, Swietlik began the practice of law in Milwaukee and the following year joined the Marquette law faculty on a part-time basis. At the time Swietlik registered for the draft on June 1, 1917, he was a cadet at the Reserve Officers Training Center (ROTC) at Camp Sheridan, Illinois. Swietlik entered the regular army later that year. He eventually attained the rank of captain of artillery and later served in France. From 1934 to 1953, Francis X. Swietlik was the dean of the Marquette College of Law and "was a nationally recognized leader of the American Polish community from the early 1930s until the 1960s."[3]

With Swietlik's help, Gutowski selected fifteen bilingual immigrant soldiers at Custer, "who had sufficient education and language skills," to join his staff. Camp officials "cited" these highly capable individuals "as loyal and intelligent." In his February 1, 1918, report submitted to FSS Chief D. Chauncy Brewer, Gutowski explained how the team had placed the non–English-speaking soldiers "in the hands of competent bilingual comrades of the same nationality who translated orders and reported the needs of the foreign troops to the commanding officers." The individuals selected by Gutowski, Ford wrote, "were the best and the brightest of the foreign privates from the various nationalities to become interpreters within each brigade, regiment, battalion, and company." By "promoting from within the ranks," Gutowski believed this "new plan ... would improve the morale of the ethnic units."[4]

Over the next two weeks, Gutowski and his staff reorganized Custer's foreign-born soldiers into what he described as "ethnic specific units." "At the brigade level," Gutowski chose "Private [Stanley?] Chylinski," also a lawyer prior to entering the military, "to act as an interpreter and intermediary representing the Slavic troops." Next he appointed "Corporal Steiman" (possibly Henry Charles), "a Jewish soldier," to represent the Jewish and German men of the 169th Infantry Brigade. Gutowski assigned interpreters to the four newly formed ethnic-specific regiments, segregated into the following nationalities—the 337th, consisting of Poles and Russians; the 338th, of Bohemians, Slavs, and Bulgarians; the 339th, which included Germans and Jewish soldiers; and the 340th, Hungarians and Romanians.[5]

Gutowski and his team commenced the project at Camp Custer by interviewing individual foreign-born soldiers in the depot brigade (see below), in an attempt to gather pertinent information about existing training deficiencies and to gauge the immediate worries and concerns of the troops. Team members entered into an intense discussion about the heretofore unworkable situation, exchanging viewpoints and discussing possible strategies designed to accelerate the development of the non–English-speaking immigrants going forward. Gutowski and Swietlik conferred regularly on any additional changes the command staff needed to make to improve the current state of affairs. The goal of the team was to transform the immigrant recruits, previously considered "unfit" and "un-trainable," into productive soldiers able to play a combat role, or be useful to the war effort in some other capacity, commensurate with their background and/or previous experience.[6]

Gutowski and Swietlik also came to realize that to better facilitate immigrant recruit training, the trainees needed to have at the least a basic working knowledge of the English language. This would, of course, require FSS officials to establish English-language education programs at each of the camps as an integral part of the basic training process. Lt. Gutowski made this recommendation to his superiors at FSS Headquarters, and he begin laying plans and making the necessary arrangements to incorporate a comprehensive instruction program "in the reading and writing of English" by foreign-born recruits at every training camp "before joining regular units" (see Chapter 19).[7]

* * *

Gutowski and his support staff decided to establish three separate and distinct classifications for the grouping of non–English-speaking recruits: (a) development battalions, (b) labor battalions, and (c) noncombatant battalions. After making their determination based on individual interviews, the officers proceeded to categorize the men for placement into one of the designated units. Interviewers assigned all "physically able men" to a development battalion; those classified as "disloyal" or an "enemy alien" to a labor battalion; and those "physically unfit" but proficient in some skill or trade to a noncombat battalion. Officials either discharged all individuals with physical disabilities ("cripples") and those with chronic (heart disease, diabetes, and arthritis, among others) or debilitating diseases ("venereal such as gonorrhea and syphilis"), or otherwise sent them to base hospital for care and treatment until they recovered.[8]

Initially, Gutowski recommended the recruitment of qualified bilingual privates and privates first-class (PFCs) to help facilitate the training process. The candidates would translate orders and commands from English-speaking officers and relay these instructions to the foreign-born trainees. With proper instruction and training, these individuals eventually became first-rate assistants conducting basic combat training that included physical fitness, weapons proficiency, and military tactics and procedures. Many among their number were military veterans in their country of origin, a number of whom had served in past European wars. As experienced soldiers, these individuals possessed special qualifications and skills that were a valuable asset to the reorganization and training efforts. FSS officials would later modify this aspect of the plan.[9]

14. FSS Recruit Training Efforts at Camps Custer and Grant 119

Immediately following the changes recommended by Gutowski, staff members implemented the new procedures at Camp Custer and immigrant training began in earnest. Officers in charge of the program reported to superiors how well the revised course of instruction proceeded and how remarkably effective and efficient the strategies worked. Thereafter, the troops drilled with precision and accuracy and, as expected, there was a significant improvement in morale among the foreign-born troops. Almost immediately, the staff detected a fierce intensity in the competition with each of the different ethnic groups striving to out-drill one another. The atmosphere at the camp "passed rapidly" from one of "pessimism to extreme enthusiasm," eventually to the point "that the foreign units could compete with any in camp." A keen sense of pride and accomplishment developed initially between the Slav and Italian trainees for proficiency, and later among the other ethnic groups. The outcome was that the companies "developed faster than the average American company of recruits."[10]

Within a short span of six weeks, the highly efficient training reorganization plan transformed the foreign-born recruits into organized units consisting of what Capt. Edward R. Padgett of the general staff described as "first-class fighting men." Following the training cycle, army officials placed units in regular divisions eventually slated for overseas assignment. In a letter to MIS chief Col. Ralph H. Van Deman dated January 24, 1918, Major Crawford praised Gutowski and described his work as "extremely important."[11]

Lt. Gutowski's report to D. Chauncy Brewer at FSS Headquarters, dated February 1, proclaimed the "reorganization" at Custer "a complete success." The lieutenant "justified the change and assured [Brewer] that these companies were not designed to encourage immigrant 'clannishness.'" In view of the current circumstances, Gutowski stated that his actions "represented a necessary and temporary measure taken in" what he emphasized was "an emergency situation." Gutowski informed Brewer that military authorities at the camp "were perfectly satisfied with the changes." It was Brewer and Gutowski's intention that the reorganization efforts at Custer would eventually become a model for the other cantonments around the country.[12]

* * *

In early February, Gutowski and his team moved to Camp Grant, named in honor of President Ulysses S. Grant, where the lieutenant implemented a reorganization of that cantonment's training procedures to accommodate the non–English-speaking trainees. Located on the southern outskirts of Rockford, Illinois, Grant was home to the 86th "Black Hawk" Division, composed primarily of recruits from Illinois and Wisconsin. Black Hawk was a war leader and warrior of the local Sauk Tribe that originally inhabited territory in the western Great Lakes region, then moved west of Lake Michigan to present-day Wisconsin. Black Hawk held high status among his people as a war chief or captain by leading raiding and war parties as a young man. During the war, the infantry replacement center became one of the army's largest military recruit training facilities, with approximately 43,000 officers and men. The camp had a large population of Polish and Slavic troops, drafted out of the Chicago metropolitan area in northeastern Illinois.[13]

Maj. Gen. Thomas H. Barry, the division commander, requested that Gutowski appoint Major Joseph E. Barzynski, "a regular officer of Polish ancestry," who was fluent in the language, to the position of "division intelligence officer." As such, he would be "in charge of meeting the needs of the foreign-born troops." Barzynski, the camp's supply officer with the Quartermaster Corps, was very popular with the Polish and Slavonic soldiers, who looked up to and admired the major.[14]

Gutowski and his team of assistants completed the training reorganization work at Camp Grant "by the end of February, 1918." This is a key date. Camp Grant, it turned out unexpectedly and for reasons not completely understood, would be the last immigrant training reorganization effort for approximately five months (see next chapter). Gutowski and his staff had tested the concept of "ethnic specific units" at the camps (Devens, Custer, and Grant) and proved it workable beyond all expectations. In view of this fact, why then did War Department officials choose to abandon the revised immigrant training measures at this particular time?

15

Restructuring Plan Canceled
An Unexpected Reversal of Direction

Under D. Chauncy Brewer's tenure as chief of the Foreign-Speaking Soldier Sub-section (FSS), the agency had successfully reorganized the immigrant training programs at Camps Custer and Grant. Shortly after completing the work at Grant in late February 1918, for reasons that are not entirely clear, the reorganization program stalled. "Additional establishments of new 'foreign legions,' and the promotion of ethnic officers," Nancy Gentile Ford wrote, "would have to wait for new FSS leadership." Unfortunately for all concerned, this did not occur for more than four months. This turn of events seems very surprising, since the revolutionary new training and education measures initiated and refined by Lt. Stanislaw A. Gutowski and his staff had worked exceptionally well, actually beyond everyone's expectations. Camp officials, by all accounts, appear to have received and embraced the changes and expressed their satisfaction with the newly adopted measures.[1]

By February, just prior to the cessation of the immigrant training program by FSS officials, the subsection's mission, Ford wrote, had evolved to include "a major reorganizing" of the depot brigades at the various camps "into ethnic-specific companies." Primary aspects of the program involved "promoting and training immigrant officers, increasing efforts at English education, and improving the morale of nonnative soldiers." Implementation of the modifications to existing programs, designed to accommodate the non–English-speaking immigrant trainees, seemed to have been the perfect solution to the army's training dilemma. Oddly enough, the next major reorganization project did not take occur until July 1918, at Camp Gordon, Georgia (see next chapter). The reason for the sudden suspension of the program at that particular time is somewhat of a mystery and leads to the questions: who was responsible, and why?

Corroborating evidence surrounding the controversial policy changes at this particular time is presented here in chronological order.[2]

There are several indications in the historical record that Col. Ralph Van Deman, chief of the Military Intelligence Section (MIS) of the general staff established in May 1917 (renamed Military Intelligence Division in June 1918), may have been behind the abrupt cessation of the new and innovative training procedures. Ford provides one of the clues when she wrote that "soon" after the formation of the Foreign-Speaking Soldier Sub-section (FSS) in January, Brewer and Van Deman, his immediate supervisor, "tangled over policies." Apparently, each man had his own respective ideas regarding the purpose and direction of the FSS. Brewer, it seems, was unable to convince Van Deman to continue with restructuring efforts following the obvious progress at Custer and Grant. The FSS chief had initiated the changes and by all indications, he was satisfied with the results.[3]

We can reasonably assume that the agency had abandoned these objectives under direct orders from above. But who was responsible and why are not clear. Evidence points to Col. Ralph Van Deman as one of the major players in the scheme and is open to much speculation. It may be that the intelligence chief was not about to allow Brewer, a civilian, to dictate Army policy and procedures. Discussed below are several possible reasons why the director chose to suspend the new program after early trials proved so successful. Van Deman, it appears on the surface, was the person responsible; however, another question to ponder is, did the order come from higher up in the chain of command?

The War Department appointed Colonel Van Deman to the directorship of the MIS in May 1917. Van Deman enlisted in the U.S. Army in 1891, and received a commission to the rank of 2nd lieutenant. In early 1895, Lt. Van Deman attended the Infantry and Cavalry School at Fort Leavenworth, Kansas. Two years later, Van Deman became an intelligence officer with the Military Intelligence Division (MID), predecessor to the Military Intelligence Section (MIS). As director of the MIS, Van Deman laid the groundwork for the agency's expanded intelligence operations and established effective code-breaking methods and technology. He is widely regarded as the "Father of American Military Intelligence."[4]

The mounting friction between Van Deman and Brewer regarding the direction of the FSS continued for several months, with the intelligence chief imposing his will over the agency. In a letter to Raymond B. Fosdick, chairman of the Commission on Training Camp Activities (CTCA) on May 7, 1918, Brewer had "expressed his frustration with Van Deman. It was Brewer's contention that Van Deman focused too much effort on espionage matters and counterpropaganda work ... instead of [concentrating] on developing 'constructive' methods of training the foreign-born soldier." Later that month, in another memo to Fosdick, "Brewer lamented ... that like a troublesome child I am spanked, ... and moved into a far corner, so that my howls will be unobjectionable." From Brewer's impassioned pleas to Fosdick, we can assume, with reasonable certainty, that Van Deman was the force behind the agency's abrupt change in direction from its original intended purpose.[5]

Was Van Deman acting on orders from a superior? Interference by the MIS director was keeping Brewer from continuing with the original goals and objectives of the Foreign-Speaking Soldier Sub-section. Training and morale issues appear to have been of secondary importance to Van Deman, thus allowing the program to remain in a state of limbo. Why did Van Deman object to the changes and subvert the program on the eve of its adoption and widespread acceptance?

In April 1917, Secretary of War Newton D. Baker commissioned Fosdick, a "former settlement [social] worker," to study military training for the United States Army and Navy. Shortly after the U.S. entered the war, Baker created the CTCA and personally chose Fosdick to head up the new agency. "At the start of the conflict, the War Department hired a number of well-known Progressive reformers," Fosdick among them, to assist the military in providing for "the socialization of both native and Foreign-born troops." Fosdick had an "excellent reputation as a municipal reformer," one of the qualities that attracted Baker to him. The Secretary "charged" Fosdick "with 'the responsibility of cultivating and conserving the manhood and manpower of America's fighting forces' by providing a 'clean and wholesome' environment."[6]

Prior to the war, Fosdick and Baker had a close personal relationship. Fosdick's autobiography indicates that the two men "had been in intimate contact since 1916." Like himself, Baker was a former progressive reformer during his days as mayor of Cleveland. There is no direct evidence that Fosdick contacted Baker directly concerning the agency's sudden change in direction, which may or may not have been the case. If he did, the Secretary of War most likely advised Fosdick to bring the matter up with Assistant Secretary of War Dr. Frederick P. Keppel (see below), thus keeping himself from being directly involved in the fray, which, because of the personal relationship, might give the appearance of a conflict of interest. Baker was responsible for the establishment of the Foreign-Speaking Soldier Sub-section (FSS), placing the agency under the direction of the MIS, headed by Van Deman.[7]

D. Chauncy Brewer believed that counterintelligence operations by the MIS were essential, but not to the degree that Van Deman's agency was pursuing the matter, while abandoning the original objectives of the FSS. MIS agents spent an inordinate amount of time and energy investigating the loyalty of both the immigrant soldiers and the interpreters, an important clue in understanding what went on behind the scenes. Brewer butted heads with Van Deman, who was obviously skeptical of the value and aims of the FSS—

to turn immigrants, especially those from one of the belligerent nations, into trained soldiers. Following the change of direction imposed on the FSS by Van Deman, Brewer wanted to refocus the mission of the FSS away from stepped-up counterintelligence work, to which it had turned, and concentrate once again on training and morale issues.

As alluded to earlier, Col. Van Deman was suspicious of all foreign-born soldiers, especially those enemy aliens from one of the Central Powers or the territories under their control. Large numbers of immigrants arrived in the United States between 1870 and 1917, seeking greater economic opportunities for employment that would ultimately lead to a better life. This great wave of immigration stimulated an anti-immigrant backlash leading to a policy of "Nativism," protecting the interests of native-born inhabitants against those of immigrants. Following the turn of the century, the social policy became widespread. The outbreak of war led to even greater anti-immigrant sentiments and outright hostility toward the new arrivals. It is very possible that Van Deman found himself caught up in this wave of intolerance and bigotry.

Beginning in 1917, Van Deman ordered his intelligence officers to set up a wide surveillance network "to spy on immigrant recruits," in an effort to determine their loyalty. There were of two types of agents on the MIS payroll, "'inside camp' agents," whose "main job was to assist in the training camps"; and "field agents," those working in urban ethnic neighborhoods and communities. Initially, the function of agents assigned to the training camps "assisted with the very early stages of the reorganization efforts [and] studied questions of morale," but also "investigated the loyalty of [immigrant] soldiers and interpreters." During the period from January to November 1918, the MIS "employed some forty-seven full-time paid agents." The majority of these leaders worked undercover to gather intelligence.[8]

* * *

On April 5, 1918, Raymond Fosdick sent a "confidential memo" to Assistant Secretary of War Frederick P. Keppel, with a request that War Department officials place the Foreign-Speaking Soldier Sub-section (FSS) under the aegis of the Commission on Training Camp Activities (CTCA), of which he was head, and away from Van Deman's negative influence and control. Fosdick's specific purpose was to get War Department officials to agree to return the FSS to its original aims and objectives, specifically to improve immigrant training methods and morale, from which it had veered. This move, he hoped, would prevent any future interference by Van Deman.

In the memo, Fosdick explained to Keppel that "instead of focusing on developing 'constructive' methods of training the foreign-born soldiers," the work of the MIS and the FSS under Van Deman "was largely of a detective nature." "Early reports" submitted by FSS field agents, Ford added, "demonstrate" that Fosdick's appraisal of the situation was "correct." Keppel wrote back three days later on April 8, promising to hold a meeting with department officials to discuss the issue. Ford's research indicates there is no record of a meeting ever having taken place.[9]

* * *

Fosdick's intercession apparently had a positive effect in Brewer's favor. A little more than a month later, on May 9, 1918, a key date, Secretary of War Newton D. Baker's headquarters issued "General Order 45," an official mandate calling for an immediate renewal of the immigrant training program initiated and established by Lt. Gutowski. Specifically, this order called for the immediate formation of ethnic training companies "organized by native tongue" at each of the camps throughout the U.S. The directive instructed camp commanders to transfer all "foreign-speaking servicemen with difficulty in receiving, executing, or transmitting spoken and written orders," from the camp's depot brigades "into special Development Battalions." Baker ordered officials at all cantonments to "expedite" the restructuring plan forthwith and with due deliberation. The order provided detailed specifics for the organization and management of the training battalions. This move is a clear indication that top military officials were in agreement with Brewer's assessment of the situation.[10]

General Order 45 called for just two classifications of "special training battalions," as opposed to three originally proposed by Lt. Gutowski. The first would be for "non–English speaking servicemen," and the second for "illiterates." The first category would include military training according to the guidelines developed under Gutowski's direction, combined with "intensive instruction in the reading and writing of English before joining regular units" (see below); and the latter was for the formation of "special development battalions" for men "who were physically, mentally, or morally incapable of performing their duties" (expressed in an unsigned *Infantry Journal* article as those "unfit and venereal"). The latter would contain men deemed by military officials as being, for the most part, untrainable. This was, Ford explained, "an efficient way" for the War Department "of either getting rid of or reclaiming 'unfit men.'" The war department stipulated that officials separate the two types, training and developmental battalions "geographically" (different camps?). The order called for the separation and transfer of all soldiers in the depot brigades accordingly.[11]

* * *

Historians can only assume that after receiving the official order (G.O. 45) in mid–May, commanding officers at the camps around the country began once again to incorporate the necessary changes to their training programs as specified by the directive, especially since the order came down from the very top. Considering the importance of getting men to the front as quickly as possible, camp commanders should have called for a maximum effort to execute the order as soon as possible. Historical evidence indicates that this does not appear to have been the case. An inordinate amount of time elapsed between the issuance of the directive and the next reorganization effort at Camp Gordon, which took place approximately two months later. For unknown reasons, camp officials failed to heed the order during this particular time period. Why they did not do so is a matter of conjecture, which leads to some interesting possibilities. Was this an indication that some leaders disagreed with the directive, or might there have been other factors responsible? Did someone order camp commanders to ignore the order?

There is a distinct probability that Col. Van Deman may have ordered commanders to ignore the directive. No proof of this exists. Remember, Secretary Baker, like Brewer, was a civilian appointee, who previously had absolutely no experience whatsoever in military matters, for which he was widely criticized. As Maj. Gen. Peyton C. March, who became Chief of Staff on May 19, 1917, put it, "When we entered the War [Baker] knew little about the business of war." In a rebuke of this bit of criticism, March countered his own statement with, "But neither did anyone else in America." Gen. March continued, "As his responsibilities increased, he developed with them. He visibly, almost from day to day, became a bigger man, with a complete and comprehensive grasp of the whole military purpose." In closing, he paid Baker the ultimate compliment: "It is my considered opinion that Newton D. Baker is the greatest Secretary of War this nation has ever produced ... no Secretary ever solved his difficulties with more success. Secretaries of War who have followed him have found his state papers models of clearness, justice and freedom from error."[12]

Secretary Baker also received high praise from President Woodrow Wilson, who wrote that as Secretary of War, Baker had "performed a task of unparalleled magnitude and difficulty with extraordinary promptness and efficiency." He later remarked, "My association and constant conferences with the secretary, have taught me to regard him as one of the ablest officials I have ever known," a statement that Baker "accepted ... with infinite gratitude." When Baker left the position after the close of the war, President Wilson informed him "that he hoped he would follow him to the White House in 1920," the ultimate compliment.[13]

As Law Director for the city of Cleveland, Baker had had years "of continuous experience before the courts as a trial lawyer." His biographer, C.H. Cramer, Dean of Adelbert College (Cleveland), described him as a "talented lawyer." While serving as mayor of Cleveland, he had been involved in negotiating contracts for the purchase of materials and supplies for the city, many of which, Cramer noted, "ultimately involved billions of dollars." President Wilson selected Baker to head the War Department, "partly" because of his experience in this area that would be extremely useful when it came to approving large defense contracts. "In these negotiations," Cramer wrote, "he had dealt with, and had come to know well, most of the prominent industrialists and financiers of the nation."[14]

After the war, both Generals John J. Pershing and Douglas MacArthur issued "subsequent statements" to the effect that Newton D. Baker "was the ablest Secretary of War the country had ever known." A *New York World* editorial declared, "His success in sending two million men to Europe in less than two years, was the most remarkable achievement of its kind known to military annals." The *New York World*, published in New York City from 1860 until 1931, was one of the most widely read newspapers of its day. The Sunday edition could sell as many as half a million or more copies around the United States.[15]

Despite all the behind-the-scenes maneuvering with regard to restoring the revised immigrant training measures, and in spite of the War Department's issuance of G.O. 45 on May 8, absolutely nothing changed, indicating that many camp commanders may have been ignoring the directive. There is no documented evidence of a single reorganization effort having taken place at any of the camps until July 1918, at Camp Gordon. Were they under orders from a superior? Foreign-Speaking Soldier Sub-section (FSS) officials took orders from and reported to Van Deman. The only conclusion historians can come to when considering this evidence is that Van Deman had continued to impose his will over the subsection's programs and policies. It seems his motive may have been to prevent foreign-born soldiers, most notably those from one of the Central Powers or their allies, from becoming an integral part of America's fighting forces, primarily because of a perceived suspicion that some soldiers might commit acts of sedition under combat conditions.

At some point in the ongoing controversy, a major shake-up took place at MIS Headquarters. Sometime in June or July, Secretary of War Baker, in an unexpected and dramatic turn of events, removed Col. Van Deman from his position as head of the MIS. This is a possible indication that he may indeed have been responsible for subverting Baker's wishes, by willfully and intentionally circumventing the implementation of G.O. 45, as ordered by the War Department. This amounted to what Baker deemed an act of insubordination on the part of his intelligence chief, that subsequently cost him dearly. He intentionally and inexcusably refused to obey a direct order from a superior, which was, in this case, related to his job function.

General March ordered Van Deman to France "with vague orders" to "inspect the intelligence operations of the AEF," an obvious demotion. Attached to Gen. Pershing's AEF Headquarters at Chaumont, he remained idle for six months before receiving a meaningful assignment, no doubt further adding to his embarrassment. "The official Army version" for Van Deman's removal was "that [his] involvement in general staff politics and his constant finagling for the advancement of Military Intelligence cost him his job," wrote Historian Roy Talbert, Jr.[16]

If true, Van Deman's attempt to exert his influence over FSS programs and policies by preventing subordinates from carrying out a direct order, in this case G.O. 45, was most likely responsible for his ultimate downfall. Talbert, for some reason, disagreed with this assessment, stating, "There is considerable evidence" that Colonel Van Deman "had an excellent relationship with Baker and his key assistants." This contention may or may not have been factual, but Secretary Baker likely deemed his apparent refusal to carry out a direct order inexcusable. The question remains, was Van Deman egotistical enough to think that, as director of the Army's intelligence operations, he was indispensable to the agency? In this instance, it appears, he went too far and overstepped his authority. Possibly, he was under the mistaken impression that Baker would never relieve him from his post. Apparently, he overestimated the importance he placed upon himself. Van Deman was certain that it was Maj. Gen. Payton C. March, described by Talbert as "his nemesis," who was responsible for his ouster. "Professionally," for Van Deman, Talbert wrote, the demotion "was a disaster."[17]

Quite possibly, Fosdick's personal relationship with Baker played a major part in the change of leadership within the MIS. Van Deman's name, Talbert wrote, "was pushed down" the promotion list "some forty spaces." It would be nearly a decade before he would receive his next increase in rank to brigadier general. Lt. Col. Marlborough Churchill (promoted to major general in August 1918) succeeded Van Deman as chief of the MIS. It appears that Churchill had a direct hand in affecting the return of the agency to its original mission.[18]

At this juncture in the controversy, War Department officials decided also to replace D. Chauncy Brewer as head of the FSS, much to his dismay. Ford states that after Brewer "failed" to convince Col. Van Deman to return to the sub-section's original goals and objectives, proven a success during trials at Camps Custer and Grant, he "quit out of frustration." In any event, Brewer submitted his resignation in June 1918. War Department officials named Capt. Herbert A. Horgan as his replacement and ordered him to report directly to Perkins, head of the Military Morale Section (MMS). "Both Perkins and Horgan signed most of the correspondence," with "a significant amount" of the agency's directives also coming directly from the office of the new chief of MIS, Brig. Gen. Churchill. In the future, the new FSS leadership would have "a more direct link to the War Department."[19]

Very little is known about Horgan, a native of Brookline, Massachusetts, who received a commission as a second lieutenant on November 27, 1917. Appointed as head of the FSS in June 1918, Horgan began signing agency correspondence beginning that month. FSS paperwork and correspondence indicates he was still head of the agency in October 1918.

After Capt. Horgan took charge of the FSS, the "'primary purpose'" of the subsection once again became the "'improvement of conditions' of foreign-born soldiers in the U.S. Army." Immediately thereafter, Horgan resumed all operations in place prior to the shift in policy that began following the Camp Grant reorganization, specifically, the formation of immigrant soldiers into ethnic-specific companies, the training and promotion of bilingual officers, and increased efforts at promoting education. This was a plan of action FSS personnel carried out for the remainder of the war. "Ironically," as Ford put it, "the FSS did change its mission, just as Brewer had suggested." Captains Horgan and Perkins were in apparent agreement with Brewer about reverting the direction of the FSS to carry out the agency's original goals and objectives.[20]

Shortly after taking control of the FSS, Capt. Horgan immediately "de-emphasized the investigation of 'suspicious persons' as a 'by-product' of the [ethnic] agents work." In June 1918, Horgan "'released most' of the ethnic agents from the service except twenty men." FSS officials instructed the remaining Military Intelligence Section agents that in the future they were to work strictly on issues pertaining to the improvement of morale and training. Under Van Deman's leadership, many of the reports submitted by the intelligence agents, Ford reported, "contained vague accusations" against foreign-born soldiers. "Perkins and Horgan," Ford wrote, "repeatedly warned agents" to discontinue reporting "'rumors' about foreign soldiers." In memorandums and other correspondence to ethnic leaders, the two men stressed that the agency could not, for obvious reasons, "take as quick action on matters in the absence of definite proof."[21]

* * *

As an afterthought, one can ponder the question as I have: If the FSS had continued and expanded the revised training measures after Gutowski initially developed and tested the innovative modifications that proved so highly effective, might the war have ended sooner? Certainly, there would have been fewer lives lost. This is an important topic to speculate upon. My great-uncle Matthew Guerra died on October 7, from wounds received in the battle of the Meuse Argonne two days earlier. The fighting ended a little more than a month later on November 11, 1918. What if?

16

The "Camp Gordon Plan"
June 1918

To conduct the training reorganization experiment on "a big scale," Foreign-speaking Soldier Sub-section (FSS) officials chose Camp Gordon, the largest camp in the Southern states, with approximately 23,600 soldiers. "Almost half" of this number, historian James J. Cooke reported, "were fairly fresh from Ellis Island, New York." Located near Atlanta, Georgia, Gordon was home to the 82nd "All-American" Division commanded by Major General Eban Swift. The 82nd consisted of trainees from every one of the 48 states, but principally those from the eastern states, the majority from the camp's home state. Camp officials estimated that of the total number at Gordon, a *New York Times* editorial reported, "Not more than one in a hundred of them knew the English language well enough to understand the instructions required to make them first-class fighting men." "Indeed," Capt. Edward R. Padgett of the General Staff wrote in an U.S. Army *Infantry Journal* article titled "The Camp Gordon Plan," "many of them were openly indifferent, discouraged, discontented, [and] rebellious." Capt. Padgett reported that "75 percent" of the immigrant troops at the camp since the previous fall "had neither learned English nor obtained even the most elementary knowledge of the art of war." All this was about to change drastically.[1]

The War Department's choice of this installation came about in response to a request from Capt. Eugene C. Bryan, the camp's "intelligence and morale officer" (date unknown), to assist with a "'distressing problem' involving non–English speaking soldiers." Military planners designed and staffed the facility "to provide a three-month intensive training course" that would produce soldiers ready to go overseas "at the rate of 10,000 a month." The inability of cadre to adequately train non–English-speaking recruits had "severely delayed" the process, preventing camp officials from meeting projected quotas. Pressure may have been forthcoming from Washington for camp officials to adopt the reorganization measures as soon as possible per

16. The "Camp Gordon Plan"

General Order 45, to increase the number of graduates for overseas assignment.[2]

Lt. Stanislaw Gutowski reported for duty at the Georgia camp sometime in late June (exact date unknown) to take charge of efforts to revamp existing training procedures. Lt. Eugene C. Weisz, "an Italian-born officer" stationed at Gordon, who was "fluent in seven different languages," joined Gutowski as his immediate assistant. Gutowski selected "a number of other experienced line officers" at the camp to assist with the project. War Department officials also ordered the immediate transfer of a number of bilingual officers from other camps around the country to provide leadership for what an *Infantry Journal* article (September 1918) described as "'Foreign Legion' Companies" soon to be established within the development battalions. Meanwhile, the FSS continued to search for additional qualified bilingual rank-and-file soldiers, primarily foreign-born and second generation individuals, to attend OCS for future service as part of the training modification efforts.[3]

During the first two weeks at Gordon, Gutowski and his team of assistants began their work with the men of the 5th Training Battalion, 158th Depot Brigade. Over the next several days, the staff of interpreters personally interviewed every man in the brigade, "either in their own respective languages or in a combination of dialects." The team "noted, classified and either explained or adjusted ... thousands of questions and complaints," wrote Capt. Padgett. "In turn," staff members also "classified" the "reasons for the disaffection of these men" with the people in authority and existing conditions. The biggest problem, of course, he noted, was a "lack of knowledge of the English language, "since it cut [the recruits] off from all chance of improvement." Gutowski and his staff assured the men that Army officials would act on all legitimate grievances to remedy or rectify the currently intolerable situation to the satisfaction of all.[4]

Interviewers then classified each of the men according "to his nationality, loyalty, intellect, citizenship, and fitness for military service." Gutowski assembled a cadre of bilingual Slavic and Italian commissioned and noncommissioned officers to act as drill and training instructors. Initially, the lieutenant formed a battalion of non–English-speaking immigrants consisting of two companies—one a Slavic unit of Russians and Poles, the second comprised of "pure-blooded Italians." "Three officers of Polish extraction and one of Russian" commanded the first company, and "two officers of Italian extraction, the second." Next, the staff set to work creating a company of Greeks and another of Russian Jews. Each of the initial four ethnic-specific companies consisted of approximately 258 officers and men. An unsigned U.S. Army *Infantry Journal* article, "'Foreign Legion' Companies," published in September 1918, reported that by the middle of July the development battalion at

Gordon was "expected to have over a thousand strong, capable fellows, who in a couple of months will be developed into first-class fighters."[5]

During the initial interviews, many of the camp's foreign-born soldiers expressed "bitter resentment" over the humiliating and degrading treatment they had received at the hands of Gordon's officers and noncoms. They were especially critical of graduates of the Officer Training Corps (OTC) and Central Officers' Training School (COTS), "labeled 90 day wonders," generally used in a "derogatory" or "sarcastic" manner, as opposed to regular or career army officers commanding units at the camp, who were generally more tolerant and respectful toward these men. Morale issues, caused by the "verbal and physical abuse of foreign soldiers" at the hands of the cadre at Gordon and the other camps, were prevalent. Captain Bryan "noted that several of sources on the post reported that 'trouble and ill feelings' were being created by the propensity of the post's native-born leaders calling foreign-born soldiers 'various epithets'" such as "'Guineas,' 'wops,' 'squareheads,' etc." Bryan "recommended" that authorities at the camp prohibit the use of all ethnic slurs.[6]

Military historian Dr. Richard S. Faulkner, in his book *The School of Hard Knocks: Combat Leadership in the American Expeditionary Forces,* indicates that the verbal abuse of trainees at the camps by officers and "hardboiled" noncommissioned officers was a common occurrence. The consensus among enlisted men awaiting demobilization following the war, who responded to a U.S. Army survey at Camp Devens, was "that OTC officers tended to abuse their authority and take an unnecessarily strict and unbending approach to discipline." Devens became a "demobilization camp" or "separation center" following the Armistice of November 11, 1918, for more than 150,000 (all from the New England states) of the more than 1,000,000 returning doughboys that underwent the discharge process at the termination of hostilities. Many of the servicemen at other camps echoed similar sentiments.[7]

FSS officials lauded the overall success of the restructuring plan at Camp Gordon in official correspondence, explaining how members of the FSS preferred staffing of units by "commissioned and non-commissioned officers of similar race." On August 17, 1918, Gutowski wrote to Capt. George B. Perkins, chief of the Military Morale Section (MMS), to inform him that commissioned officers and noncoms of the same nationality, "knowing the habits, language and psychology of their respective companies, drilled and turned out splendid Polish, Greek, Italian, etc. companies," adding "thousands of foreign-born fighters ... to the army and sent to the front."[8]

Capt. Bryan sent a memorandum to Chief Perkins on July 22, in which he reported that "after the plan went into effect," he witnessed "a dramatic improvement in the morale of immigrant soldiers." Almost immediately, the staff noticed a remarkable turnaround in the attitude and spirit of the foreign born relegated to the new training companies. "Straightaway," a *New York Times* article reported that among the foreign-born soldiers "50 percent of the discontent disappeared, and real enthusiasm was evident." An atmosphere of cooperation and mutual respect ensued among the men as well as a strong determination to succeed. Thereafter, a fierce competitive spirit evolved "between the Italians and Slavs for proficiency." Both Perkins and Horgan proclaimed that of all the units at Gordon, the Polish company was "the best-drilled unit, a credit to all Americans of Polish ancestry."[9]

Four weeks after the intensive training of the foreign-born recruits began, which was halfway through the cycle, Camp Commander Major General Swift reviewed the companies of the Second Development Battalion participating in close-order drill on the parade ground. Drill procedures included the formal movements and formations used in marching and in the handling of arms for ceremonial parades and guard. Reports indicated the general and his staff "were highly pleased" by the impressive showing.

The following week, Colonel Elvid Hunt, an officer of the General Staff from Washington, came to the camp to conduct an inspect the troops, and was likewise "impressed" by the results. He addressed a company of Slavs and asked, "How many of you men are ready to go abroad immediately?" "In response," Padgett wrote, "92 percent ... stepped forward with spirit and enthusiasm." Capt. Bryan reported to Capt. Perkins that one month prior to the initiation of the reorganization plan at Gordon, "all of the foreign-speaking soldiers had refused go overseas." The captain also pointed out in his report that the majority of the remaining eight percent, those who had refused overseas duty, did so "to avoid possibly fighting their relatives in Germany." Col. Hunt, along with Maj. Gen. Swift, Camp Gordon's C.O., "expressed their 'entire satisfaction' with the reorganization."[10]

Once training was complete, the army shipped the immigrant soldiers overseas as replacement troops and, in some cases, "together as companies," where they joined AEF divisions. FSS officials generally "preferred" to divide the companies up "into smaller platoon-sized units ... accompanied by their foreign-speaking officers whenever possible." This "proved beneficial," Ford explained, "since the immigrants could converse in their native language and still be in contact with English-speaking soldiers in the larger companies." FSS officials, Ford noted, "believed" that the transfer of immigrants "in larger units would encourage them to associate only with members of their own nationality and result in their loss of newly acquired English-language skills."[11]

In late August or early September of 1918, War Department officials disseminated information to the news media "applaud[ing] the 'extraordinary' efficiency" of the new training measures intended to prepare thousands of foreign-born men for overseas duty. Press releases "noted the amazing increase in morale" among the immigrant troops. News reporters immediately dubbed the new training measures the "Camp Gordon Plan." Print and non-print media sources—broadcasting and newsreel companies, newspapers, magazines, and other periodicals—presented stories and accounts detailing the success of the adopted changes to the standard training procedures used to transform immigrant soldiers into "efficient fighters." Following its incorporation at Camp Gordon, the FSS "used" the plan "as a training prototype" for immediate adoption by other army cantonments across the country.[12]

A September 1918 unsigned *Infantry Journal* article mentioned above, the earliest to report on the revived reorganization efforts, gives sole credit for the innovative changes to a single individual (not named): "The [training] problem was too big to settle in Washington or on theory, so an officer who spoke many languages and who had specialized on the problem of the foreigner was sent there [Camp Gordon] to take hold on the ground." Unmistakably, this was Lt. Stanislaw Gutkowski.[13]

The articles written by Captains Padgett and Perkins, both quoting from a single (unknown) source, stated: "Then came to the fore two officers [not named] with a plan which they believed would solve the problem, a plan so simple that now it seems it should have been obvious." The two officers were undoubtedly Lt. Stanislaw Gutowski and Lt. Francis X. Swietlik. They had a plan that military officials were previously unable to conceive of, to organize foreign recruits into ethnic units. The basic premise of the plan "was to segregate according to their nationality the foreign speaking soldiers who could not understand commands, army orders[,] and regulations in English" into separate and distinct companies. "A simple plan! Indeed yes," both articles declared, "looking backward! But not quite so simple as it seems, even now." At Camps Custer and Grant, Gutowski and his staff had tested the strategy and not only proved it workable, but found the concept to be highly efficient. Swietlik and Gutowski worked together to refine the concept during the initial stages of implementation, consulting on the best methods for resolving any unexpected issues and problems that arose.[14]

In an FSS report on the success of the training measures dated September 17, 1918, officials "bragged" that the agency "was able in only three months' time to make efficient soldiers of these nonnatives." Previously, the article stated, "these soldiers were practically lost to the Army and many of them classed as disloyal and unfit." In Capt. Edward R. Padgett's October 1918 *Infantry Journal* article, he likewise praised the Camp Gordon Plan, "which," Ford wrote, "he believed completely and quickly resolved the tremendous problem of the ethnic soldiers." Padgett stated that graduates of the plan "will add thousands and thousands of virile, efficient soldiers to our armies on the battle lines." "Truly," Padgett closed, "the soldier of foreign extraction is to be an important part of our overseas forces."[15]

There are several questions that remain unanswered. Probably the most puzzling is the suspension of the revised immigrant training procedures by War Department officials in February 1918, considering the apparent successes recorded at Camps Custer and Grant. Second, what would the overall benefits have been if officials had not terminated the revamped training measures and waited approximately four and a half months before resuming the program at Camp Gordon? Might the war have ended sooner? A distinct possibility.

17

FSS English Education Program

Capt. Edward R. Padgett, a member of the General Staff, estimated that among the number of incoming foreign-born recruits, there were "not more than one in a hundred" who "knew the English language well enough" to participate in existing training procedures "necessary to make them first-class fighting men." Camp commanders had no choice but to assign the majority of these men to the camp's depot brigades, where they languished. Depot brigades processed new draftees for placement—the army organized the brigades into numbered battalions: 1st Battalion, 2nd Battalion, etc., that consist of lettered companies: Company A, Company B, etc. One source describes these units as "a military clearing house for soldiers, a continuous training-school, a repair-shop for the deficient, a source of supply of manpower for the line regiments."[1]

Non–English-speaking recruits, unable to take part in the training process, were relegated to work parties and often performed some of the most strenuous, often back-breaking labor, that can be described as grueling and exhausting. As Ford phrased it, "Immigrants had been indiscriminately assigned to 'pick and shovel work' to keep them active." Cadre assigned many of the immigrant men to "duties and [other] menial tasks around the camp," such as, for example, kitchen police, garbage collection details, the care and maintenance of the campgrounds, and/or clearing ice and snow during the winter months. They often toiled under extreme weather and climate conditions. Among the immigrant troops, these often demeaning work assignments created much discontentment, evoking a sense of outright anger and resentment. This caused the men in the labor battalions to grow sullen and down-hearted. "Subsequently," Capt. Padgett "reported that their 'morale had been 'shattered to pieces.'" A considerable number of these men were more than "willing" to go to war. They "were," "Padgett explained, more than "anxious to fight to free their homeland from the 'hated' Central Powers," to their growing frustration and annoyance.[2]

17. FSS English Education Program

Following D. Chauncy Brewer's departure as head of the Foreign-speaking Soldier Sub-Section (FSS) in May 1918, War Department officials appointed 1st Lt. Herbert A. Horgan as his replacement. Previously, the officer had served with the Military Intelligence Division (MID) of the General Staff from January 1918 through May 1918. Chief Horgan came to the stark realization early on that the subsection needed to come up with a viable solution for dealing with the existing "communication handicap," heretofore a serious impediment to the immigrant training process. And it was extremely crucial that he develop a plan for reversing the situation and that it be carried out immediately.

In order for the non–English-speaking inductees to be able "to communicate and understand military orders," Nancy Gentile Ford explained, it was "imperative" that they have at the very least a working "knowledge of the English language." Once Lt. Horgan came on board, the scope of the subsection's plan of action, first and foremost, was to emphasize the need for "increasing efforts at English education." Horgan and his staff immediately set about to develop a specific strategy for instituting a remedial English education component as an integral part of the regular training regimen.[3]

In an attempt to accomplish the agency's intended purpose, Chief Horgan concentrated all efforts toward eliminating or greatly reducing the number of existing limitations related to the language barrier that were imposing a serious negative effect on the immigrant training process. Horgan and his staff were in agreement that the best way to accomplish this would be a major reorganization of the various nationalities. Essentially, the initial strategy called for all immigrants to be divided up into "ethnic specific companies." This plan of action was likely proposed by Lt. Stanislaw A. Gutowski (see Chapter 12), appointed by Brewer to the FSS staff shortly after he became head of the agency. Gutowski, with his experience and prior background, was charged with initiating an investigation into "the crucial language and cultural barriers exiting in the multiethnic army." Each of these units would be placed under the command and direction of a contingent of qualified bilingual commissioned and noncommissioned officers. The team's senior ranking officer would be responsible for getting the program up and running, and would then act in a supervisory capacity to ensure each phase of the training process ran smoothly as intended.[4]

Another major problem that existed was the serious shortage of bilingual officers and noncoms within the ranks at many of the camps. FSS Chief Horgan came to the realization that the only way to alleviate the situation was through the immediate promotion of qualified bilingual enlisted "immigrants and second generation immigrant soldiers" to these vital positions. "This new plan," Ford explained, "would end the need for interpreters" and thereby "improve the morale of the ethnic [soldiers] by promoting from within the ranks." Horgan sent a communiqué to camp commanders exhorting them to encourage qualified candidates from the rank and file to volunteer for enrollment in Officers Training School (OTS), where they would be given the opportunity to earn a commission as 2nd Lieutenants.[5]

"With the reorganization of the FSS," Ford wrote, "the agency refocused most of its attention on issues of soldier morale," another aspect of deep concern. "The new military approach" adopted by Horgan, she added, "reflected a more pragmatic method of training immigrant soldiers," as MID officials came to recognize "the vital link between creating an effective fighting force and the need for a high level of morale." Thereafter, one of the subsection's primary goals was "stimulating and maintaining the morale of the army, not only as a whole but with special references to the various races."[6]

Horgan's philosophy regarding the Army's previous waste of manpower was that the primary purpose of the FSS should be to focus on improving the conditions faced by the foreign-born soldiers. This would enable these men to complete the training process to become part of the manpower pool (referred to as a "'ready pool' of replacements") from which qualified men fit for immediate overseas duty as replacements are drawn. Due to the number of casualties in France, the supply of potential replacements was rapidly dwindling. There were also acute manpower shortages at this particular time as a result of the catastrophic influenza epidemic of 1918–19, then raging around the world. The special August 24, 1918, "supplemental draft registration" ordered by Congress at the request of the War Department, for those men who turned turning 21 after June 5, 1918, attests to the need at the time for more men to replenish losses by AEF forces in France. In addition, Congress amended the law for subsequent drafts that expanded the age range from 21 to 30 to ages 18 to 45.[7]

Brig. Gen. Marlborough Churchill, the new chief of the Military Intelligence Division (MID) and Horgan's immediate supervisor, had a great deal to do with affecting the proposed changes. Churchill, a graduate of Harvard University in 1900, joined the army the following year as a 2nd lieutenant and began his career in the coast artillery at Fort McHenry (Baltimore, Maryland). Following his promotion to captain in 1912, Churchill was an instructor at the School of Fire for Field Artillery at Fort Sill, Oklahoma, for four years (1912 to 1916), and from 1914 to 1916, he edited the *Field Artillery Journal*. Following that assignment, he shipped out in January 1916 to France, where Major Churchill "served as an observer with the French Army," until June 1917. From February to May 1918, Col. Churchill "was detailed" to Gen. John J. Pershing's First Army Headquarters as "acting Chief of Staff." In June 1918, he returned to the U.S. to replace Van Deman, at which time he received a promotion to the rank of brigadier general. Churchill worked closely with Lt. Horgan, providing a great deal of guidance and direction.[8]

In a move designed to "standardize" the English-language education program "so that the plan could be easily duplicated in camps throughout the United States," Horgan's staff "quickly designed and distributed written instructions" for use as a guide by camp commanders and staff officers. The directive put forth a detailed plan for the reorganization and development of the Foreign Legion companies into ethnic-specific units and outlined the proposed measures related to the training and education of personnel. "The FSS staff," Ford wrote, "also selected a foreign born or second generation [bilingual] officer to head each company." After careful review, Assistant Secretary of War Frederick P. Keppel, himself an educator, on leave as dean of Columbia University, approved the proposed English education program submitted by Horgan and his department. In his attempt to hasten the training and development process, Horgan ordered camp commanders to implement schools at every camp forthwith.[9]

Horgan's staff also designed lessons to teach American history and government as well as to provide "classes in civics and citizenship" that "focused on the country's democratic objectives." Instructors "not only taught the history of the United States," but also made it a point to include "some reference to the countries from which groups have come."[10]

Another major objective of the FSS was to organize a slate of "counterpropaganda" measures aimed at enlightening skeptical and, in many cases, somewhat apprehensive camp commanders and other officials, "about the benefits" to be realized "through the newly developed policies." The primary goal of military leaders, in this instance, Churchill noted, "was to create an efficient fighting force and make 'non–English speaking soldiers ... a permanent part of the camp machinery.'" Horgan "assured" camp officials, Churchill wrote, that "'men of foreign races' generally were 'ready pupils, capable of concentration and quick progress.'"[11]

An outline of the English Education program guidelines prepared and issued by FSS officials called for immigrants to receive classroom instruction for a minimum of "three hours per day," as a regular "part of their mandatory military duties." "This instruction normally lasted" for a period of "four months, although," Ford noted, "some programs were shorter." A possible factor may have been that some trainees progressed at a faster rate than others and were therefore deemed by the teaching staff to be ready for overseas duty sooner. Following the completion of the combined programs—physical fitness, weapons training, and English-language education—the staff would "assess" each of the candidates "for duty [or] transfer." At any point during the training cycle, men determined by a member of the medical staff not to be physically able for any reason due possibly to a disability or handicap, described by Ford as "the 'sick' and 'cripple,'" were summarily discharged from military service. Likewise, after a meeting with line officers and a psychologist, men found to be unqualified for reasons relating to mental health were awarded a medical discharge.[12]

The overall scheme was a very efficient and practical solution designed to address the problems related to the immigrant training issue resulting directly from the existing communication difficulties. A basic knowledge of the English language would, of course, facilitate the training process by creating a system of conveying orders and commands that was more efficient. Basically, this would enable training camp personnel to effectively impart orders and information and would allow trainees to be able to understand those commands, previously not possible. More importantly, it now became achievable, within a relatively brief period of time, to train and prepare thousands of non–English-speaking men for combat or in some other vital or necessary capacity, who otherwise would have and had been lost to the army for duty overseas. Prior to this, the deployment of these men to the battlefields of France could ultimately have resulted in instances of miscommunication and confusion, a direct result of the language barrier. In some instances, while under fire for example, this might possibly have resulted in a misinterpretation of orders and commands, creating a perilous and unsafe situation that could have disastrous consequences.

* * *

Initially, camp commanders appointed a bilingual officer to the position of program director to oversee the implementation of the English education component of the revised training procedures. These individuals were responsible not only for establishing school facilities at their respective camps, but for the management of the program as well. Secondly, the director needed to assemble the necessary teaching and support staff at the company level to accomplish a predetermined number of set educational goals and objectives. Educators recruited by the director to staff the schools included a number of trained bilingual teachers, assisted in the classroom by a cadre of first- and second-generation bilingual officers, noncoms, and qualified trained bilingual privates, as well as members of the Chaplain Corps (clergy who are commissioned officers). The staff also included a number of native-born and foreign-born civilian volunteers.

To accomplish the enormous task at hand, Keppel and his department enlisted the help of a number of outside educational agencies including the U.S. Department of the Interior's Bureau of Education, many of the nation's major colleges and universities, the Young Men's Christian Association (YMCA), the Jewish Welfare Board (JWB), and other national organizations to procure qualified instructors for the education programs. In addition, Keppel and his staff designed and implemented an elaborate and innovative plan of English instruction and study so that the foreign-speaking trainees could acquire the necessary skills as quickly and effectively as possible under existing circumstances, which included time restrictions.

In an article titled "Uncle Sam's Adopted Nephews," published in the June–November 1918 issue of *Harper's Magazine*, Fred H. Rindge, Jr., Secretary of the International Committee of the YMCA, outlined the work of the association in the various army cantonments across the country. The committee, under Keppel's direction and guidance, devised a program designed to instruct soldiers in English and in the duties and privileges of American citizenship. "Every regiment," Rindge explained, "has a general educational officer, often the chaplain, who helps supervise the work," and "each company generally has an educational representative." The officer selected bilingual instructors from the ranks, many of whom had prior "experience and ability, who possessed the necessary teaching skills to assist with the work." The YMCA staff also made available "classroom space" in the organization's "huts and auditoriums" and scheduled classroom time for various subjects.[13]

After a proper orientation and training period, members the bilingual teaching staff were ready to conduct individual English classes, basically to provide "intensive instruction" in speaking the language, by first learning the words—how to pronounce them, then their meaning, and finally, using them in a simple sentence. YMCA staffers also designed lessons to teach "history, geography, American government, civics, and citizenship." Instructors were equipped with all the necessary essentials for carrying out their teaching duties—lesson sheets, charts, books, and other educational materials and teaching supplies to conduct the classes. In a camp with a population of approximately 4,000 non–English-speaking immigrant soldiers, there were on average thirty to forty basic courses of instruction as well as specialized classes running on any given day.[14]

During the first week of the program, bilingual educators provided recruits with an outline of the preliminary training procedures they would undergo in the coming weeks. Initially, teachers devoted the course of instruction to include lectures in their native tongue pertaining to military discipline, the Articles of War, and military justice. Beginning in week two, instructors commenced a series of basic English lessons in which they "painstakingly taught, first the English alphabet, then words, then sentences." Next, teachers concentrated on "nouns, verbs, [and] adjectives—'I write,'—'I wrote'—'I will write,'" until students had a basic understanding "of the elementary principals of the tenses of English grammar." Eager students wrote the words and sentences out on pads of lined paper that they turned in to the instructor at the end of each lesson to be corrected and graded. Once the program succeeded in bridging the communication gap, the education and military training of the foreign-born recruits continued rather smoothly.[15]

During every phase of each course, the teaching staff made extensive use of "picture text-books" and magazines such as *National Geographic*, *Harper's*, *Popular Mechanics*, *Popular Science*, and other similar publications, "to teach English by using the 'universal language' of pictures." Also utilized were maps found in *National Geographic* and in atlases to show the location of France and the other European nations in relation to other world countries involved in or affected in any way by the war.[16]

The U.S. Bureau of Education provided participating instructors with a variety of standard lesson plans and teaching aids, plus a number of instructional publications that included a number of specifically designed and prepared textbooks. One series, *Enlisted Men Schools*, included among other subjects a "vocabulary and phrase book" titled *Topics for Instruction*, that concentrated on key "military-related" terms and vocabulary words—such as, for example, "rifle," "guard," "bayonet," "march," "drill," "reveille," "inspection," "saluting," and "double-time." Teachers used the series to teach English reading and writing skills. The bureau based the series on the teaching methods designed and prepared by Capt. Emery L. Bryan, the intelligence officer at Camp Upton, New York. Officials at the War Department "directed" teachers "to relate English-language instruction to military life so the soldiers" could adjust "to their "new surroundings and to the new national ideal and purpose."[17]

Also provided by the U.S. Bureau of Education was a pamphlet titled *Teaching English to non–English Speaking Selectives*, adapted from the publication *Education of the Immigrant: Teaching of Modern Languages*. This proved to be a "valuable" instructional aid. Teachers utilized special publications made available by the bureau, such as *The Soldier's Text Book*, by Cora Wilson Stewart, a prominent social reformer and educator during the American progressive era noted for her campaign to eliminate adult illiteracy. Another popular textbook was the *Camp Reader* by Professor J. Duncan Spaeth, a member of the National War Work Council who served as educational director at Camp Wheeler, near Macon, Georgia. The Young Men's Christian Association provided qualified teachers with a number of instructional manuals and other relative publications. These valuable teaching aids included, among others, *Spelling Book for Soldiers*, as well as a number of pamphlets specially prepared to introduce immigrant soldiers to the government and history of the United States. They proved very useful.[18]

Instructors also utilized a series of lessons developed Dr. Peter Roberts, known among educators as the "Robert's Method" of instruction, lauded by Rindge as an "efficient method of teaching English to foreigners." The approach takes a group of immigrant recruits, consisting of a number of different nationalities, and teaches them all English "equally well." At the time, the "method" was "recognized by experts as scientific, accurate, and particularly rapid." YMCA personnel had previously used this simple but efficient technique to teach foreign-born workers in industry. There were, according to Rindge, "three fundamental principles" behind the process. First, the instructor teaches the students "how to speak." The premise behind the concept is "that the ear and not the eye is the organ of language." Initially, Rindge noted, humans "learned [their] native tongue by hearing it spoken by our parents and others." Reading and writing English "came later in the course." "We did not learn from books until long after we learned to speak," Rindge explained. "Second, ... each lesson must deal with a common experience of every-day life." "Third, the sentences" taught by the instructor "must be logically arranged and bear on the main theme," and "each sentence suggest[s] what the next sentence shall be."[19]

Next, the teachers concentrated on pronunciation. The students repeat each word after the instructor in unison. For example, one lesson begins with five words—all verbs—awake, open, look, find, and see. Students then learned the definition of each word. Next, teachers then used these verbs in a series of sentences that are sequential, "acting [out] each sentence slowly and with dramatic precision"—"I awake from sleep." "I open my eyes." "I look for my watch." "I find my watch." "I see what time it is." Pupils then memorize a second set of words and sentences—"It is six o'clock," "I must get up," and so on. Rindge wrote, "It is amazing how quickly the men ... understand and can repeat the lesson without the teacher's help." Next, the teacher "exhibits a large chart on which the lesson is printed." This way the men "then connect what they have seen dramatized and what they have memorized with what they now see in print."[20]

Each lesson consisted of 15 to 20 sentences and lasted approximately an hour to an hour and a half. Everyone in the class received a "copy-book" in which they wrote out the lesson and submitted to the teacher for grading and correction. This allows every member of the class, "many nationalities, to understand the objective of each lesson, memorize a number of words in English, while learning to read, write, and understand the grammar." Classroom teachers wrote a list of objectives for each lesson on the board, to make the students aware of what he intended them to accomplish. Educators used a series of prepared lessons on various military topics, for example: "A Soldier's Duty," "Reveille," "The Commanding Officer," "Commissioned Officers," "Non-commissioned Officers," "The Salute," "Drills," "Exercises," "Rifle and Bayonet," "Care of the Rifle," and "Inspection of Arms." Prepared teaching aids include specialized lesson sheets, "one side ... in print and the reverse side in script," that are read aloud in class and are accompanied by a number of "charts." Next, Rindge explained, teachers covered "some simple grammar with immediate application to the lesson learned, and close[d] each lesson with a review."[21]

* * *

The American Library Association's (ALA) Library War Service established small libraries in various social welfare buildings at camps across the country—a total of forty-three, including thirty-six built with funds from the Andrew Carnegie Foundation. These libraries, each with "a uniformed Librarian" and a number of assistants, provided a selection of reading books of general interest, primarily works of fiction, in various languages. Librarians made every attempt to procure books requested by the soldiers on a timely basis. The ALA also provided camps with "Americanization books" as well as other popular publications such as foreign-language newspapers and magazines. Library collections also included a wide selection of "'purely literary material' along with books," again in a variety of languages, "that would educate the immigrants about the American government and history." Camp libraries contained hundreds of titles in Yiddish, Russian, Italian, Romanian, Spanish, Polish, and a number of other languages. The YMCA also provided its own library services to the soldiers.[22]

The Military Morale Section (MMS) issued a memorandum to all librarians "that the libraries' book selections should include items that that discuss American 'war aims' to reinforce why soldiers were fighting." Each of the camp libraries contained "as complete a collection of reference books, on every conceivable subject as can be assembled in the space available."[23]

* * *

Over the course of the war, the training camps' special development battalions processed "over 209,000" non–English-speaking immigrant recruits. Of that number, "almost 20 percent" went on to full duty with front line units, 42 percent received limited duty in one capacity or another, while the army discharged 17.4 percent. When the war ended, 19.4 percent were still participating in the program (total 98.8 percent) stateside. These figures attest to the efficiency as well as the effectiveness of the new training and education procedures adopted by the Foreign-speaking Soldier Sub-Section (FSS). A September 1918 article in the U.S. Army *Infantry Journal*, published less than two months before the end of the war, reported, "Finally, the foreign-speaking soldiers are happy, the camp officers are released from an intolerable burden, and the work thus started can be conducted wisely and perfected by the officers who have been chosen for it."[24]

18

Resurrection of the Immigrant Training Program at Other Camps

Initially, the War Department reported that following the successful reorganization at Camp Gordon, fifteen additional camps had implemented the plan. On August 31, 1918, Secretary of War Newton D. Baker issued a memorandum calling for the formation of "development battalions" at the remaining twenty of the thirty-five training camps across the country. The order included a request for a list "of the number of foreign-born soldiers (classified by mother tongue) along with the name, rank, organization and language of all foreign-speaking line officers." Foreign-speaking Soldier Sub-Section (FSS) chief Lt. Herbert A. Horgan and his staff "quickly designed and distributed written instructions" that camp commanders could use as a guide "for the development of 'Foreign Legion' training companies so the plan could be easily duplicated in cantonments throughout the United States." An integral part of Horgan's directive on that date "called for an intensive study program in conversational English and military terms." He also recommended that in the future instructors conduct classes "in the morning and afternoon," as opposed to the current practice of holding them during the evening hours, "since the men would be too tired after drill."[1]

Following the successful reorganization at Camp Gordon, Lt. Horgan ordered Lt. Stanislaw Gutowski to increase his staff to address the expanded efforts at the other camps. Gutowski personally handpicked all of the appointees. First, he chose Lt. Eugene C. Weisz, who worked with him at Camp Gordon, to serve as his immediate assistant. Also selected by Gutowski for assignment with the team were Russian-born 1st Lt. Constantin Walczynski, with a command of the Russian, Polish, and Lithuanian (Baltic) languages. His career in the U.S. military spanned seventeen years. Walczynski's linguistic skills and prior experience working with immigrant soldiers at Camp

Custer made him an essential and indispensable part of the FSS program. Selected next were Lt. Walter S. Przybyszewski, the son of Polish immigrants, fluent in Russian and Polish, who joined the army in 1915 as a private and rose to the rank of 1st lieutenant in June 1918 (Przybyszewski had served in the Mexican Expedition against Francisco "Pancho" Villa in 1916); 1st Lt. Louis Washington Zara, able to communicate in Italian, French, and Spanish; Ignatius Prylinski, who "spoke Italian, Magyar, Serbo-Croatian, Russian, Polish, and several other languages"; Lt. Felix Mateia, who had a command of the Slavic languages; and Lieutenants Michael Angelo Viricola and Frank J. Kracha.[2]

* * *

In early August, Lt. Col. Marlborough Churchill, the new chief of the MID, informed assistant chief of staff Maj. Gen. Peyton C. March that "an officer was urgently needed" at Camp Meade, Maryland, to help "create ethnic platoons ... and assist in the 'upbuilding of the morale' of the foreign-speaking soldiers." March immediately dispatched Lt. Gutowski and his team to the training facility to assess the situation and implement the necessary measures to get the training program up and running as quickly as possible. Brig. Gen. Henry Jervey, acting assistant chief of staff, instructed Gutowski to begin with the creation of "a model development battalion" at the camp, for the express purpose of testing the "efficiency" of the new program "before implementing it in other Meade units." Apparently, there were still some nonbelievers among the upper echelon of the military establishment. Secretary of War Baker ordered thirty-four foreign-speaking officers from other camps around the country to proceed to the Maryland camp "to observe ... and help coordinate the activities" of the new program so they would be able to direct the implementation of the plan at their respective cantonments.[3]

At the same time, Lt. Horgan again put out the call for camp officials to seek out all qualified bilingual soldiers within the ranks and select the best qualified to be considered for promotion as commissioned and noncommissioned officers "to assist ... with the growing percentage of immigrant draftees," wrote Ford. This included a significant number of individuals with prior service in their country of origin, many of whom "were veterans of past European wars." Horgan reminded camp commanders that some of these experienced individuals possessed "special qualifications" and would be valuable assets in the instruction and drill of the foreign infantry units.[4]

After having received a number of reports alleging "supposed disloyalty" among the foreign-born recruits, Lt. Horgan ordered the formation of "a board of foreign-speaking officers" on August 23, 1918, to conduct an investigation into the matter. Apparently, this was still of some concern to a number of skeptical military officials.[5]

18. Resurrection of the Immigrant Training Program

Horgan also "suggested" that officials at each of the camps initiate several measures in a concerted effort "to help raise the spirit of the foreign troops." Changes included providing ethnic entertainment, recruiting "prominent ethnic speakers" to "host" a number of patriotic lectures, showing popular foreign-language motion pictures, and providing appropriate reading and learning materials. The purpose of these presentations was to inform the immigrant soldiers why the U.S. was fighting the Great War.[6]

According to historian David Laskin, one of the major changes made by the War Department that vastly improved morale among the various nationalities was to issue a directive ordering "mess sergeants" at the camps to "prepare ethnically appropriate food." In essence, as the author of an unsigned *Infantry Journal* article titled "The Camp Gordon Plan" phrased it, "Give them their own mess sergeants to feed them what they were used to [eating]." Officials at some of the camps promoted a number of qualified foreign-born chefs and cooks to prepare ethnic meals. Historian Richard Slotkin noted that somewhere "between 30 and 40 percent of the enlisted men" in the 77th "Statue of Liberty" Division at Camp Upton "were Jewish." "Representatives of the Jewish community" met with Capt. Perkins, head of the MMS, "to discuss the possibility of establishing a store" on the grounds of the camp "for the sale of Kosher food." Jewish leaders also proposed "the building of a Kosher restaurant" at the Long Island training facility. Secretary of War Baker "had previously turned down a … request to serve Kosher food at the camps." Army officials did allow unknown persons, possibly the Jewish Welfare Board (JWB), to set up a Kosher restaurant just outside the gates of Camp Upton, within walking distance, that the men could frequent during off-duty hours.[7]

Immediately following Gutowski's completion of the reorganization at Camp Meade, he returned to Camp Devens for his next assignment. It had been eight months since his original visit where he began his initial investigation into the morale and training problems. FSS officials ordered Lt. Frank Kracha, a member of Gutowski's team, to remain at Meade to oversee and coordinate the work. Lieutenants Walter S. Przybyszewski and Louis Zara received special orders to assist Gutowski at Camp Devens. During Gutowski's first visit in December, there were 17,932 trainees at the facility, and of that number, 4,735 were foreign-born (26 percent). Following the second national draft registration of June 1918, the number of ethnic soldiers at Devens had more than doubled "to some 10,000." Churchill's office arranged for the rapid transfer of two bilingual Italian and two Slavic officers to report to Devens from other camps and sent out a memorandum for Capt. Ernest J. Hall, the camp's Intelligence Officer, to search for two Armenian and two Greek officers. Due to the shortage of foreign-born officers, the MIS "recommended" that some of the bilingual soldiers "be considered for commissions to assist with the growing percentage of immigrant draftees."[8]

Before Gutowski left Devens, there were eighty bilingual officers who spoke the following languages: Ukrainian, French, German, Hebrew, Italian, Norwegian, Polish, Portuguese, Spanish, Swedish, and Yiddish. Twenty-one of the eighty were of "foreign extraction" and the remainder were second-generation Americans. Within ten days of Gutowski's arrival at the camp, the FSS was reporting that the foreign-born troops "were in 'excellent shape'" and that morale "had improved '100 percent.'" Captain Hall submitted a report to MIS Chief Churchill, in which he declared that the reorganization "proved to be a complete success."[9]

* * *

After completing the reorganization at Devens in late August, Lt. Gutowski headed to Camp Upton, New York, to "install" the "Camp Gordon Plan" at that facility. Upton was the home of the 77th "Statue of Liberty" Division, with approximately 23,000 draftees, primarily from New York City and some of the surrounding counties. In October, Gutowski reported to Camp Dix, New Jersey, while FSS officials assigned members of his team to other camps around the country. An MIS bulletin titled "'Foreign Legion' Companies," issued on July 15, 1918, explained how "the non–English men ... can be grouped, handled and controlled together, and the wastage which has existed, time, money and foreign human material can be brought to an end." FSS chief Lt. Herbert A. Horgan concluded that the plan "would save the military great numbers of soldiers of proved fighting stock and capability.'" Lt. Gutowski "received continual praise" from officials at his assigned camps as well as from FSS superiors for his reorganization work. In November 1918, Gutowski's contributions to the training restructuring efforts resulted in a promotion to the rank of captain. A letter to Churchill, from Capt. J. Joseph Lilly, the Camp Dix Intelligence Officer, on November 9, 1918, reported that Gutowski "had been of immense assistance in 'clearing up the foreign soldier situation.'" Lt. Horgan also praised Lt. Walter S. Przybyszewski for his assistance with initiating the training modifications at the camp.[10]

In October 1918, following the implementation of the "Camp Gordon Plan" at Camp Lee, Virginia, by Lt. Eugene C. Weisz, Gutowski "reported a vast improvement in the morale of the Foreign-born troops." Lee was the home of the 80th "Blue Ridge" Division (and later the 37th "Buckeye" Division). A report titled "Camp Lee Situation Survey," an appraisal of the FSS reorganization efforts submitted to (now) Capt. Horgan, reported that "the drill and march" of the troops "was 'exceptionally good and the execution of their movements very precise.'" The report noted, "The men go to their work ... with a song on their lips."[11]

* * *

18. Resurrection of the Immigrant Training Program 149

There were an "unknown number" of soldiers of Spanish-speaking origin or descent, particularly from Spain, Latin America (Central and South America—also referred to as Latinos), where the population speaks primarily Spanish and Portuguese, at several cantonments around the country. According to Fred H. Rindge, there were a total "5,794 Mexicans" taken in the first draft of June 5, 1917. Utilizing the Camp Gordon Plan, the army eventually organized approximately 4,000 Hispanics into the immigrant training program. Officials sent "most" of the approximately 600 Mexican-American recruits from New Mexico and west Texas, the greatest number from Albuquerque, to Camp Cody (New Mexico). Named in honor of Buffalo Bill Cody (1846–1917), the camp was home to the 34th "Sandstorm" Division, a name based on the region's desert climate, where temperatures of 120+ degrees were not uncommon. The camp was located northwest of the town of Deming (pop. 3,000), approximately 216 miles from El Paso, Texas, and thirty-three miles north of the Mexican border. Deming was a whistle stop on the route of the Southern Pacific R.R. The division, numbering approximately 10,000 in October 1917, consisted of National Guard units from the Dakotas, Nebraska, Minnesota, and Iowa. By early 1918, the total population at the camp had jumped to nearly 25,000.[12]

"The FSS detailed Capt. J. Mott Dahlgreen" of Camp Travis, Texas, "to reorganize" Camp Cody's "Spanish speaking soldiers into [ethnic-specific] training companies." He arranged to have five bilingual officers transferred to the camp to assist with the necessary changes to the training procedures to accommodate the Spanish-speaking recruits. This reorganization, however, did not get underway until November 1918, just as the war concluded. Prior to that, Travis officials had relegated the majority of Hispanic recruits to labor details. Associated Press writer Russell Contreras, quoting another source, stated that soon after the declaration of war against Germany, "tens of thousands of Mexican Americans fled Texas to Mexico to avoid being drafted."[13]

19

The 76th Division Overseas
The St. Mihiel Offensive

The 76th "Liberty Bell" Division began the move overseas from Camp Devens on July 3, 1918. It took until July 15 before the last of the vessels carrying the troops of the 76th Division shipped out. During this period, approximately 28,000 men departed the cantonment. Between July 4 and July 15, 1918, units of the 301st Infantry Regiment ("Boston's Own") departed Devens for England, port of departure unknown. By the latter date, the last of the 76th Division troops had shipped out. For security purposes, newspapers held the story until the 24th. Matthew Guerra's regiment, the 304th Infantry (Connecticut), sailed "from Boston Harbor" on "July 8th, 1918" (*History of the 304th Infantry Regiment* states the 7th) arriving in England on the 15th, where the unit "rested."[1]

William J. Robinson, in his *History of Camp Devens*, noted that several "last-minute weddings" took place at the camp just prior to shipping out. A small crowd of well-wishers, "not more than friends and families happened to be on hand to kiss their soldiers goodbye." The group followed behind the procession as the troops marched smartly down the road to the "railway siding" in the town of Ayer. As "the trains rolled swiftly out to 'that somewhere,'" wrote Robinson, the crowd "waved farewells." The men, he closed, "went out singing, 'Hail, Hail the Gang's all Here,' and all the rest of it."[2]

U.S. Navy destroyer escorts protected the convoys from enemy submarines as they steamed across the North Atlantic. To confuse German "wolf packs" lurking offshore, the troopships zigged and zagged, often changing speed (a method first tested in World War I). Most men had never been to sea and suffered from frequent bouts of violent seasickness, especially during rough weather and high seas. All units of the division arrived at English ports between July 12 and August 8, 1918. After a brief delay in rest camps in Great Britain, the units of the 76th proceeded across the English Channel to either of three French ports, Bordeaux, Cherbourg, and

American soldiers in France.

UNE VISITE DANS UN CAMP AMERICAIN EN FRANCE
13. Prends patience brave poilu voilà de solides renforts qui nous arrivent

American soldiers in France.

Le Havre. On July 27, 1918, Guerra's 304th regiment boarded a troopship for Le Harve.

Upon arrival in France, the 76th Division established its headquarters in the commune of St. Amand-Montrond, near Bourges, France, approximately 120 miles due south of Paris. On July 14, while en route, the War Department changed the designation of the 76th to the 3rd Depot Division, which meant the men of the 76th would not fight as a complete unit. Once in place in France, "the unit served as a replacement regiment, providing officers and enlisted men to the units ... fighting on the front line." On August 3, 1918, the AEF transferred 7,000 men from the 76th to line divisions as replacements known as "fillers." Additional transfers followed. Guerra joined the 4th Infantry Division on August 8, 1918.[3]

* * *

Just prior to going overseas, 76th Division Headquarters posted a bulletin that every man would receive a five-day furlough. Most of the men, those who lived within a reasonable distance from Camp Devens, managed to get to their homes just before departing for France. Robinson related, "They had told the home folks that this would probably be their last visit for some time." Family members were painfully aware that their farewell could be a final parting. Their boys were embarking on a journey that might possibly end in death and bereavement.[4]

19. The 76th Division Overseas

There were two possible scenarios regarding Matthew Guerra's last visit with his sister Lucia, his brother-in-law Antonio, and his four-year-old niece, my aunt Victoria, before shipping out to France. One is that the family traveled to Camp Devens by passenger train on a weekend visiting day or on the 4th of July holiday to see Matthew shortly before his final departure. The second possibility is that during his five-day furlough he managed to travel to Worcester to visit the Palumbos. It would be the last time they would ever see him.

Guerra's stateside training began on April 26, 1918. His outfit shipped overseas on July 18, 1918, two months and twenty-two days later—a total of 83 days. Upon arrival in France, Guerra spent six days with a depot company. On August 18, he received an assignment with Company C, 58th Infantry Regiment, 4th "Ivy" Division, headquartered at St. Amand-Montrond.

* * *

On September 2, 1918, a meeting of the allied commanders took place at the headquarters of Field Marshal Ferdinand Foch, commander-in-chief of the Allied armies, in Bombon, France. In attendance were General Henri Philippe Pétain, commander-in-chief of French forces; Field Marshal Sir Douglas Haig, commander-in-chief, British Expeditionary Force (BEF); and General John "Black Jack" Pershing, commander of the American Expeditionary Forces (AEF). Also in attendance were a host of other high-ranking staff officers.

During the course of the meeting, Commander Foch proposed that General Pershing's First Army take on not one, but two separate combat operations in succession against the German lines. For the first, Foch charged the American commander with the mission of reducing the St. Mihiel salient, so named for the town located at its tip, 22 miles (36km) south of the city of Verdun. For the second offensive, Foch offered Gen. Pershing a choice between the Champagne and that immediately to the east from the western edge of the Argonne Forest, described as a heavily wooded plateau, and the Meuse River, approximately 22 miles to the east (see map on page 158).

The St. Mihiel offensive, scheduled to take place beginning in ten days on September 12, would be the first major campaign by the AEF in France as a completely independent force. The ultimate objective of the drive was to capture the key rail center in the city of Metz, which was not realized, as the Germans hurriedly refortified their positions. Pershing then turned all efforts toward mounting the second of his objectives, the Meuse-Argonne Offensive.

The St. Mihiel salient, a 30-mile-wide German-held position jutting 15.5 miles (25km) into the Allied-held territory (see map on page 158) was basically triangular in shape. The sector had as its three points the commune of Pont-a-Mousson on the Moselle River, at the western tip; from there due west to the town of St. Mihiel; and then continued north-northwest to a point approximately four miles northwest of Fresnes, the northernmost objective; then back to Pont-a-Mousson. Approximately thirty-three miles due north of Pont-a-Mousson was the city of Metz, held by German forces. French agents spread rumors that the Americans were planning a massive drive toward the heavily fortified city. Most importantly, if Pershing's forces did not eliminate the salient prior to the Meuse-Argonne operation, German forces would threaten the flank of any offensive the Allies might undertake to the north and west. German artillery batteries located within the salient could blanket the target area with incessant and deadly fire against advancing American units in the sector.

Field Marshal Foch proposed an attack on the south and west face of the salient. Pershing could, he suggested, reduce the size of his assault force, employing a minimum of nine U.S. and five French divisions—deemed by Foch to be of sufficient strength to produce the required result of eliminating the German-held sector. "The general plan," Pershing wrote in his final report, "was to make simultaneous attacks against the flanks of the salient." The advance would stop at a line running from Vigneulles, on the west, through Thiaucourt, to Regniéville. A small force would then hold the line until the beginning of the Meuse-Argonne Campaign.[5]

Pershing's U.S. First Army attack force for the St. Mihiel offensive included three American and one French corps, composed of the following units:

>I Corps—2nd ("Warrior") Division, 5th ("Red Diamond" or "Red Devils") Division, 82nd ("All American") Division, 90th ("Tough Ombres") Division. Reserve: 78th ("Lightning") Division.
>
>IV Corps—1st ("Fighting First") Division, 42nd ("Rainbow") Division, 89th ("Middle West" or "Rolling W") Division. Reserve: 3rd ("Rock of the Marne" or "Marne Men," a nickname attained in World War I following the Aisne-Marne Offensive of July 15–August 6, 1918).
>
>V Corps—4th ("Ivy") Division, 26th ("Yankee") Division, 15th French Colonial Division. Reserve: Units of 4th Division.
>
>II French Colonial Corps—2nd Dismounted Cavalry Division, supported by the American 320th Infantry and 315th MG Battalion detached from the 80th ("Blue Ridge Mountain") Division. Reserve: the 26th and 39th French Colonial Divisions.

The strength of Pershing's First Army in this battle totaled approximately 660,000, including 550,000 U.S. and 110,000 French troops. Gen. Pétain had placed all French units involved in the offensive under Pershing's "personal command." On the German side, Commander General Max von Gallwitz had 197 divisions, 113 on the line consisting of 75,000 German and Austro-Hungarian troops. Sixty-six-year-old Gallwitz, "a crafty veteran" who had fought in Russia, Verdun, and on the Somme, commanded the German front

19. The 76th Division Overseas

west to the Argonne Forest. This would be the first combat experienced by the 4th "Ivy" Division.[6]

Supporting the operation was an arsenal that included approximately 3,000 Allied artillery pieces, as well as 430 tanks commanded by Col. George S. Patton. Tanks did not fare well, primarily because of weather conditions. American aircraft totaled 640, commanded by U.S. Col. William "Billy" Mitchell, to become known later as the "father of the United States Air Force." The British, French, and Italian military provided approximately 841 additional aircraft, and the RAF nine bomber squadrons, giving the Allies overwhelming air superiority on paper (see below). Foch felt that Pershing should be able to accomplish the mission within a time span of no more than three to four days, which, as the situation played out, was an accurate assessment. Once forces completed the operation, Pershing would then shift the remainder of his First Army west to take part in Foch's much larger offensive in the Meuse-Argonne sector. General Pershing was satisfied with the decision and readily accepted the challenge. Regarding the matter, he expressed his personal view later in his Final Report: "It was only my absolute faith in the energy and resourcefulness of our officers of both staff and line and the resolute and aggressive courage of our soldiers that permitted me to accept such a prodigious undertaking." The consensus among French military leaders was very pessimistic, believing that the Allies could not possibly win a final victory against Germany before the summer of 1919.[7]

* * *

At H-Hour on September 12, 1918, American and French troops, supported in the initial onslaught by more than 1,400 aircraft and 267 light tanks, attacked the German defenses of the St. Mihiel salient. A massive barrage preceded the advance beginning at precisely 1:00 a.m., described by Capt. George L. Morrow as "the greatest artillery concentration ever brought together on the western front." The two American and one French divisions of V Corps, supported by six divisions of the Second French Army on their right flank, would attack the western face of the salient. Six American divisions of IV Corps and I Corps would advance against the southern face, while three French divisions of the II French Colonial Corps would assail the tip of the salient toward the city of St. Mihiel. As Pershing expected, the American offensive caught German commanders completely off guard.[8]

Fortunately for the Allies, General von Gallwitz, deeming the salient untenable, had issued an order for his forces to evacuate the sector on September 8, five days prior to the assault. On that date, the bulk of the enemy forces began a general withdrawal, leaving only a small defensive force in the forward positions. Intelligence reports received on September 13 and 14, the second and third day of the battle, indicated that the remaining enemy forces were retreating in considerable disorder.

The weather, as it turned out, was a major factor during the offensive as it was throughout the remainder of the war. Rain fell off and on throughout the early days of the battle, with heavy downpours during parts of the day and night accompanied by driving, bitter cold winds. Torrential rains had turned the terrain into a quagmire of ooze and muck, impassable in many places to both infantrymen and vehicles. Another detriment to advancing troops were swollen and unfordable streams that greatly impeded the forward advance of many units that had to detour around impassible sectors.

American and French forces had to endure cold, miserable conditions in drenched wool uniforms (despite wearing raincoats) with soggy shoes and leggings. Chilled to the bone and shivering uncontrollably, they suffered much discomfort. Doughboys carried their "lightly stuffed" combat pack (as opposed to the M-1910 "long-pack" or "haversack" with "bedroll extension"), that held a blanket, shelter-half, and other pieces of clothing as well as personal items. Adding to a doughboy's burden was a canteen kit, gas mask, shovel, and an "11-pack grenade pouch" that hung over the left hip. Many men spent the night prior to the attack standing knee-deep in water-filled foxholes and shell craters. Their teeth chattered and their bodies shivered uncontrollably, preventing any kind of meaningful sleep. Squad-mates snuggled together for warmth in their mud- and slime-caked uniforms, providing some small measure of personal comfort.

H-hour began at first light. A heavy mist combined with fog and low clouds made for poor visibility at times. Fortunately, these adverse conditions worked to the advantage of Allied forces, often concealing the presence troops in the advance. Infantrymen struggled to cross water-soaked muddy terrain that had turned into a sucking quagmire. Frequently the men had to pull mired comrades out of treacherous water-filled trenches and foxholes. One can find numerous accounts in the historical record and in personal narratives and memoirs of men who told of squad-mates, buddies, who struggled and became exhausted and were eventually sucked down into the mire and slowly drowned. Troops later discovered the bodies of these poor souls.

Unfavorable weather conditions hampered Allied aviation as well, forcing flight commanders to cancel a number of planned sorties. For those missions that managed to get airborne, low clouds and high winds posed serious impediments to formation flying and made accurate bombing difficult. It was not until late in the day of September 14 that the weather finally cleared up enough for Col. Mitchell to send aircraft aloft.

Despite these horrid weather conditions, American and French troops managed to obliterate the salient within four days. Upon reaching the Vigneulles-Thiaucourt-Regniéville RR line, one of the operation's fixed objectives, the American advance halted. The St. Mihiel offensive turned out to be an "easy victory" for Pershing and the Americans. During the brief battle, Pershing's forces captured more than 15,000 German prisoners, 443 artillery pieces, and scores of machine guns, while suffering fewer than 7,000 casualties.[9]

* * *

During the St. Mihiel Campaign, the 58th and 59th Infantry Regiments, 8th Infantry Brigade, 4th Division, were situated in an area south of Verdun, on the western face "or northernmost sector" of the salient (see map). AEF General Headquarters (GHQ) assigned the division to V Army Corps, commanded by Major General George H. Cameron. Captain George L. Morrow's *History of the Fifty-Eighth Infantry*, indicates the unit was "in support of the 59th Infantry." The 59th and the attached 12th Machine Gun Battalion moved into an area previously occupied by the French, deploying along a five-and-one-half-mile (9 km) front, while the 58th "held the support position." First Battalion headquarters "sent various details of officers and men" into the front-line positions. While "in the trenches in this sector," Morrow's history reported, the battalion came "under shell fire." This was Pvt. Matthew Guerra's "baptism of fire."[10]

U.S. soldier in France. Typical uniform.

Beginning on the night of September 9–10, units of the 58th and 59th Infantry Regiments moved into their assigned positions, "in concealment in the woods east of [the village of] Haudainville," just south of Verdun, where the 4th Division had established its headquarters. Between September 12 and

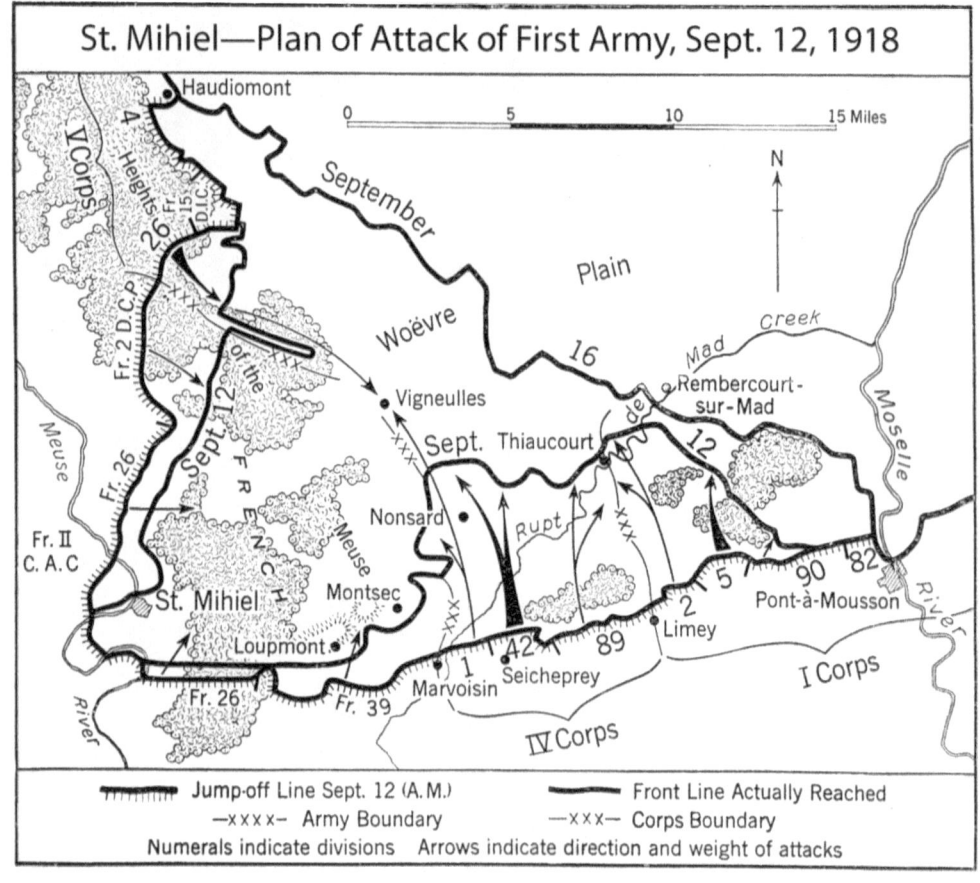

Source: General John J. Pershing, *My Experiences in the World War* (2 volumes), 1931.

15, V Corps held the 7th Infantry Brigade (39th and 47th Regiments) of the 4th Division, in reserve. The brigade did not participate in the action. A drizzling rain and mist continued throughout the afternoon of September 11, eventually turning into a heavy downpour later that evening.[11]

On September 12, the day of the scheduled attack, plans called for V Corps to push in a southeasterly direction and join with IV Corps advancing toward the northwest, in an attempt to trap the Germans in the town of St. Mihiel proper. Fifth Corps headquarters directed the 59th Infantry to remain in place, "holding its front" and not to attack without express orders. During the early afternoon, the order came down from 8th Brigade headquarters for the 59th to send out patrols to conduct a series of raids and "a general harassing of the enemy." At 4:10 p.m., another patrol followed with orders to reconnoiter the nearby town of Manheulles, where "heavy machine gun fire greeted them." Having little cover, the lieutenant leading the patrol ordered his men to pull back to the protection of nearby woods. All that night and the next day, the regiment sent out additional patrols "endeavoring to determine the exact movements of the enemy."[12]

At 10:00 a.m. on September 14, units of the 59th Regiment moved out of the trenches, advancing behind an artillery barrage to attack the Germans' forward line. Later that morning, Company D entered Manheulles and captured three enemy soldiers among the many fleeing from the rear of the town. In their haste to escape, German cooks preparing the noonday meal left behind their mobile kitchens. The Americans managed to enjoy a sumptuous hot meal consisting of "roast beef, fried potatoes, sauerkraut, coffee, loaf sugar, bread and beer," bringing much comfort to the men in rain-soaked uniforms with temperatures at that time of the year likely in the low 40s.[13]

During the engagement, between September 12 and 15, the enemy wounded 10 men of the 58th Infantry, while the 59th, which saw most of the action, suffered 35 casualties, with one man killed. Five more later died of their wounds. Machine gun battalions suffered an additional 14 dead and five wounded. On the morning of September 15, units of the 4th Division withdrew from the St. Mihiel sector and marched to a point two kilometers north of the town of Sommedieue. Units assembled on Hill 360 in the le Tremblais Woods to await further orders to commence the move west to the Meuse-Argonne sector.[14]

* * *

Following the initial stages of the St. Mihiel offensive, plans for a shift of operations to the Meuse-Argonne front were already in full swing. General Pershing and his staff were acutely aware of the fact that this sector of the western front contained a portion of the German-held territory "which the enemy could least afford to lose." Located within the bounds of the attack zone was a critical railroad hub near the city of Sedan, 35 miles (53 km) north of the jump-off point, connecting the tracks of the Carignan rail line with those of the Mézières Railroad. This important rail line supplied the majority of the German units in France and Flanders. General Pershing emphasized the "strategical importance" of this portion of the region's rail supply network for the German Army in France, describing it as "second to none on the western front." In a single day, more than two hundred fifty supply trains traveled over the Carignan-Sedan-Mézières rail net to supply units in the field. The city of Sedan, situated on the Meuse River approximately 80 miles (128 km) northeast of Paris near the French-Belgian border, served as a crucial German supply center for the units in the Meuse-Argonne region.[15]

More importantly, the Carignan-Sedan-Mézières rail system was likewise essential to the German Army for the rapid movement of troops and heavy artillery. The severing of this important artery would render the German positions, wholly dependent upon the line for supplies and munitions, untenable. It was even more critical, should the combined Franco-American offensive in the Meuse-Argonne sector succeed, for the evacuation of German troops through Belgium and across the Rhine River into Germany. Here, safe from attack, the German armies could hold out through the winter months and regroup, with the possibility of launching a new offensive the following spring. Pershing emphasized that should the Allies cut this railway supply system before Germany could withdraw its forces from the region, "the ruin" of the German armies "in France and Belgium would be complete."[16]

Given the critical importance of the Meuse-Argonne region, General Pershing was highly cognizant of the fact that "nowhere" on the western front "were the German defenses stronger" and that no other sector "would be more solidly held and more desperately defended." Pershing wrote that he "planned to use all available forces of the American First Army, including such divisions and troops as we might be able to withdraw from the St. Mihiel front." The First Army commander "counted on surprise to overwhelm the outnumbered defenders," before the German command could move reserve forces into the Meuse-Argonne to strengthen their positions, wrote historian Dr. Paul F. Braim.[17]

General Pershing was confident and determined that his forces would be able to break the German resistance before the onset of winter. Completion of preparations necessary to commence the drive by AEF General Headquarters (GHQ) within a ten-day time span was essential for units to be ready for H-Hour at 5:30 a.m. on D-Day, set for September 26. Foch and Pétain were highly skeptical. Pershing placed the responsibility for this seemingly impossible task in the hands of a young staff officer from the operations section at AEF Headquarters, thirty-seven-year-old Colonel George C. Marshall, Jr. The battle of St. Mihiel marked the first time that American commanders used the terms "D-Day" and "H-Hour."[18]

* * *

The "immediate problem" facing Headquarters First Army following the success of the St. Mihiel offensive, historian Frank Freidel explained, "was to move most of [the participating] divisions northward to the new battlefield." All units had to be in position along the jump-off point, a line between the Meuse River on the east and the western edge of the Argonne forest, within a ten-day span. This force included 15 U.S. divisions, consisting of approximately 400,000 men; an additional 220,000 French troops; aviation and balloon units; and other auxiliary troops, plus 90,000 horses and mules. Of these 15 divisions, seven took part in the St. Mihiel drive. Add to this the redeployment of American Army and Corps artillery, plus French artillery, which alone totaled 3,980 pieces. Lastly, the operation would necessitate the movement of 40,000 tons of supplies and approximately 850,000 tons of ammunition.[19]

Marshall later reported that to accomplish the stated objectives he was up against "two great difficulties." First, as in conjunction with any large-scale movement of troops, weapons, and supplies, he had to deal with a number of associated logistical problems and requirements. Second, Marshall had to coordinate plans to move the bulk of the divisions scheduled to take part the offensive from east of the Moselle River, "across the rear zone of the corps engaged in the St. Mihiel battle during the period when all roads were congested with the movement forward of ammunition, rations, and engineer material." This case was a unique logistical situation as well as a monumental undertaking.[20]

As with the St. Mihiel campaign, Col. Marshall also had to contend with the height of the fall rainy season. "Bivouacking in sodden woods, plodding at night along muddy roads in utter darkness with clothing soaked and no prospect of dry blankets or a cheering fire, the [4th Division] Ivy men felt, more than once, that when it came to bad weather during combat their luck was certainly against them," commented Bach and Hall.[21]

These inherent problems were coupled with the fact that unit commanders had to execute all movement of men and materials under the "utmost secrecy" and "cover of darkness." GHQ issued strict orders that troops and support personnel suspend all activity in the open during daylight hours and remain concealed in wooded areas. These precautions were an attempt by the American command to avoid attention and suspicion by enemy aerial reconnaissance aircraft, thus alerting German intelligence of the impending change in strategy by Pershing to discontinue the drive toward Metz, a continuation of the St. Mihiel offensive, as originally expected by the Germans. In anticipation of an impending attack against the city of Metz, German commanders had made extensive plans and preparations.

Throughout the impending operation, the Allies endeavored in every possible way to conceal all activities and movements up to the jump-off point. Divisions moved up to the front "by successive stages." One unit would leave its bivouac area after dark and advance forward to a pre-determined location, then another would move up to occupy the vacated space. This strategy enabled units to settle in just before daybreak. Commanders did not move troops into the front-line trenches until the night preceding the attack (September 25–26). Artillery brigades moving up to the front located and camouflaged their guns from prying eyes in the sky before first light. Marshall's plan of deception completely fooled German intelligence.[22]

The second major difficulty, explained Col. Marshall, involved the limited number of roads used to transfer the large mass of troops to the new positions on the Argonne front. In this case, there were a total of three, described as "deep rutted … muddy farm roads": the Toul-Void-Bar-le-Duc Road, referred to in accounts as "the motor highway"; and two others, employed primarily for the movement of foot troops and animal-drawn vehicles, "except in a few instances where tractor artillery had to be sent over them." Fourth Division historians Bach and Hall provide a vivid description of this tenable situation:

> The routes of all were bound to cross more or less. The ammunition necessary for the tremendous artillery concentration that was to precede the attack, had to be brought up on truck trains whose routes threaded in and out through the mass of moving men and transport. For each a road must be determined that would least interfere with others. Every night the entire area south of the front line and west of the Meuse was a wriggling, seething, ant-like mass of men, animals, wagons and trucks. They covered every road, trail and footpath. All this was in utter darkness; not a light was shown; and night after night it rained.

Troops and supplies in many places "moved forward" over these routes at an incredibly slow "two-mile-an-hour pace," due primarily to a number of massive traffic jams and tie-ups. In some instances, the congestion was so great it took units as long as 16 hours to cover the 50-mile distance from St. Mihiel to predetermined locations in the Meuse-Argonne sector.[23]

Engineer battalions had to work continuously rebuilding the decimated and limited transportation network. In addition, during the entire period of this operation, Bach and Hall explained, "[a]ll work was done at night, [and] all the nights were inky dark." Road crews "toiled in pouring rain, and all the roads were bad." Rain fell continually from September 8 through the 13th. Workers had to complete all work at the same time before sunup on the 26th, under complete concealment and making very little noise lest they be detected by German intelligence.[24]

Within a 16-hour time span, engineers rebuilt five kilometers of the road from Esnes to Malancourt across No Man's Land. Engineers used anything and everything available for road construction material, including stone and rubble from abandoned buildings, and filled sandbags, forty thousand in number, to fill the shell holes. The remains of many shattered buildings were "pulled down" while at Malancourt, the ruins of the local church as well as all the stones in the graveyard, disappeared.

The myriad of seemingly insurmountable challenges and obstacles notwithstanding, by the night preceding H-hour at 5:30 a.m. on D-Day, every unit was in place "ready to begin the fight." "Despite the haste with which all the movements had to be carried out, the inexperience of commanders in movements of such density, the condition of the animals and the limitations as to roads," unit leaders managed to complete the entire operation "without a single element failing to reach its place on the date scheduled." Col. Marshall boasted afterwards that this incredible feat occurred "one day earlier" than Marshal Foch "considered possible." It was to Marshall's "great credit that the displacement succeeded in the time required," wrote Dr. Braim.[25]

20

The Meuse-Argonne Offensive
Phase One (September 26–October 3, 1918)

The U.S. First Army, personally commanded by Gen. John J. Pershing, included an assault force comprised of 15 U.S. infantry divisions, totaling approximately 600,000 men. Providing support for the infantry divisions were 821 aircraft, 604 piloted by Americans ("in contrast to nearly 1,500 available for the lesser St. Mihiel campaign"), and two tank battalions, the 326th and 327th of the U.S. Tank Department (later the Tank Corps), under the command of Lt. Col. George S. Patton, Jr. Col. Patton's battalions consisted of 144 French-built FT-17 light tanks. "Impressed by the mercurial young captain's intelligence and devotion to duty," wrote military historian Edward G. Lengel, "Pershing confirmed his appointment and ordered him to establish the First Army Tank School at Langres, France." Assisting the U.S. tank force during the battle were an additional 275 French tanks (216 Ft-17s and 59 Schneider CA1 heavy tanks) of the French 1st Assault Artillery Brigade.[1]

Unfortunately, during the battle, tank support failed to live up to expectations, due primarily to the difficulty of the terrain, made worse by the fall rainy season. Many bogged down in a sea of mud, muck and watery mire, which was typical of existing battlefield conditions. Tank drivers experienced a host of mechanical and other problems as well. The first day of battle saw a considerable number of the machines knocked out or otherwise rendered inoperable. Lengel reported that "most" of the tanks in Patton's force "toppled into ravines and shell holes," and either "broke down, or got lost without ever seeing combat." German commanders had only 20 tanks (Model A7V) in their arsenal, and commanders in the Argonne had none at their disposal.[2]

On September 26, the main American front line ran from the Meuse River, near the village of Regniéville on the east, westward to the commune of Vienne-le-Chateau on the western edge of the Argonne Forest (see map).

20. The Meuse-Argonne Offensive

Streets of Seringis, France, crowded with infantry and artillery from the (Guerra's) 4th Division on the way to the front. August 4, 1918.

From east to west, the jump-off line covered a distance of twenty air miles. Fourth Division historians Col. Christian A. Bach and Henry Noble Hall noted that "the actual length of the line was much greater, owing to its winding character." Bach was chief of staff of the 4th Division. Pershing planned to commence the attack with three corps abreast, each with three attacking divisions, while retaining three divisions in general reserve. Corps commanders held one division in reserve.[3]

Units on the front line from left to right included I Corps on the left, commanded by Major. Gen. Hunter Liggett, comprised of the 77th ("Metropolitan" or "Times Square"), 28th ("Keystone"), and 35th ("Santa Fe") Divisions; V Corps in the center, under the command of Maj. General George Cameron, included the 91st ("Wild West," "Far West," or "Powder River"), 37th ("Buckeye"), and 79th ("Liberty") Divisions; and III Corps on the right, commanded by Maj. Gen. Robert Bullard, consisted of the 4th ("Ivy"), 80th ("Blue Ridge Mountain"), and 33rd ("Prairie") Divisions.

Plans for the initial assault on D-Day included a force of approximately 100,000 infantrymen, plus support troops. Only three of the nine divisions on the line—the 4 (Matthew Guerra's division), 28th, and 77th—had seen action previously, the remainder were inexperienced. Lengel noted that the 28th and 77th were "worn-out" and in need of rest and replacements.[4]

Pershing's master plan called for a "three-pronged attack": I Corps "to press northward" on the left side of the main line to clear the Argonne Forest; III Corps, positioned on the far east, would advance up the Meuse Valley west of the river to its western boundary with V Corps in the center. V Corps, flanked by I Corps on the west and III Corps to the east, would attack in the direction of Montfaucon ("Mount of the Falcon").

Pershing assigned the 79th Division, described as the "central prong" of the advance, the important mission of seizing the height of Montfaucon. This strategic German stronghold, a fortified hill 1,222 feet (342 meters) above sea level, stood "squarely in center of the Army's zone of action." The heavily defended position provided German artillery spotters with an exceptional vantage point to observe and adjust fire against advancing American troops. To accomplish its objective, the 79th would bypass the high ground by advancing north on both sides of the prominence avoiding a frontal assault. This strategy would allow Pershing's forces to seize the commanding position in a flanking maneuver (see below).[5]

Field Marshal Ferdinand Foch and General Henri Philippe Pétain expressed extreme skepticism of Pershing's plan and predicted that AEF forces would not be able to capture the Meuse-Argonne sector before the summer of 1919. A decidedly more confident Pershing was certain that his forces could and would accomplish far greater gains than predicted by French commanders. His set goals and objectives for the massive campaign reflected that sense of optimism. Primarily, what General Pershing counted on for the overall success of the operation was surprise and the weakness of the German front-line divisions.

* * *

The German Army had occupied the Meuse-Argonne region since the fall of 1914, more than four years. Facing American forces were three major east-west German defense lines or "Stellungen," named after witches in Richard Wagner's operas—Giselher, Kreimhilde, and Freya. Stellung was the German term for a fortified defense line. In addition, there were "several minor" defense lines (see map, p. 175). The Meuse-Argonne defenses, wrote historian Edward G. Lengel, "had long been considered impregnable." During the occupation of this sector, German engineer battalions had constructed a strong network of field fortifications that took advantage of the east-west ridges extending from south to north throughout the region. The "net result," Pershing stated, was the creation of a "defensive system of unusual depth and strength and a wide zone of utter devastation, itself a serious obstacle to offensive operations."[6]

The first of these defensive positions, the Etzel-Giselher Stellung, was located approximately three miles north of the American front line. This defense line ran just to the south of and included Montfaucon, described as a "rocky butte," an elaborate and heavily defended German stronghold and observation post, heavily fortified with bunkers, tunnels, and a maze of interconnected trenches (more below). French commanders deemed Montfaucon "impregnable" and dubbed it the "Little Gibraltar of the Western Front." German commanders "boasted" the position "would never be taken" by the Allied armies. Located in the center of the line that dominated the sector, the steep-sided hill, 500-feet above sea level, was an exceptional vantage point to observe the movement of advancing troops and adjust artillery fire. Between the American-French front line and the first of these positions was No Man's Land.[7]

Four miles beyond the Etzel-Giselher Stellung was the Kriemhilde line, a part of the larger Siegfried Stellung (referred to by the Allies as the Hindenburg Line), considered the strongest of the Stellungen. From the west, the position extended from the Bois de Forêt, ran along the Heights of Cunel and Romagne, and encompassed the high ground north of Grandpre. Robert Laplander describes the Heights of Romagne as "a ridgeline of whaleback hills that form the strongest natural barrier in France." The Germans had "thoroughly organized" the first two stellungen and constructed numerous intermediate lines and switch positions, a succession of trenches that laced the area interconnecting each of the main positions to further strengthen the defenses.[8]

Five miles farther north lay the Freya Stellung, "not yet fully organized," considered the weakest of the three lines. Lengel described the stellung as a "last-ditch position." This defense line ran from the town of Buzancy on the west, through Andevanne and Dun-sur-Meuse, and on to Lissey and beyond. Beyond the Freya there was nothing left to stop American and French forces.[9]

Throughout the sector, the Germans had constructed an intricate maze of deep trenches, concrete dugouts, and command posts, interconnected by numerous machine gun positions. Along the main defense line were well-placed observation posts with powerful telescopes with which the enemy could observe every square inch of the battlefield. Observers could direct and adjust accurate and deadly heavy mortar and artillery fire on advancing American troops. German troops occupying the positions lived in very comfortable accommodations with electricity and lighting and well-stocked with provisions and supplies. The defensive network included the most up-to-date means of communication, including telegraph, telephone, and radio (referred to at the time as "wireless").

German regiments positioned "many thousands" of machine gun sections, armed with both light and heavy Maxims at strategic points along the line that "anchored" the sector's defense system. Machine gun companies averaged 12 sled-mounted heavy Maxims (Model 08/15) and approximately four times as many light Maxims. Lengel described the Maxims as "magnificent and reliable weapons with an astonishingly high rate of fire," 400 to 500 rounds per minute. Heavy Maxims had an extreme range of about 4,400 yards and fired a 7.92mm round. The lighter version of the 08, fitted with a bipod, shoulder stock and pistol grip, also fired a 7.92mm round. German machine gunners were highly trained elite troops. Heavy artillery batteries, considered "the best in the world," were "manned by superbly trained crews." Supporting "air formations" of the Kaiser's Imperial Flying Corps (Deutsche Luftstreitkräfte), the air arm of the German Army, Lengel reported as being "strong and vigorous." German air forces operated conventional aircraft, fighters, light and heavy bombers, balloons, and Zeppelins.[10]

Within the Meuse-Argonne region, there was "a series of rolling hills" with "small but dense patches of woods here and there, each hill and each wood well adapted to sustained defense." When units in the advance encountered fierce resistance in one of these heavily defended forested areas, the forward movement of a section of the frontline often stalled for days. The flank of an adjacent unit, unimpeded by this type of obstacle, would become subjected to fire and maneuver by opposing forces, sustaining heavy casualties. These wooded areas were choked with a thick undergrowth (see description below), and were virtually impassable. Pinned-down troops, unable to advance, were subjected to murderous machine-gun fire as well as exploding trench-mortar shells and artillery rounds. Violent opposition by defending troops caused the number of dead and wounded to mount precipitously. It was in one of these dark and dismal places—the Bois de Fays—that Matthew Guerra met his fate. American commanders were well aware that the Meuse-Argonne region "would be more solidly held and desperately defended than any other part of the front for if it were broken through, the retreat of the German Armies to the Rhine would be cut off and forced to surrender," wrote Bach and Hall.[11]

Controlling the portion of the German front from Verdun to the Argonne Forest in this region of France was General Max von Gallwitz, commander of the namesake German Army "Group Von Gallwitz." American and French forces faced the German Twelfth Army (part of "Group von Gallwitz")—consisting of five German divisions and part of a sixth, totaling approximately 70,000 men in the main positions. German commanders were "under orders to stop the Americans at all costs." AEF planners rated the "fighting quality" of the German troops in the first sector "as poor," a factor in General Pershing's decision making. German commanders placed "the elderly, underage, or infirmed soldiers" in the front lines and temporary positions, and relegated their best troops in the well-fortified second and third lines.[12]

The watershed divide separating the Meuse and Aire River valleys, on the west and east respectively, formed a north-south hogback. Atop this divide sat the butte of Montfaucon, "not to be confused" with the town of the same name at its base a few miles behind enemy lines. Located on the summit of the steep-sloped prominence was a strategic German command and observation post that stood amid the ruins of a Benedictine monastery (founded in the 6th century). Within the center of the town of Montfaucon was a significant road junction—one road ran in a northwest direction to the village of Romagne, and the other northeasterly to the commune of Brieuelles on the Meuse River.[13]

Historian John S.D. Eisenhower in the book *Yanks* ("with Joanne T. Eisenhower"), wrote that Montfaucon "was not a towering eminence." The butte, he noted, "stood only about three hundred feet above the floor of the valley." However, its strategic location, "squarely in the middle of the center of the army's zone of action," midway between the heights east of the Meuse and the Argonne Forest on the west, "gave it overriding importance." Eisenhower provided the following detailed description: The outpost atop its crest gave German artillery excellent observation for accurate fire adjustment, thus transforming the Meuse-Argonne Valley from one twenty-mile corridor into two corridors of ten miles each. Distance to the target was a prime factor in maintaining or increasing accuracy. The town and the butte of Montfaucon were two of Pershing's three original objectives for the first day of the attack.[14]

Fifth Corps commander Major General George Cameron assigned the important task of seizing the strategic objective of Montfaucon to the 79th Division, which lay within the unit's attack zone. Maj. Gen. Joseph Kuhn, commander of the 79th, was "a capable, highly respected officer," who graduated at the top of his class at West point in 1885. "Unfortunately, Eisenhower explained, because of considerations beyond his control, the general pursued this all-important mission with one hand tied behind his back." Kuhn was inexperienced in commanding infantry troops. Previously he was the commanding officer, 1st Regiment of Engineers. His division consisted largely of inexperienced troops, with 60 percent of the infantrymen and 50 percent of the artillerymen having entered the army after May 25, 1918, a mere four months earlier. Further compounding Kuhn's problems was the fact that the majority of the troops under his command had not completed the training most other AEF divisions had received before going into the line. In spite of these handicaps, Kuhn's division took Montfaucon on the second day of the drive.[15]

The German high command considered the garrison on the summit of Montfaucon impregnable, and vowed the Allies would never seize the heavily fortified stronghold. This boast did not seem to deter Pershing from predicting its downfall on the first day of the drive. As mentioned earlier, General Pétain himself "was not optimistic" regarding the success of the Meuse-Argonne operation. He was convinced that the Americans would not be able advance farther north than Montfaucon, and predicted that they would be "lucky" to do so by Christmas. Eisenhower alluded to the fact that Pershing and his staff were of "the mistaken belief, that the seizure of Montfaucon ... would be easy," and ordered his V Corps commander, General George Cameron, to take the German fortress by the end of the first day (see below).[16]

After capturing Montfaucon, American forces would drive all the way to the Heights north of Romagne and Cunel 4.5 miles beyond. The positions were two key strong points along the Kriemhilde Stellung, the eastern portion of the strongly fortified and defended Hindenburg Line. Pershing scheduled capture of the positions for the afternoon of the second day, before the Germans could rush in reinforcements. "Achievement of that ambitious objective," Eisenhower stated, "was dependent on capturing the Butte of Montfaucon."[17]

In conjunction with the American advance, General Henri Gouraud's French Fourth Army would attack simultaneously to the west of the Argonne forest between the watershed divide of the Aisne and the Suippe River, while protecting the U.S. First Army's left flank. French forces would link up with the Americans near Grandpré at the northern tip of the Argonne forest.

* * *

Marking the western limits of the American sector was the far edge of the Argonne Forest, bounded on the west by the headwaters of the Aisne River. Within the Argonne Forest itself was a succession of rugged east-west ridges, some as high as 750 feet in elevation, separated by steep-sided ravines. A dense growth of trees and underwood, combined with a maze of vines, limited visibility to not more than twenty feet, making it extremely difficult to advance. Adding to this were fallen trees that littered the forest floor, from an attempt by the French to retake the forest from the Germans in 1915.

The rapid movement of troops northward could only take place along the few good dirt roads and/or paths and trails that traversed the interior. German machine gun positions and trenches, camouflaged and concealed by the thick foliage and dense underbrush, covered every possible approach. Attacking parties could only push into the woods by crawling from tree to tree seeking out the invisible enemy. Here and there were swamps and muddy morasses flooded by the constant rains of the wet season that began in mid-September.

Major General Hunter Liggett, Commander of I Corps, provided an apt description of conditions faced by American forces advancing north through the forest:

> It was masked and tortuous before the enemy strung his first wire and dug his first trench.... The underbrush had grown up through the German barbed and rabbit wire [wire mesh], interlacing it and concealing it, and machine guns lurked like copperheads in the ambush of shell-fallen trees. Other machine guns were strewn in concrete pill boxes and in defiles. On the offense, tanks could not follow, nor artillery see where it was shooting, while the enemy guns [artillery], on the defense, could fire by map.

Based on this intelligence, Liggett determined, "Patently it would be suicidal to attack such a labyrinth directly; it must be pinched out by attacks on either side."[18]

20. The Meuse-Argonne Offensive 171

The strategy of First Corps (77th, 28th, and 35th divisions in line; 1st and 92d divisions in reserve) commanders was for the 28th Division to move up the Aisne Valley on the west and the 35th in the Aire Valley to the east of the Argonne Forest, acting "as the two wings," methodically clearing the western and eastern portions of the forest as they advanced. Both divisions would eventually join up near the town of Grandpré. Units of the 77th Division would push directly through the Argonne forest itself, "following up" at a designated distance rearward so as to prevent troops from mistakenly firing on their own troops moving up on their right and left flanks or accidently interfering in any way with other units.[19]

It was deep in the Argonne Forest that German forces isolated 554 men of the 77th Division in an incident known as the "Lost Battalion." Units of the 307th and 308th Infantry Regiments moved ahead of the rest of the Allied line and found themselves cut off and surrounded by German forces for six days. Amid the putrefying corpses of their fallen comrades, the 77th repelled several attacks by the Germans until other Allied units came to their rescue. Only 194 members of the unit were able to walk out alive, with 197 killed and 150 missing or taken prisoner.

* * *

The "un-fordable" Meuse River bordered the Meuse-Argonne battle area to the right of advancing American troops. On the east bank of the river is a steep-sided valley wall or palisades, the Côtes de Meuse (Meuse Heights), a 1,600-foot-high ridgeline that extends between Saint-Mihiel and Verdun and beyond to Mézières. This steep rock face, which has historically functioned as a natural defensive barrier, rises abruptly to the Heights of the Meuse, a plateau some five miles broad that slopes gently to the east. Possession of the heights afforded the Germans commanding ground from which to observe and to blanket the battlefield with intense artillery barrages of high explosive and gas shells that rained death on advancing American infantry troops as they advanced.[20]

Pershing made note that the dominating heights east of the Meuse River "not only protected" the Germans' left flank "but gave him positions from which powerful artillery could deliver an oblique fire on the western bank [of the Meuse River]." Batteries "located in the elaborately fortified Argonne forest" covering the Germans' right flank allowed gunners to "cross their fire with that of the guns on the east bank of the Meuse." The American III and V Corps in the center of the main front line, which included Matthew Guerra's 4th Division, were subjected to this murderous artillery fire, and, Pershing wrote, "had suffered heavily."[21]

* * *

Part of Pershing's plan was to trick German intelligence into believing the next push would be a further advance toward the east, a continuation of the St. Mihiel offensive (September 12–15) toward the city of Metz. This stratagem, known as the "Metz Feint," began on September 25, 1918, one day before the start of the Meuse-Argonne operation. The offensive was part of a conceived plan of deceptions by General Headquarters to confuse German intelligence into thinking the main attack would be a continuation of the drive to the east against the outer defenses of Metz. If successful, the Germans would maintain the bulk of its reserve forces near that city instead of reinforcing the Argonne front.[22]

The ruse proved successful. As a result, General Georg von Marwitz, commanding the Fifth German Army at Verdun, part of Army Group von Gallwitz, was certain that the bulk of the U.S. forces would continue the attack eastward in the direction of Metz, as an exploitation of the St. Mihiel success. He remained convinced that the Americans' primary objective was to capture the key rail center in that city. Once American commanders established new bases closer to the Rhine, von Marwitz knew there was more than a distinct possibility the Allies would then launch an offensive into the heart of Germany. In anticipation of a renewal of the advance, von Marwitz positioned all available units in the St. Mihiel sector—eighteen divisions, with 12 in reserve—most clustered around Metz.[23]

Prior to the expected attack, General von Marwitz issued a communiqué exhorting all units "to 'fulfill their duty to the utmost as the Fifth Army may have to bear the brunt of the fighting expected in the coming weeks, on which the security of the Fatherland may depend." The "fate of a large portion of the western front, perhaps of the nation," he implored them, "depends on the firm holding of the Verdun front."[24]

To further confirm the "impression" that the St. Mihiel advance would continue to the east, the Intelligence Section of Pershing's General Staff fabricated a number of "very clever and ingenious wireless messages." These were sent out "by a fictitious army commander in charge of a phantom American [Tenth] army to the east of Verdun." German wireless stations picked up these misleading communications and relayed them to intelligence codebreakers for decryption. This ploy, part of the overall scheme, "resulted in a sudden increase of anxious information-seeking raids by the Germans on that front." French agents in towns occupied by the Germans "spread gossip that the Americans planned a big drive toward Metz."[25]

* * *

Beginning at 2:30 a.m. on September 26, a joint force of American and French troops launched the Meuse-Argonne Campaign. Preceding the attack was a massive three-hour-long barrage by American and French artillery. At precisely 5:30 a.m., officers blew their whistles, signaling the start of the battle. Thousands of men scaled the ladders with fixed bayonets and scrambled forward out of the trenches into the void of No Man's Land. They advanced "behind a rolling barrage about 100 yards to the front." Fortunately, "a heavy fog mixed with cordite smoke" cloaked the entire battlefield, and aided in masking the initial advance of the infantry units. Initially, Eisenhower reported, "some of the troops mistook this smoke for an enemy gas attack, and in their struggle to don gas masks many lost contact with one another." Another downside was that with sunrise more than an hour away, the predawn darkness, combined with the mist-shrouded forward zone, caused many difficulties in maintaining liaison and communication.[26]

Paul F. Braim provides a vivid description of the initial stages of the advance: "The 'doughboys' climbed in and out of great shell holes, bunching up at the enemy barbed wire," while others "in the lead assault became lost." A number of the men collected in "low ground" safe from enemy fire. Pushing "the line of contact forward" was "the pressure of those advancing from behind." Troops "quickly" overran the "lightly" manned "initial German defenses," retreating to "the first prepared Stellung." By 9:15 a.m., a slight wind dissipated the fog and mist and the sun shone brightly.[27]

Initially, the "Yanks" in the Meuse-Argonne outnumbered the Germans "on the order of eight to one, depending on who and what is counted," wrote Braim. Once von Gallwitz realized that the attack was the main American effort, he reacted by pouring every reserve formation at his disposal in defense of the sector. Strong opposition and counterattacks by German defenders forced a number of American assault divisions to retreat. The drive had also rendered other divisions "exhausted and depleted." Despite these setbacks, Pershing, known to rely on costly frontal assaults, ordered the drive to continue. By September 29, the American attack force "had pushed forward to an average of eight miles" before its "forward momentum ceased." Pershing then ordered a temporary halt in the attack until his veteran divisions, the 1st ("Fighting First"), 2nd ("Warrior"), 26th ("Yankee"), and 42nd ("Rainbow") Divisions, en route from St. Mihiel, could arrive.[28]

21

Meuse-Argonne
Second Phase (October 4, 1918)

During the brief period between Phases One and Two of the Meuse-Argonne Offensive, the 4th Division utilized every conceivable means possible to correct all deficiencies experienced during the initial phase that would ensure the smooth functioning of all rear echelons going forward. By October 3, an "extreme effort" on the part of division ammunition and supply trains resulted in the accumulation of sufficient munitions and materials "for the maintenance of the division's fighting strength." Medical Department personnel with the division Sanitary Train, consisting of an ambulance section, a field hospital section, and a medical supply unit, "systematized" all policies and procedures to ensure the prompt evacuation of casualties from the battlefield to a medical facility farther to the rear for more definitive care.[1]

Fourth Division Headquarters took steps to relieve congestion experienced by trucks and other vehicles during Phase One on the main Esnes-Malancourt-Cuisy Road, approximately 5 miles long, so that "traffic flowed to and from the line more smoothly." All roads in the division sector were "constantly under repair by two regiments of engineers; the 4th Engineers, the engineers of the 79th Division and the Corps engineers." To keep order and control the movement of troops and supplies in the zones of operation, American Expeditionary Forces (AEF) GHQ established traffic control posts manned by Military Police (sometime referred to in accounts of the period as "Battle Police") units "at various points," including "the Esnes and Malancourt forks" and at all at crossroads. Tragically, during Phase One many ambulatory cases died on the way to a medical facility due to a "lack of sufficient attention" while held up by traffic jams and stoppages of long duration. Staff ordered that all vehicles with engine or mechanical trouble, or having one of the team animals pulling wagons (two pairs of horses or mules) become injured or dropped dead, be "ruthlessly ditched."[2]

Headquarters deployed Military Police patrols in the trenches to deal

Source: General John J. Pershing, *My Experiences in the World War* (2 volumes), 1931.

with men who had refused to go over the top and following an attack to cope with the large number of "battle stragglers." This included men who were lost and wandering around in an attempt to find their units or moving to the rear to evade fighting on the front lines. M.P.s rounded up or collected stragglers "loitering in the rear area" and returned them to their units. "One officer described these stragglers as "shell-holers," men who remained there "while their comrades advanced unsupported by them."[3]

Engineers, working "tirelessly," managed to widen the main road through the 4th Division sector, the Cuisy-Béthencourt Road, along its entire length. Heavy rains had reduced the clay soil adjacent to the road to "muck," preventing trucks and wagons carrying needed supplies from maneuvering around a disabled vehicle. Crews had to haul crushed rock from Esnes, Malancourt, and Haucourt, to stabilize the shoulders. Later, Corps made the road one-way for southbound traffic only, facilitating the delivery of the more seriously wounded to field hospitals. Engineer battalions labored around the

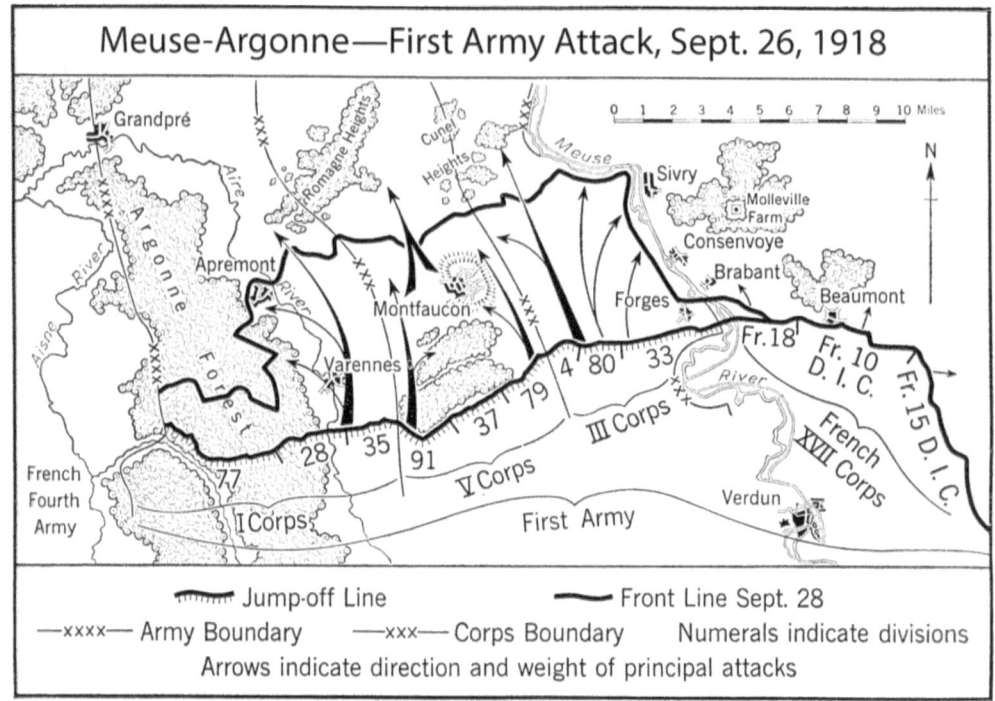

Attacking U.S. and French divisions on jump off line. Source: General John J. Pershing, *My Experiences in the World War* **(2 Volumes), 1931.**

clock to repair and improve all back roads, farm roads, and makeshift routes crudely built across what had been No Man's Land. Capt. George L. Morrow, 58th Infantry, described the roads at the beginning of Phase Two as being "in good condition," with traffic flowing "to and from the front lines more smoothly." Crews worked continuously to widen the Esnes-Malancourt-Cuisy and Malancourt-Montfaucon roads (3.5 miles). During the "later stage of the operations, … the road had been so widened that it could be used for two-way traffic."[4]

* * *

During the 2nd Phase of the battle, AEF forces were up against the last of the German defenses—the Kriemhilde Stellung, the eastern end of the famed Hindenburg Line. The line began east of the Argonne Forest just south of Romagne and continued east to a point on the Meuse River just north of the village of Brieulles. Part of the line ran north of the Bois de Ogons, and then followed the southern and eastern edge of the Bois de Fays, turning north and east along the edge of the Bois de Forêt, then on to the Meuse River (see map on previous page).

21. Meuse-Argonne

Traffic (3rd Div.) congestion on road passing through Esnes, France, northwest of Verdun. The town has been destroyed. The congestion of traffic on the roads in back of the American lines in the Argonne is at places so great that the stream of vehicles are unable to move faster than two miles an hour. September 19, 1918.

On the night of October 3, the AEF attack force along the main jump-off line was as follows: Third Corps, situated on the far right, consisted of the 80th, 4th, and 33rd Divisions, from left to right respectively. Fifth Corps in the center included the 91st, 32nd, and 3rd Divisions. I Corps, comprised of the 77th, 28th, and 1st Divisions, was on the left. The following is a diagram showing the placement of AEF forces:

```
A                                                      M
p                                                      e
r           I Corps       V Corps       III Corps      u
e         77th 28th 1st / 91st 32nd 3rd / 80th 4th 33rd s
m                                                      e
o
n                                                      R.
t
```

The line extended from village of Apremont on the west, just north of Nantillois, then due east to a point on the Meuse River. It ran approximately 2 to

3 miles south of the Kriemhilde Stellung and more or less parallel with that defense line.⁵

Third Corps assigned Guerra's 4th Division the task of carrying out several primary objectives. From positions on the northern edge of the Bois de Brieulles, division forces would advance across an open expanse, described as a "ravine," to attack the Bois de Fays (sometimes written Bois du Fays), translation "Woods of the Fairies." At the bottom of the slope, troops had to cross a small stream (Le Wassieu) flowing east into the Meuse River.

Once division forces managed to gain a foothold inside the Bois de Fays, units would drive the Germans from that wooded area. This proved to be a greater undertaking than initially expected. Division Headquarters ordered unit commanders to avoid the open ground between the Bois de Fays and Bois de la Côte Lémont (Fr. Laimont) to the east "because of the perfect observation and annihilating fire that could be brought to bear on it by the Germans." After securing the Bois de Fays, units of the 4th Division would drive north through the Bois de Malaumont, then turn east in the direction of the Meuse River and "sweep" the Germans from the Bois de Forêt. The "success of this movement," division believed, "would have compelled the evacuation the village of Brieulles," thereby forcing defending units to withdraw across the Meuse River "without the firing of a shot." This proved far more difficult than originally anticipated.⁶

The front line of the 4th Division attack force "extended from Hill 280," located in the eastern part of Bois de la Côte Lémont on the east, then "along the northern edge of the Bois de Brieulles," to the western edge of the Bois de Fays, where it met with the right flank of the 80th Division. Units of the 33rd Division protected the "eastern flank of the 4th Division."⁷

On the morning of October 4, the 4th Division attack force along the jump-off line consisted of the 3rd Battalion, Companies I, K, L, M, 58th Infantry Regiment in the lead, with the 1st (Companies A-D) and 2nd Battalions (Companies E-H) in support. During the initial drive, the 59th Regiment followed behind the 58th, approximately one kilometer to the rear, later shifting over to the right flank. The forward line stretched out approximately two miles in length. Division preceded the attack against the Bois de Fays with an "intense" artillery bombardment beginning at 5:25 a.m., which continued uninterrupted for a full 24 minutes. French heavy artillery batteries placed "destructive fire" into the southern edge of the woods "and upon all known enemy artillery positions within the 4th Division sector." "Tanks assisted" in the advance, Morrow noted, "but were soon put out of action by hostile artillery fire." These were either the Model 1918 3-ton light tank (M1918), developed by the Ford Motor Company, or the (M1917) 6-ton light tank, an American license-production copy of the French-designed Renault FT-17.⁸

The infantry advance, which began at 5:49 a.m., followed "behind a heavy rolling barrage" let loose by 2,700 artillery pieces. Infantrymen of the 58th Regiment left their holes and proceeded toward the north "across open ground in the direction of the southern edge of the Bois de Fays," a distance of approximately 850 yards. A heavy morning mist hung over the forward area leading to the objective, obscuring enemy observation. Machine gunners of the 10th M.G. Battalion, along with Companies A and D of the 12th M.G. Battalion, delivered a high volume of concentrated fire on the southern edge of the woods.[9]

Unfortunately, during the latter part of the advance, the haze that shrouded the open ground leading to the edge of the woods lifted, disclosing American lines. Exposed troops "were met with a storm of projectiles" before lead elements could reach the cover of the woods and establish a foothold inside the tree line. Hostile German machine gun and small weapons fire coming from the Meuse on the right, and from "cleverly concealed positions" along the front facing edge of the Bois de Fays and from the Bois des Ogons, forced the men of the 3rd Battalion to halt. Bach and Hall described the scene:

> Artillery from the east of the Meuse swept the entire front, deluging it with gas, shrapnel, and high explosive. Machine guns poured a stream of lead into their lines from every conceivable direction. There was [artillery] fire from the Meuse on the right, [and rifle and machine gun fire] from the Bois de Fays in front and from the Bois de Ogons on the left.

Men flopped down in the high grass and scrambled to find low spots, "dips and hollows," or if lucky, a ravine, that afforded any manner of protection at all. Up and down the line could be heard screams for a medic.[10]

During the interlude between the first and second phases of the campaign, Bach and Hall explained, the Germans "had taken full advantage" of the opportunity by bringing up reinforcements to shore up the forward trenches as well as to "select the best positions" for resisting the expected assault. German troops resisted "along the entire Army front with a tenacity that was not altogether expected." In closing, the authors stated that the "struggle was to be bitter and costly."[11]

When the advance began, German troops subjected battalion forces to machine gun and sniper fire, as well as intense, concentrated artillery fire "from 77's up to the massive 210's," in an attempt to stop the progress of the AEF and force a retreat. Many of the incoming projectiles were antipersonnel artillery shells that burst in the air and rained down deadly spherical pieces of metal on advancing troops. In the afternoon of October 4, an unknown number of German aircraft began strafing and bombing the troops caught out in the open without cover. Antiaircraft machine gun fire succeeded in bringing down five of the planes.[12]

An unrelenting hail of artillery fire from batteries east of the Meuse

River swept the entire front with gas, shrapnel, and high explosive shells, holding up forward progress of advancing infantry units. The open field over which division forces made the advance, Bach and Hall related, "became wreathed with smoke and gas" from chemical shells, forcing the men to fight in their gas masks.[13]

* * *

In January 1919, a small staff of officers and men from the 77th "Statue of Liberty" Division compiled a history of the unit from "Division records, maps and personal writings." Major Julius Ochs Adler, 306th Regiment, served as "Editor in Chief." One of the contributors related that the doughboys referred to "the various assortment" of incoming artillery projectiles "sent over by the Boche" (French slang word for "rascal"), as "stuff." It was either "light stuff or heavy stuff, slow stuff or fast stuff; but all of it is undeniably mean stuff."[14]

Shell types included the "whizzbang (whizz-bang)" or as the troops liked to call them, "Herr Wizzbang," fired by an Austrian 77mm field gun. In flight, the high-velocity shell gives off "a shrill whistle" that arrives "almost simultaneously ... as its explosion." As the shell "came towards you," it "sounded ... like 'whizz' and then 'bang.'" The shell traveled faster than the speed of sound; consequently, it exploded with little or no warning. Of all the artillery thrown at them, the whizzbang was the most feared by infantrymen because there was virtually no time to take evasive or protective action from the blast. Many a poor soul suffered a direct hit, instantly blowing him to pieces, leaving nothing to bury. Detonation heaved a geyser of dirt skyward, raining loose soil and clods of earth down on forward positions. Advancing troops caught without cover while crossing No-Man's Land during a barrage learned that "the best manner in which to receive [a whizzbang] is by lying prone on the stomach," minimizing the chance of a hit by deadly shrapnel.[15]

Next was the "Minnie Werfer," derived from the German *Minenwerfer*, a "mine launcher" or "mine thrower," defined as a class of different caliber short-range trench mortars employed extensively by the German Army. Engineers used the weapons "to clear obstacles including bunkers and barbed wire that longer range artillery would not be able to accurately target." American troops referred to the incoming shells as "Herr Whizzbang's ... ladyfriend." These "are peculiarly disconcerting," Adler wrote, "as they come through the air with a wailing sob-like whistle, something like a mixture of a locomotive whistle and siren," getting louder and louder as it bore down on a man's position. The trajectory of the projectiles was an extremely high arc coming almost straight down toward the intended target. "Iron Mermaid" was another colorful term used by soldiers to describe this type of the shell, so named "because of the fish-like tails that keep them straight on their course." It was difficult for the troops to be able to "judge" where the shell was going to hit.[16]

"Tons-of-Coal," "Whimpering Willies," and "Jack Johnsons" or "Crumps," were just a few of the pet names adopted by the U.S. troops for the larger "eight-inch and ten-inch howitzer and rifle shells." Major Adler referred to them facetiously as "German long-range greetings." Doughboys also applied the nickname "G.I. Can" to the large German artillery shells after the 20-gallon galvanized iron garbage cans used in army camps. Some accounts have described the noise of these huge shells as sounding like a "roaring freight train" bearing down on them when tumbling through the air. Upon impact, the shell made a characteristic "crump" noise, hence the nickname "crumps." When they hit, the resulting explosion could create massive craters, some "as large as eighteen feet in diameter and ten feet in depth."[17]

The British used the name "Jack Johnson" to describe the power of the impact and the large amount of thick black smoke produced by the powerful explosion of a German 90-lb. artillery shell from a 15cm heavy field howitzer, after the famous American boxer "Jack" (John Arthur) Johnson (1878–1946). Johnson was the name of a popular heavyweight boxer born in Galveston, Texas. The 6'2" Johnson, known as "the Galveston Giant," captured the World Heavyweight title in 1908, the first African American to win the crown. Johnson held the title until 1915. He continued to box until the age of 50, compiling a lifetime record of 73 wins (40 KOs), 13 losses and 10 draws. The big guns could throw a shell for distances of up to 4.66 miles (7,500 meters). Authors Ronald Haycock and Keith Neilson described the 15cm Howitzer as the "the backbone of Germany's artillery during World War I."[18]

One popular contemporary World War I trench song, "'I Want to Go Home,'" anonymously composed, provides one Englishman's unique view of the German shelling at the front:

> I want to go home, I want to go home.
> I don't want to go in the trenches no more,
> Where whizzbangs and shrapnel they whistle and roar.
> Take me over the sea, where the Alleyman can't get at me.
> Oh my, I don't want to die, I want to go home.
> I want to go home, I want to go home.
> I don't want to visit la Belle France no more,
> For oh the Jack Johnsons they make such a roar.
> Take me over the sea, where the snipers they can't get at me.
> Oh my, I don't want to die, I want to go home.

The term "Alleyman" referred to a German soldier. The British corrupted the French word Allemagne, meaning "German."[19]

To protect themselves on the line while in the advance during a defensive artillery barrage, "each man," Adler wrote, "would dig himself [in], as fast as

Corporal Erland Johnson, 4th Division, in the Bois de la Côte Lémont, October 2, 1918.

he could." Men burrowed through the soil like moles. When there was no time, they scrambled into a convenient shell crater or depression in the landscape, if they were lucky enough to find one. When the unit happened to remain in place for any length of time, men "dug shallow ditches and 'foxholes' to crawl into for the night." The latter was described "generally" as a hole or pit "suitable to size, either into the flat surface of the ground or into a protecting bank, into which he would crawl, maintaining a sitting posture or prone position according to the nature of the terrain." Foxholes varied in size and shape and usually held one or two men.[20]

In an effort to provide further protection from the hail of shells, men dug "funk-holes" or "cubbyholes," which they scraped into the forward or side wall of a trench or foxhole. The latter term was "possibly derived from *cupboard*." Sources describe a funk-hole as a "small dugout or shelter, just big enough to accommodate one or two men." Men propped up the roof using a combination wooden posts and boards or corrugated iron. "A funk-hole," Adler wrote, "worked very well and afforded good protection against everything but a direct hit." What had come to be "a popular saying among the troops," he related, was that "'[e]verything is bomb-proof until it is hit.'"[21]

* * *

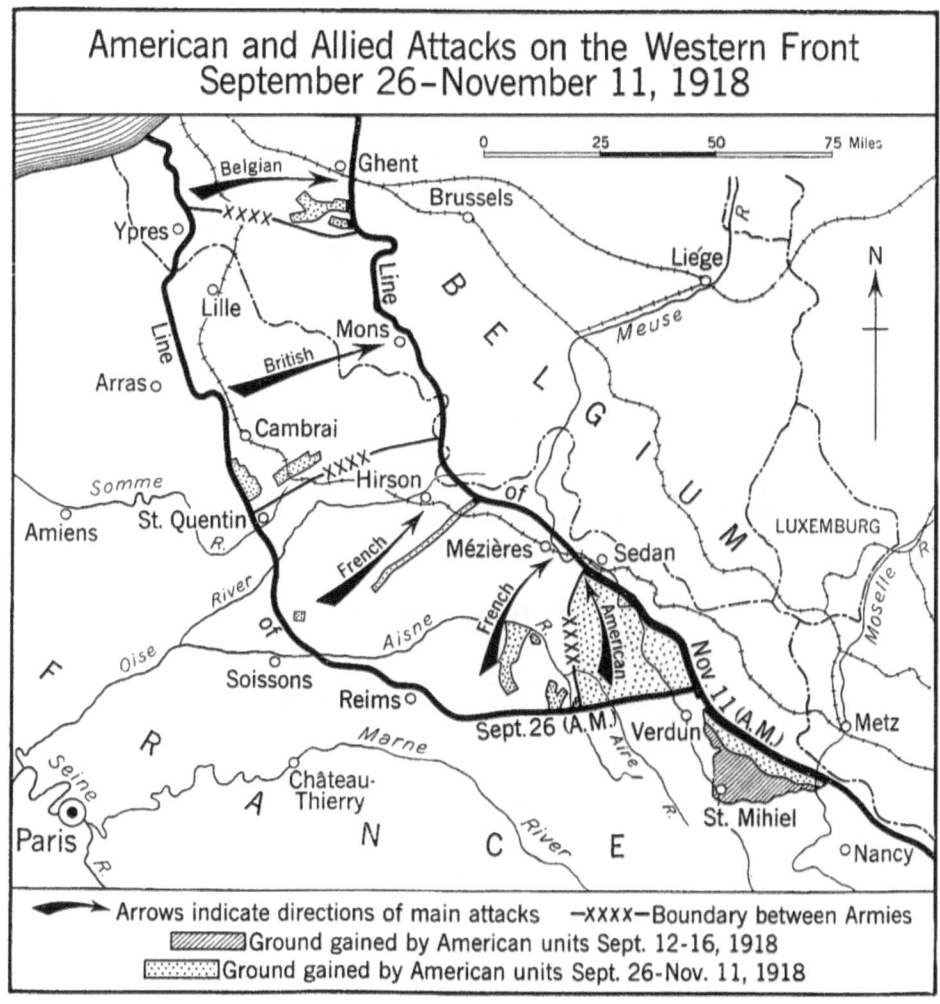

Source: General John J. Pershing, *My Experiences in the World War* (2 volumes), 1931.

The Germans had strategically placed a number of fortified machine gun nests inside the forward edge of the woods to provide interlocking or overlapping fire that impeded the progress of the Allied troops advancing on the objective. Lead elements had to reduce these hostile emplacements with the utmost dispatch. For this purpose, advancing units used whatever means available, including rifle fire, machine guns, automatic weapons (Chauchet— French machine rifle or light machine gun), and grenades, to drive the defenders from the nests. Artillery observers accompanied infantry units to provide supporting fire. Infantry or machine gun units had to silence these positions one by one.

Inside the edge of the woods was a mass of barbed wire entanglements running through the undergrowth and around the trees, so dense as to make forward movement practically impossible. Officers sent out small patrols to maneuver around and come in behind German machine gun nests and wipe them out, allowing the advance to continue. During this stage of the operation, the forward units suffered a high number of casualties.

By 10:49 a.m. on October 4, units of the 58th and 59th regiments of the 8th Infantry Brigade had penetrated the Bois de Fays and established a foothold along the southern fringe of the woods. Once inside the tree line, troops were able to take advantage of the cover and concealment afforded them by the heavy tangle of undergrowth and that furnished by low-lying mist or fog combined with smoke, creating a thick haze that remained into the late morning hours.

Lengel noted in *To Conquer Hell* that the doughboys "slashed forward through the Bois de Fays." The staccato of machine gun and rifle fire, combined with the crash and roar from exploding artillery shells, reverberated among the trees echoing and re-echoing. Whenever the shelling finally stopped for a brief period, one could hear the agonized screams of wounded men. The 58th Regiment on the left and 59th Regiment, which had moved over to the right, continued to gain ground, albeit slowly, forcing the Germans to retreat deeper and deeper into the interior of the wood.[22]

U.S. Marine Col. Frederic M. Wise, commander of the 59th Infantry, who watched the advance through his field glasses from the crest of a ridge, described the action as the troops entered the woods: "The minute the artillery ceased, ... I heard the German machine guns in the woods take up the chorus." Wise was a veteran of Battle of Belleau Woods a few months earlier. The brigade, forming a line that stretched across a two-mile front, started "down the slope, across the brook, [and] up the exposed half of the opposite side of the valley." As the line went ahead, Wise continued, "their path was marked by the men who fell." He commented, "You can't drive troops out of the woods by artillery alone," so the objective "had to be taken by hand-to-hand fighting."[23]

Wise watched as "the line vanished in the woods." Once out of sight, he could hear, "as so many times before," he wrote, "the spasmodic bursts of fire" to indicate that "desperate hand-to-hand fighting was going on about those German machine-gun nests." After a time, Wise could see the "walking wounded" as they "began to limp back across the valley on their way to the rear. Poor devils who couldn't walk were trying to crawl."[24]

About midafternoon, Col. Wise and Major Wilson (?), 1st Battalion commander, "proceeded down the hill, across the valley, up into the woods ... to inspect the new front lines." Upon entering the thick growth of trees and brambles, Wise wrote, "I saw again the old, inevitable story of woods fighting where men take machine-gun nests by frontal attack. Out in front of those nests lay our dead. About the guns lay the German dead. They had fought to the finish." The brigade had taken the objective, but had suffered "very heavy losses." For the remainder of the day the Germans shelled the American positions "steadily." At this point, German units began a series of counterattacks, stalling the advance.[25]

* * *

Edwin L. James, a war correspondent "with the American Army," sent a "Special Cable" to the New York Times Company at "11:30 p.m." on October 5, describing his firsthand account of the events of the previous two days. The *Times* published his story the following day. James's report contained details of the fighting, specifically that which occurred in the assault on the Bois de Fays by the 4th "Ivy" Division on the previous day. "The German high command, by means of new troops, artillery and additional aerial forces," he wrote, "threw terrific resistance against the First American Army on the Meuse-Argonne front ... in an effort to check the American advance." James observed the battle from "on top of the hill which the ruins of Montfaucon perch," overlooking the 4th Division sector to the east. He described the battle as it unfolded before him: "I watched the artillery and machine gun duel this afternoon. The air was filled with German shells, and more than an equal number of ours returning." From his lofty observation point atop the Butte of Montfaucon, James related that he could clearly see the "German attack on our lines three miles ahead" and "could hear the rat-tat-tat of dozens of machine guns going at the same time."[26]

During the morning of the 4th, the troops of the 4th Division, James noted, "pushed up to the Bois de Fays, the southern edge of which was strongly held by the Germans with machine guns." The correspondent's report contained an interesting item relating an encounter west of the Bois de Fays in which the Germans "used tanks, the first they have put in the line against our drive." "These," he informed his readers, "did not meet with much success." American artillery units "used seventy-fives [75mm artillery pieces] against them effectively." Bach and Hall mention the capture of two tanks by 4th Division forces during the drive, but provided no other details.[27]

The Imperial German Army Air Service (*Luftstreitkräfte*) was "most intense" throughout the day, with both American and German aircraft "venturing far over one another's lines and precipitating scores of combat." James commented, "The German aviators were very daring." The correspondent told of "heavy swarms" of German airplanes, coming "over our lines in large aggregations, sometimes as many as thirty machines in a group." "In one corps' front," the correspondent observed "forty aerial combats." German aviators, he said, "showed the utmost daring in their work against our balloons." One German fighter strafing a line of infantry troops "was brought down by rifle fire and the pilot killed."[28]

"Starting at an early hour this morning" (October 5), James wrote, "German heavies [heavy artillery] shelled our roads and villages, paying special attention to the roads out of Montafucon, Nantillois, Cierges, the Bois de Septsarges, and Bois de Forges." German pilots flying reconnaissance aircraft over the battlefield helped coordinate the artillery barrages. An observer in the rear cockpit used a one-way wireless telegraph transmitter to direct artillery adjustments by Morse code.[29]

"The day," James wrote in his closing paragraph, "was marked by the liveliest aerial fighting." He reported that American aircraft "carried out sixty reconnaissance missions back of the German lines," and that "our pursuit planes strafed the German roads, breaking up at least one heavy counterattack." James personally observed American antiaircraft fire bring down six planes, adding, "It is very seldom these guns actually bring down a plane, being used most largely to keep them off." Air Corps fighters also "had a large number of victories," with ace Lt. Eddie Rickenbacker getting credit for three of his 26 kills.[30]

* * *

On the morning of October 5, the 517th Infantry Regiment of the 80th Division occupied a position on the left flank of the 4th Division, approximately 0.6 of a mile to the south of the Bois de Ogons and one mile north of the town of Nantillois. Advancing troops of the 80th, Bach and Hall wrote, encountered "violent resistance." German units "stoutly defending forward positions" along the wood-line kept the division forces pinned down and unable to press the attack. The lack of forward progress by the 517th allowed the unprotected left flank of the more rapidly advancing troops of the 58th Infantry Regiment to be "decimated by fire" from several directions, causing heavy casualties.[31]

Company D, Matthew Guerra's unit, was on the far-left flank of the 58th Infantry when this occurred. The only course of action left open for the units of the regiment was to fall back "from their hard won position and retreat to the Fond de Ville aux Bois" (the ruins of a small farm located in "a hollow" between the Bois de Fays and the Bois de Malaumont), "half a kilometer to the rear" (see photograph of the Fond de Ville aux Bois, Bach and Hall, facing p. 197). There, the regiment established a "temporary line of defense" and dug in while waiting for units of the 517th to come alongside.[32]

A "Field Message" received by 58th Infantry field headquarters at "Hour 11:30 a.m." from Captain Vic K. Burris, a native of Kansas City, Missouri, with the 12th M.G. Company, 4th Division, reported: "Our left is still up in the air but an officer from the 517th Inf. tells us two companies from his regiment are moving forward to connect up with our left."[33]

22

Bois de Fays
"Woods of the Fairies"
(October 5, 1918)

The 4th Division occupied the Bois (Woods) de Fays (sometimes "des Fays" or "du Fays"), located a little more than a mile southeast of the village of Cunel, from October 4 to 18, 1918. The Bois de Fays adjoins the Bois de Malaumont to the northwest. Separating the two is the Fond (English trans: bottom) de Ville au Bois, that appears on a map (see note 1) to be a low-lying area separating the two woods with a road coming from the Route de Brieulles (to Cunel) and a small stream running west to east between the two. A short distance to the west is La Ville-au-Bois, that appears to be a cluster of buildings. Just to the west of Cunel is the Meuse-Argonne Cemetery, Matthew Guerra's final resting place.

It was Bois de Fays that division troops "suffered" what Edward D. Lengel described in his history of the Meuse-Argonne Battle *To Conquer Hell* as "unremitting torment." This patch of woods was located along and considered a part of the Hindenburg Line of defenses (see Lengel, p. 319—Map: "Heights of Cunel and Romagne"). What were conditions like for the men of the 58th Infantry on the date of October 5, the day my great-uncle Matthew Guerra received shrapnel wounds that ultimately led to his demise? The best way to describe the dire predicament and horrific circumstances these men were up against inside the Bois de Fays is by using the words of the participants themselves. Numerous vivid and graphic firsthand accounts and reports are included that attest to the horrors and paint a disturbing and gruesome picture of what the officers and men of the 4th "Ivy" Division experienced in what one member of the regiment described as those "hellish woods," that drove many to despair and often madness.[1]

Included as well are vivid descriptions of the brutal hardships faced by division forces in the process of trying to advance within this particular patch of woods facing entrenched German units (many in underground bunkers

22. Bois de Fays

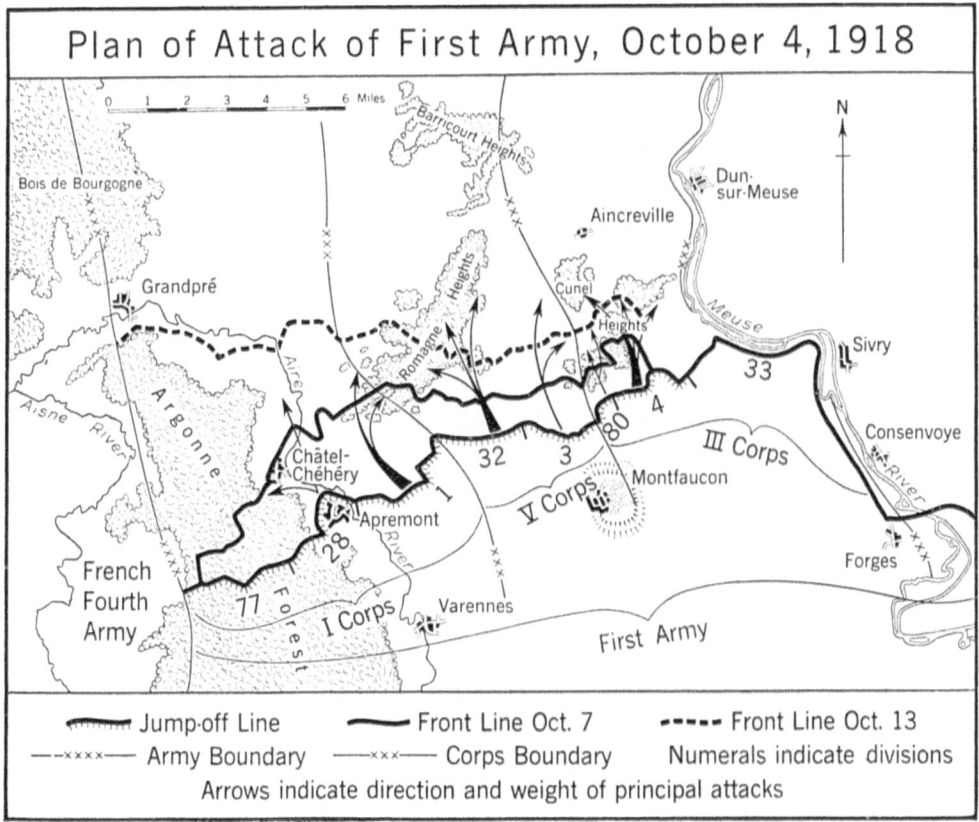

Meuse-Argonne Offensive, Second Phase. Source: General John J. Pershing, *My Experiences in the World War* (2 volumes), 1931.

and blockhouses). It was in these forested areas that units of the AEF "encountered hard fighting." The struggle to capture the Bois de Fays was typical of similar such heavily wooded areas encountered by other units in the Meuse-Argonne, such as the Bois de la Côte, Bois de Forêt, Bois de Cunel, and Bois de Ogons.

Col. Fredric May "Fritz" Wise (USMC), commander of the 59th Infantry Regiment, described the German tactics in the Bois de Fays:

> Their infantry counterattacks, though not very heavy in numbers, were extraordinarily vicious. Parties of fifty to a hundred of them would worm their way through the underbrush and behind trees close to our line of fox holes, with a couple of machine guns. After a few bursts of machine-gun fire, they would attack with fixed bayonets.

"Every night," Lengel wrote, German patrols, "snipers and machine-gun teams entered the woods in small parties, penetrating gaps in the American lines on either flank." At first light, "they opened fire from every direction." He added, "Nowhere was safe." "Survivors recalled the broken, the hysterical, and the shell-shocked: more than anything they remembered how the men's eyes grew dull, their movements mechanical." Wise commented, "The life of my men in that salient [Bois de Fays] was plain hell." The colonel railed about the hardships they had to endure—"cold food, cold weather, steady rain, constant enemy fire, patrols feeling out the line all the time, shelling, gas." He closed, "Yet they never gave an inch." Col. Wise was one of two U.S. Marine officers who commanded American units in World War I (see note).[2]

Toward dusk on October 4, the 3rd Battalion (Companies I, K, L, M), 58th Infantry was dug in along an east-west line in the northern part of the Bois de Fays with Company E of the 2nd Battalion positioned on the right. Next, the 1st Battalion (Companies A, B, C, D) established itself to the rear of the 3rd Battalion in the middle and southern portion of the woods. "On the night of October 4th–5th the [front] line of the Division extended from Hill 280 [on the east] along the northern edge of the Bois de Bruielles, eastern edge of the Bois de Fays, Fond de Ville aux Bois to the western boundary of the Division, thence south ... to where it joined the right of the 80th Division."[3]

Wise described what conditions were like for the troops of the 4th Division on the dreary night of October 4:

> In cold and a steady rain, without blankets or slickers, [the men] lay in the wet fox holes they had dug.... Parts of that line were in woods so thick that even in daytime they couldn't see one hundred yards ahead. They hadn't had a cup of hot coffee or a mouthful of hot food since they had started. Hard bread, canned salmon, canned corned beef, eaten out of the can, were all their rations.

"That was," according to Wise, "the program ... and the menu for the next solid three weeks."[4]

"At night," wrote historians Col. Christian A. Bach, Chief of Staff, 4th Division, and Henry N. Hall, a war correspondent for the *London Times*, it was the "infiltration tactics" of the Germans "that caused the most anxiety among the men of the Ivy Division." Small German patrols would attempt to steal into the woods and come in behind the infantrymen up on the line and fire into their backs, creating much consternation and strife among jittery troops who got little rest. "These tactics," the authors noted, "demanded strict vigilance, particularly from the units guarding the flanks." There would be long periods of silence, shattered suddenly by the occasional "whang" of a sniper's rifle fire and then the whizz of the round as it cuts a path through the air very near a person. What often followed were the panicked calls for a medic.[5]

* * *

The salient created by units of the division as the attack on the Bois de Fays unfolded was in the form of a horseshoe, described thusly by Col. Frederick Wise:

22. Bois de Fays

Our attack had punched a pocket about two miles deep and, roughly, four miles wide at the base, in the German line. The end of the pocket toward Germany was possibly a mile long. We were due to catch hell on three sides the minute the German counterattack started. Toward the left of my line the men of the two regiments [58th and 59th] were pretty thoroughly mixed.

Wise reported, "We've taken everything we were told to take. We can hold it but we can't advance any further."[6]

The following entry for the 5th of October is from the history of the 1st Battalion, 58th Infantry, written shortly after the war by Major Ernest John, who took part in every engagement by the regiment. John reported that 1st Battalion forces "entrenched in the Bois de Fays" were "forced to halt on account of Machine Gun nests, sniping and heavy artillery fire, ... mostly Austrian 88's." German artillery shelled the troops with intermittent fire "for about ten (10) consecutive minutes ... at intervals of every thirty (30) minutes" throughout the day and night. "Many of the shells were shrapnel bursting in the air." "Enemy bombing planes flying low" made passes over the Bois de Fays "all day."[7]

Bach and Hall reported that on October 5, established lines remained stationary throughout the day. The troops awakened that morning to heavy machine gun and sniper fire, "keeping them below ground." On that day, the authors noted that artillery fire emanating from the heights east of the Meuse "was incessant and deadly." German reconnaissance patrols attempting to take advantage of weak spots along the main line of defense "were constant and aggressive."[8]

* * *

As a creeping barrage advanced across the interior of the Bois de Fays, flashes of varying intensity lit up the darkened forest. Shells burst in the canopy overhead, followed by the loud thundering crash of falling timber down through the upper branches that echoed throughout the interior of the wood. There was the snapping and splintering noise of limbs breaking that sounded much like the crack of a rifle shot. Shells exploding on the ground uprooted huge trees, causing them to come crashing to the forest floor with a terrifying roar. Shards and slivers of flying shrapnel whistled and whined as they passed through the air overhead, many striking men who were caught partially or completely above ground for whatever reason. Each bombardment keyed the highly-strung nerves of the jittery men, some not yet out of their teens, cowering in their foxholes very near to the breaking point. Some men snapped, suffering severe psychological trauma (shell shock). The worst cases lapsed into a state of shock or unconsciousness and stretcher bearers escorted them to the rear, at much danger to themselves.

The forward line of the German defenses consisted of machine gun emplacements interspersed with infantrymen in trenches or foxholes. To further impede the progress of the advancing American troops, the Germans had "bound" the underbrush and trees together with huge belts of coiled barbed wire staked in the ground. New growth vegetation had grown up and entwined itself through the coils over the years of German occupation, so dense as to make it "absolutely impenetrable." Forward movement through these areas of the wood was virtually impossible. GHQ attached a squad of combat engineers to each company of infantry. These men were specialists who performed a variety of construction, mine clearing, and demolition tasks—this included necessary maintenance and repair of roads and bridges—many times under combat conditions. Their primary duty in the Bois de Fays was to clear the tangle of underbrush to improve field of fire as well as to create paths for the infantrymen to advance. Engineers cut through the coils of barbed wire that were impeding forward progress using a pair of quarter-inch bolt cutters. Field engineers also used high explosives to blast a path through the maze of wire. A combat engineer's job was one of the most dangerous around, making them superb targets for enemy machine gunners and snipers. They were also called upon to fight as infantry when necessary.

Inside the Bois de Fays, the Germans occupied machine gun nests, usually a pillbox or, according to Lengel, "wood or earthen bunkers." A pillbox was generally a constructed fortification (metal or concrete), round or rectangular, with cut-outs or slits for the gun and of course, a rear exit if overrun. A bunker was much larger in size, with living quarters for the crew. Throughout he Bois de Fays there were many of these positions, the remains of which exist to this day. See Google images under Bois de Fays for photographs showing remnants of war era concrete bunkers and dugouts in the wood. One shows the interior of a bunker with a corrugated metal roof (likely covered over by a thick layer of soil).[9]

Lt. Col. Ashby Williams, commander of the 320th Regiment, 80th Division, on the immediate left flank of Guerra's 4th Division in the Bois de Borros, described what it was like to come under artillery fire while in a heavily wooded area on the battlefield. "Suddenly," he said, "the Boche began to shell the woods again." Williams's regiment could not pass around the companies ahead of them and there was no turning back. He ordered his men to take cover among the trees and dense tangle of undergrowth and dig in as best they could. "We could only wait and trust to the Grace of God." He provided a vivid description of the foreboding sound of that first projectile:

> We could hear the explosion as the shell left the muzzle of the Boche gun, ... like the single bark of a great dog in the distance, and you hear the deadly missile singing as it comes towards you, faintly at first, then distinctly, then louder and louder until it seems so loud that everything else has died, and then the earth shakes and the eardrums ring, and dirt and iron reverberate through the woods and fall about you.

22. Bois de Fays

Williams expressed his innermost feelings at that precise moment:

> no man can tell what surges through the heart and mind as you lie with your face upon the ground listening to the growing sound of the hellish thing as it comes towards you. You do not think, sorrow only fills the heart, and you only hope and pray. And when the doubly-damned thing hits the ground, you take a breath and feel relieved, and think how good God has been to you again. And God was good to us that night—to those of us who escaped unhurt. And for the ones who were killed, poor fellows, some blown to fragments that could not be recognized, and the men who were hurt, we said a prayer in our hearts.

As Williams related, the torrent of artillery shells caused a great deal of anxiety and fear among those exposed to incoming fire. The colonel closed, "Such was my experience and the experience of my men that night in the Bois de Borrus, but their conduct was fine.... I knew that men like these would never turn back and they never did."[10]

Maj. Julius Ochs Adler, in his *History of the 77th Division*, explained that an "exploding shell throws its fragment upward and outward at a considerable angle, and these fragments sometimes travel for hundreds of feet." Flying shrapnel searched for exposed and unprotected body parts of men, a number of whom were caught out in the open. Some men, hands on their helmets, curled up in the fetal position, head pushed face-first in the ground. Between shell bursts, one could hear agonizing cries and screams of pain from the wounded, followed by frantic shouts for a medic, who patched them up as best they could, then called out for stretcher-bearers, if available, to take them to a rear area. Men of the medical corps were exposed to shell and shot as they came to the aid of wounded and dying. The job of these men was an extremely dangerous one. While responding to a call, they had to traverse the battlefield during the height of an engagement to tend to wounded comrades at much risk to their own lives. During times like this, medical teams were stretched to their limit and beyond.[11]

Men dug in along the front during the shelling shuddered in absolute horror and fear, hoping and praying for a merciful God to spare them from a direct or near hit. Threatened with imminent death, they uttered promises to their God, many quickly forgotten once the shelling ceased. Others cursed and cried out in terror—a wailing or mournful cry. The statement "There are no atheists in foxholes," is an aphorism that first appeared in press reports dating from the end of the First World War.

* * *

Fortunately, available to historians are the Field Messages and other records of Guerra's 58th Infantry during the offensive, prepared by officers at command headquarters, located in the village of Cuisy. Presented next is a chronological account from "'WAR DIARIES,' Headquarters 4th Division,

October 5, 1918, CHRONOLOGICAL RECORD OF EVENTS," that begins with a brief synopsis of the day's activities within the Bois de Fays. These communications provide additional testimony surrounding the events that transpired on that date:

> Remarks: P.C. [Command Post at the Village of] CUISY. Activity limited to organizing positions already held and to patrolling. Enemy counter-attacked during the night and was driven off. Attacked again at 10 a.m. with 300 men, again driven off, leaving 6 prisoners and 6 machine guns in our hands. Considerable enemy machine gun and artillery activity. CUISY shelled at noon. F.O. [Field Order] #61 issued, directing an advance when the 80th Division on the left should arrive abreast of the 8th Brigade's present position [58th Infantry Regiment, 59th Infantry Regiment, and 12th Machine Gun Battalion].

2nd Lt. Wells A. Hutchins, Inf.-Asst. G-3, "reported.... Weather: Cloudy and rainy." Several Field Messages for October 5 indicate "heavy" artillery fire by the Germans throughout the day on the eastern edge of Bois de Fays. A number of entries indicate heavy shelling from the "northeast and east" at specific times throughout the day:

> From: Dixon 1
> To: Denver 1
> Date 10/5/18
> Hour: 7:55 a.m.
>
> The enemy artillery has been very active. Enemy machine guns are still numerous and owing to the dense underbrush, few twisting trails and heavy enemy artillery fire are difficult to get at. Our troops are engaged in trying to clean up their immediate vicinity.

Hour: 8:20 a.m.

> No change in position. Small counterattacks repulsed this a.m. Morale of troops and officers ... poor. Artillery barrage pretty bad this a.m. Quite a few officers and men wounded. Lt. Roby, M.G. Co., killed. Lts. Morse, Waltmire and Ash wounded slightly. Must have someone over here capable of giving first aid. Cannot spare men to evacuate wounded. Let all runners and men reporting here bring water and Chauchat [French Machine Gun] and .30 [cal.] ammunition. Companies are very depleted. We will hold though as long as required.... We need men to act as stretcher bearers. [Maj. Gilbert R.] COOK [2nd Bn. commander].

The message is a possible indication that an unusually high number of casualties and a shortage of medical personnel were taxing the normal evacuation process. This resulted in long delays before medics could provide aid to the wounded and move them out of the woods to a rear area for more specialized treatment.

Hour 11:25 a.m.

> At about 10 o'clock this a.m., about 300 Germans advancing through the N.W. edge of the Bois de Fays from the Bois de Malamount delivered a counter attack against our

left. They were driven back with losses. We captured six machine guns and six prisoners. Owing to the necessity of getting troops back to the eastern edge of the Bois de Fays to hold against a threatened counter attack an energetic pursuit of the enemy was not pushed.

Hour 11:30 a.m.

Attack still in progress. Our left is still up in the air but an officer from the 517th Inf. [80th Div.] tells us two companies from his regiment are moving forward to connect up with our left. Parts of F and H Cos., 58th Inf. are covering the Bn. right. The Bn's do not connect but the ground is open so I can see all in between our right and the 59th Bn. [Captain Vic K.] BURRIS.

Hour: 2:12 p.m.

… Intense shelling on eastern edge of Bois de FAYS. Fire coming from north east and east. Large explosion observed around buildings 2.2–4.9 [?] at 4:05 p.m. Another large explosion at same place at 4:12 p.m.

The last entry by the 58th Infantry for "Hour: 9:15 p.m., October 5," mentions one final counterattack that occurred after dark, but provided no details. "Battalion dug in fairly secure for the night. Telephone established with each battalion with one local counter attack with second battalion all went duly well."[12]

Pvt. Roy E. Mathews, Company E, 58th Infantry Regiment, 4th Division received a Distinguished Service Cross (DSC) for "heroism" with regard to an incident involving "friendly fire" that occurred on October 5.

Citation:

The Distinguished Service Cross is presented to Roy E. Mathews, Private, U.S. Army, for extraordinary heroism in action in the Bois-du-Fays, France, October 5, 1918. Acting without orders, Private Mathews went through heavy artillery fire to notify his regimental commander that our own barrage was falling short, his bravery and presence of mind thus saving the lives of many American soldiers.
General Orders No. 46, W.D., 1919
Home Town: Seattle, Washington."

This presents a somewhat distressing thought for consideration: could Matthew Guerra and others have tragically been victims of their own artillery?[13]

* * *

In his memoirs, Sgt. Major James W. Block of the 59th Infantry, 4th Division, began:

It is said the Bois de Fays means "Woods of the Fairies." Were I to name it, I would call it "The Center of Hell." Any man who ever spent any time in those woods, from the 4th to the 17th of October, knows that even that term does not adequately express the true situation.

He elaborated at length describing the conditions and relating the ordeal experienced by himself and by his fellow 4th Division soldiers:

> The shell torn woods were wet and muddy; everything was wet and damp, raw, cold and clammy. Not a breeze blew to clear the gas laden air. The sun never shone, it was always dark and murky. Down the sides of our foxholes, water trickled or seeped through the walls. From all sides came the odor of death and decay. Mangled bodies of men were everywhere to be seen. Our bodies ached from the cold and wet. The foul surroundings made one sick at heart. We were hungry, yet unable to eat but little of the food which came up. For hours at a time we were forced to be without water, for to go after it was to gamble with death. The mental strain was maddening, the physical strain exhausted us. We had to be alert. Sleep was impossible. The enemy counter-attacked time and again, but was repulsed each time…. When the Boche were not counter-attacking, they were shelling our positions. We had to lay there and hold. We had to take all the punishment with our hands tied.

Inside the Bois de Fays, the Germans had pinned down the troops of the 4th Division for days, leaving them unable to advance.[14]

Another vivid description of the Bois de Fays is provided by Bach and Hall:

> It rained nearly every day and the dampness and cold, the mud and the darkness, made life almost unbearable…. No fires could be built. Hot food could only be brought up from the Bois de Brieulles at night. Gas reeked through the woods. Aeroplanes bombed [the troops] at frequent intervals. The stench of dead bodies became unendurable, and as many as could be found in the thick underbrush were carried to the southern edge of the woods and later buried. Seldom has there been such a combination of horrors and seldom have the supreme qualities of endurance of mind and body and quiet heroism been in greater demand.

The authors closed: "The men wanted to go forward. They were tired of the Bois de Fays."[15]

Maj. Gen. Robert Lee Bullard, III Corps commander, provided the following account of the place echoing that of others who were there:

> In the Bois de Fays, … the 4th Division held a scattered line of holes in rain and cold, amid shattered tree trunks. There was mud, gas, attack from three sides, shell-fire, counter-attack, cold food if any, the stench of dead bodies, continuous horror. In one spot, 60 dead, in another 200.

Bullard closed: "The division was almost exhausted. Their food was used up and their ammunition almost gone, but they still held on—weak, scattered, and disorganized by heavy losses and repeated enemy counter-attacks, but still in the Bois de Fays."[16]

Colonel Frederick M. Wise, another participant of the battle, reiterated Bullard's remarks, stating that the "stench of death, from dozens of unburied bodies in the thick underbrush, floated everywhere," a common theme in the writings and memoirs of veterans. No matter how long they lived, the sickening smell of putrefying flesh was something the men could never erase from their memories. He related how a detail searching for bodies, a gruesome task, "found one man still living with eight bullet holes in him, too weak to move or call out. He had lain in the brush under that steady rain for a week before we found him." An incredible story about the will to live.[17]

The colonel "watched the remnants of his 59th Regiment hobbling out of the woods," which they could only do after dark. Men with "their gas-infected eyes oozing fluid" headed to the aid station in the rear for treatment. "One man who could see a little" would be at the head of the column, "leading the others totally blinded, who held onto little sticks, extending from hand to hand, to guide them."[18]

* * *

On the 5th of October, Gen. Bullard visited 4th Division headquarters at Cuisy to confer with Maj. Gen. John L. Hines, division commander. Conditions in the Bois de Fays were so dire, Hines, who was "greatly concerned," requested that Bullard allow him to withdraw his troops from the woods. The General answered, "No, ... we've got to stay there; we give up nothing. Your division has done magnificent work and shown wonderful courage." Hines "exclaimed," rather indignantly, "'Then tell them so!'"[19]

Bullard immediately dashed off a letter of commendation to the men of the 4th extolling their praiseworthy achievement and courage. He "ordered a corps airplane to fly over and scatter down to the troops in that wood (that was the only way they could be reached) a citation for their bravery and an encouragement to stick. They did stick." An "Extract" of the citation, dated October 5, 1918, reads:

"HEADQUARTERS THIRD ARMY CORPS AMERICAN EXPEDITIONARY FORCES— France, October 5, 1918.

General Orders: No. 29.

The Corps Commander, in General Orders, cites the gallant conduct of the 4th Division, especially the 7th [39th and 47th Regiments] and 8th Infantry [58th and 59th Regiments] Brigades, in the seizure against great difficulties, of the BOIS DE FAYS, and the holding of it against repeated and determined counterattacks, between September 26th and October 5. You are there; stay there.

By command of MAJOR GENERAL BULLARD: A.W. Bjornstad, Brigadier General, G.S., Chief of Staff

Wise wrote, "Copies of [the leaflet] were sent up the line. The men would have given a lot more for a cup of hot coffee. We had determined to stay there, anyway, from the day we arrived."[20]

Bullard "ordered all the artillery and airplanes that [he] could lay [his] hands on to bombard [the village of] Brieulles and the fort near it that was decimating these men with machine-gun fire, and to bombard the enemy's batteries in the hills east of the Meuse." These steps, which proved successful, "relieved the 4th Division." As a result, he wrote, "The troops on the Bois de Fays were reinforced, fed, and saved." Too late for Matthew Guerra.[21]

In Bullard's final commentary, found in his memoirs written after the war, he states that "the losses and strain upon" the troops of the 4th Division "had been very great, the greatest that I have known. I shall remember this as one of the finest if not the finest deed I have known. They were gassed, bombarded with artillery, and riddled with machine-gun fire, but they stayed." At last, the enemy was finally "pushed out of the wood" by division forces.[22]

At some point in time on the 5th of October, a shell exploded on or very near Matthew Guerra's position, inflicting severe shrapnel wounds. Medics evacuated him to the nearest dressing station, from there to an Advanced First Aid Station, and then by ambulance to Evacuation Hospital #4, at Fontaine Routon.

On October 6, the Germans had stopped the division's forward progress. October 6 through the 8th, Bach and Hall wrote, "saw no marked change" in the 4th Division's "situation." Later in the day of the 6th, III Corps relieved the 58th and one battalion of the 59th Infantry Regiments (4th) and withdrew them from the Bois de Fays "to the vicinity of Cuisy to rest." The remaining units of the 59th Regiment with the attached 3rd Battalion and the regimental machine gun company of the 132nd Infantry, 33rd Division, took over the forward positions.[23]

* * *

Fourth "Ivy" Division forces remained in action at the front during the Meuse-Argonne campaign for 24 days, the longest consecutive period of any other AEF division. Pershing withdrew the division from the battle lines on October 24, 1918. In that time, the 4th Division had lost 1,120 enlisted men and 45 officers, with another 6,048 soldiers and 199 officers wounded, gassed, or reported missing. Two officers and forty-five men had died from other causes, for a combined total loss in strength of 7,459 officers and men. Bach and Hall closed: "The men of the Ivy Division had, in truth, fought with splendid courage and devotion to duty. They had been steadfast and loyal."[24]

In his summary of the battle, Jeffrey Aarnio, assistant superintendent of Meuse-Argonne American Cemetery, wrote: "The Meuse-Argonne Offensive of 26 September through 11 November, 1918, ... remains America's largest military offensive to date with over 1,200,000 soldiers [taking] part in this continuous battle over a 47-day period." On the jump-off line, during "the early morning hours of 26 September, ... there were nine American divisions with six divisions in reserve." An American division in World War I consisted of 28,000 men, as opposed to a World War II Division of 18,000. Aarnio noted, "There were only five U.S. assault Divisions in Normandy on 6 June 1944."[25]

23

October 5–7, 1918
The Death of a Doughboy

On October 5, 1918, Matthew Guerra's company hunkered down inside the Bois de Fays while German artillery batteries blanketed the woods with their big guns from forward positions and from the east across the Meuse River ("Heights of the Meuse"). Incoming artillery rounds hammered the tenuous American positions at intervals around the clock. Terrified men crouched in their hastily dug foxholes, in a shell hole, or behind some type of protective cover such as a fallen tree or log. Soldiers curled up in the fetal position, hearts pounding and literally shaking uncontrollably from the sheer horror of knowing that a shell could literally blow them to bits at any moment and they would be no more.

As the exploding shells marched closer and closer across the woods towards the positions held by the men of the 58th Regiment, their anxiety mounted. At some point during the day, an artillery shell or mortar round exploded in close proximity to Guerra's platoon, spraying the area with splinters of deadly shrapnel. As Guerra hugged the earth, steel fragments ripped into his flesh, likely rendering him unconscious. One of three types of shells, high-explosive, antipersonnel (fragmentation), or chemical (gas), could have caused Guerra's injuries that eventually proved fatal.

When Guerra received his shrapnel wounds, the call for a medic brought members of the 58th Infantry regimental medical detachment, who rendered immediate first aid to stop the bleeding and to apply a dressing. Once Guerra's condition was stabilized, litter bearers transported him to the nearest clearing station to be sorted. Generally there were four types of cases: wounded, gas injuries, shell shock, and disease. At this medical post, medical detachment personnel administered emergency treatment prior to transport to an advanced aid station in the rear. This would have included applying an antiseptic and dressing the wound, checking for internal hemorrhaging, and administering splints if necessary. It was impossible for ambulances to come

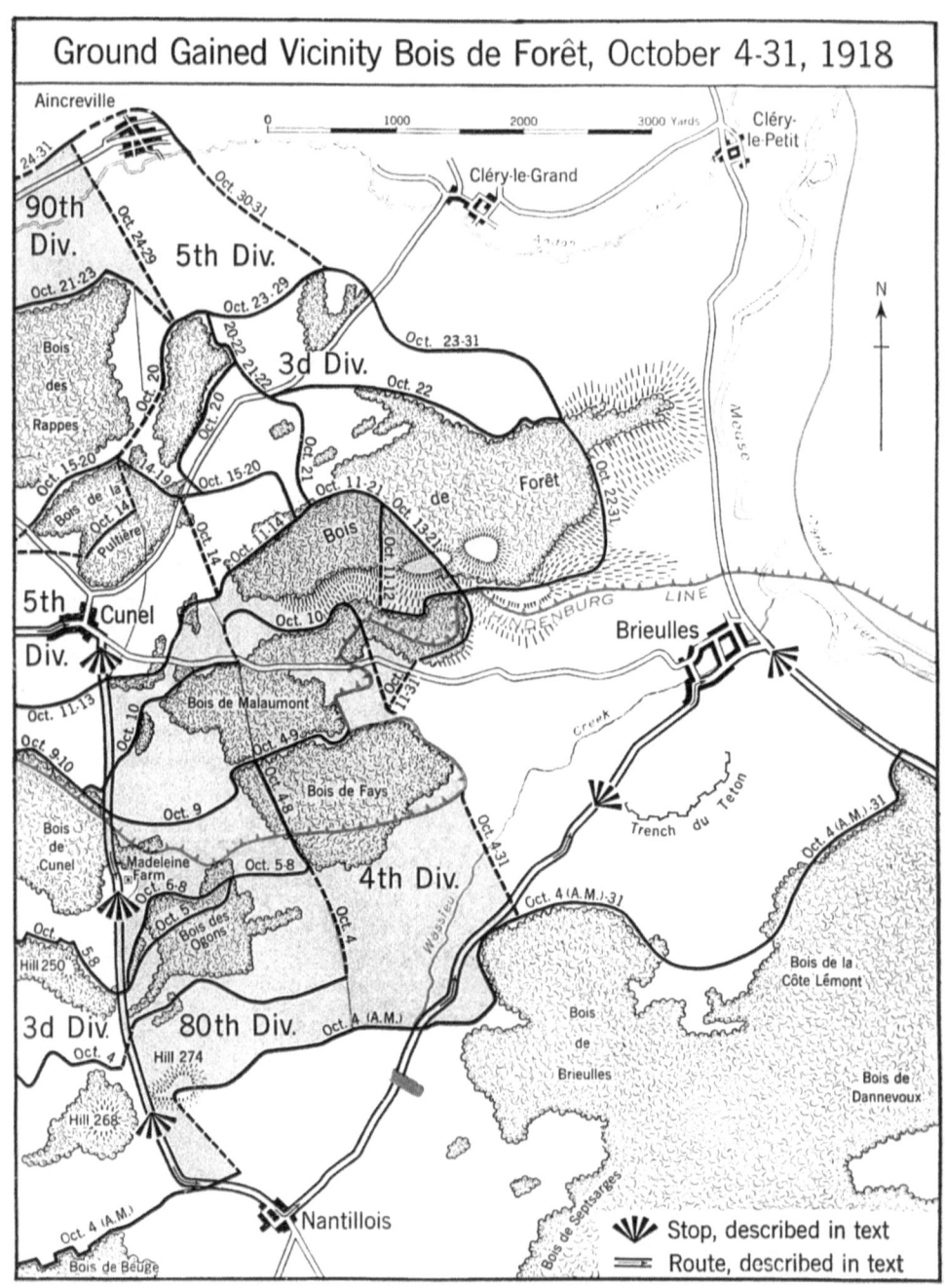

Source: General John J. Pershing, *My Experiences in the World War* (2 volumes), 1931.

nearer than one and a half kilometers to the battle lines. Stretcher-bearers succeeded in evacuating the wounded promptly under the most trying circumstances of battlefield conditions. The editors of *The 39th Infantry* (4th Division) *in the World War*, Maj. Robert B. Cole and Capt. Bernard Eberlin, wrote: "The spirit and bravery of the members of this detachment, in the performance of their duty, elicited from the soldiers the greatest praise and gratitude, and bound them to the regiment with the strongest of human ties."[1]

From the dressing station, stretcher-bearers carried Guerra to an "ambulance head or collecting station," the most advanced relay point along the system of evacuation that could be reached by ambulance. Usually, medical detachment personnel located the station in a rear area where drivers could position a vehicle safely and conveniently, generally out of the danger of direct fire and shelling. Whenever possible, ambulance drivers "went all the way to aid stations and thus reduced the heavy labor of litter-bearing." In some cases, the medical officer in charge, a doctor or surgeon, often located at an aid station or at the ambulance head, may decide to perform any necessary emergency surgery before transferring the casualty farther along the chain of medical treatment.[2]

An ambulance would have transported Guerra from the collecting station to the nearest 58th Infantry "advanced field hospital," in this case, located at Septsarges (opened September 30), approximately one mile northeast of Montfaucon, approximately 2.5 to 3 miles behind the front lines. Here, a medical officer would have, if necessary, performed a more complex surgical procedure to remove shell fragments, redressed his wounds, relieved pain, treated for shock, and prepared him for transport farther to the rear. Each station along the route was progressively better equipped and thus able to provide more advanced treatment and care.

At this particular location, the wounded man is provisionally diagnosed and provided a "diagnosis tag" (a "wire tag") before continuing the evacuation process. Corpsmen carried with them a "Diagnosis tag book." This recorded information apprised doctors at a rear area station of the severity and complexity of the soldier's injuries. It also provided medical personnel at each station along the way with a detailed record of the types of treatment performed or medication administered. The tags recorded the date, name and rank of the wounded man, his unit, the station where tagged, diagnosis, and treatment, followed by the signature of the attendant or physician. Personnel attached these tags to a front shirt button if possible or elsewhere.

After undergoing emergency treatment at Septsarges, ambulance personnel might possibly have, depending on Guerra's condition, transferred him to one of the 4th Division field hospitals, in this case No. 19 or 21. Both units were located just north of Cuisy and south of Septsarges. From this point, an ambulance transported him to Evacuation Hospital No. 4, his final destination, for more specialized medical care. "Evacuation" or "evac hospitals" are described as "the backbone of all combat hospitalization." The location of this evac hospital was Fontaine Routon, approximately two miles north of Lemmes and 12 kilometers (7.4 miles) south of the city of Verdun. Two days later, Guerra died of his wounds, most likely from complications (see below).[3]

Ordinarily, the medical corps situated these units some distance from the front lines, usually somewhere between 10 and 20 miles, purposely to avoid bombing and long-range artillery fire. These units received all cases evacuated from the field hospitals and provided "complete facilities for operation and hospitalization of sick and wounded." The medical corps staffed each facility with teams of trained specialists "for the treatment of various classes of wounds and disease." The capacity of an evac hospital could be as high as 500. Evacuation hospitals operated annexes for special treatment of gas, neurological, contagious diseases, and other cases. Evacuation hospital personnel, "as officially prescribed," according to the Office of Medical History, "consisted of 34 officers and 237 enlisted men, but in practice this number was at times greatly increased." Medical personnel retained the serious cases requiring immediate surgery or hospitalization and evacuated the remainder to another facility for more specialized treatment.[4]

* * *

Accounts relating to the situation at this time indicate that given the condition of the roads, heavily congested on October 5, it would have taken considerably longer for the ambulance carrying Guerra to arrive at Evacuation Hospital No. 4 in Fontaine Routon. Bach and Hall wrote, "The Esnes-Malancourt-Cuisy road carried all the traffic of the 4th Division, ... in addition, all the traffic of the 79th Division, and later of both the 80th and 3rd Divisions," adding, "congestion on this road can hardly be described."

> Beginning at 1:30 p.m. on September 26th there was not a minute of the twenty-four hours when the road was not covered for every yard of its length with everything it could carry. Whenever a truck broke down, an animal dropped dead, a wagon broke a wheel—and these were not infrequent incidents—the entire traffic halted. When a shell struck the road it caused a jam which could not be moved again until the road had been repaired. Consequently, when traffic did move, it moved very slowly. Frequently, it did not move at all. During the whole period this road was constantly under repair by two regiments of engineers.

Time en route had, in a number of instances, increased by as much as 24 to 48 hours or longer. In that time, Guerra's likely guarded condition may have deteriorated rapidly. For photographs showing the extent of the road congestion, see note.[5]

For most seriously wounded patients, transportation by ambulance, primitive vehicles by today's standards, with crude spring suspension systems, was long and torturous. Bouncing along over rough, crater pitted roads, the ride was a painful and extremely punishing experience. Such conditions inflicted horrendous suffering upon the wounded during transportation, further exacerbating their trauma. Pvt. Loren "Larry" Duren, Company K, a member of Guerra's 58th Infantry Regiment, 4th Division, described his ambulance ride from the aid station to the field hospital after receiving multiple shrapnel wounds to his legs:

> A bit later they loaded me into an ambulance, together with three other lads and we began the long, dark ride to the hospital. Out of the whole "Experience," I really think that night stands out vividly as being the only awful bit. Over a shell torn and muddy road we went, with jolts which sometimes nearly threw us from the stretchers. I tried hard to keep my [wounded] legs still but each jar shook them and they would pain so. One poor lad next to me would moan pitifully. His arm was gone at the shoulder. While another, above me, screamed and screamed. I slept some, or was unconscious I guess, but would come to with a start as we went into a shell hole and that poor lad above me would scream again.... And all through that long, long night as we bumped along I listened to that poor lad scream, or else drop off unconscious.

At the aid station, a doctor examined Duren and administered "a shot," then shouted to the stretcher bearers, "All right, take him on to Chateau Thierry as fast as you can."[6]

Some of the major risk factors associated with pre- and postoperative surgical patients during the war, that may (or may not) have contributed to Guerra's eventual demise, are included here. Penetrating trauma resulting from shrapnel can be very serious, especially if they strike major internal organs. The severity of these types of wounds varied greatly, depending on the part of the body involved, the type or characteristics of the projectile, the velocity, as well as the point of entry. Bursting shells, by their very nature, proved the most destructive, usually resulting in multiple injuries. Shrapnel caused 46 percent of all casualties in World War I, poison gas 31 percent, bullets (from machine guns and rifles) 17 percent, and hand grenades 3 percent (percentages are from a number of sources and are approximate). Such injuries also presented a substantial risk of shock, which increases exponentially depending on the degree of blood loss, and/or if infection set in, which, given existing unsanitary conditions on the battlefield, was generally the norm.[7]

Besides penetrating wounds from shrapnel—shards of jagged metal and other debris—a person in close proximity to a shell blast could also receive internal or external physical injuries from the concussive pressure of shock and sound waves. Neurological damage to the nervous system (brain and spinal cord) can also occur. Direct or indirect exposure to an explosion can cause tiny blood vessels in the brain and central nervous system to hemorrhage, resulting in coma and, in some instances, eventual death. Serious injuries to sensory organs are a definite possibility. Damage to the tympanic membrane can occur, resulting in permanent loss of hearing. Eye trauma can cause an inflammation or detachment of the retina, or hyphema—a collection of blood in the anterior chamber of the eye between the cornea and iris causing an elevation of pressure, possibly resulting in loss of sight.

* * *

Another possible cause of Guerra's rapid demise in such a brief time span could very well have been the outbreak of the catastrophic Spanish influenza of 1918, which occurred at the height of the American military involvement in the war—September through November. Epidemiologists cite the Spanish flu as one of the deadliest global pandemics ever recorded in human history, with an estimated 20 to 50 million deaths (some estimates are considerably higher). Worldwide, approximately 20 percent to 40 percent of the population became ill.

"The crisis of the Pandemic in the AEF's First Army," wrote Historian Alfred W. Crosby, a professor emeritus in American Studies, History and Geography, at the University of Texas at Austin, came "during the second phase of the Meuse-Argonne offensive," which began on October 4, and "took up most of the month of October." "As the number of casualties spurted upward, so did the number of flu cases," he added. Spanish flu was 25 times more lethal than ordinary flu, killing 2.5 percent of its victims as opposed to .1 percent for the latter.[8]

Seasonal flu usually strikes the elderly (people over age 65) and young children, generally under five years of age. The most puzzling aspect of the 1918 flu was that worldwide the largest segment of society affected was the adult population between 20 and 40 years of age, for the most part young and healthy individuals. Scientists are uncertain as to the underlying reason for this anomaly. During World War I, more American soldiers died from the flu than from combat, approximately 57,000 versus 53,500. In 1918 alone, the Army estimated that 36 percent of its members contracted the disease, "over 621,000, ... upwards of one-sixth of the overall number of soldiers in World War I." The total number of military deaths (Army and Navy) in 1918 alone "was over 43,000," approximately 80 percent of American combat casualties. According to Crosby, there may actually have been two epidemics raging at the same time, influenza and dysentery, resulting in a great deal of confusion. Could Guerra have been one of the epidemic's many victims?[9]

During the Meuse-Argonne offensive, the AEF reported "93,160 wounded" and another "68,700" listed as "medical cases," the majority of which "were flu or resulting complications of flu." Of this number, "about one in every three soldiers ... died." Out of every one thousand soldiers in the U.S. Army in 1918, doctors officially admitted 361 to hospitals as flu patients. Crosby concludes that this "figure should be higher, because many with symptoms of flu never reported as sick. AEF influenza and pneumonia deaths for September, October, and November, were 2,500, 5,092, and 1,552 respectively. By the time the war ended in mid-November, the flu epidemic was essentially over.[10]

The official history of the U.S. Army Medical Corps reported that the influenza epidemic "did not stop military operations," but it greatly reduced the number of fighting or support troops available, slowing operations "perceptibly." It also, according to Crosby, "threatened for a while to disrupt the evacuation system and to overwhelm the hospitals completely." Because of the heavy losses, none of the front-line divisions could sustain operations "for more than several days without requiring reinforcements." Interestingly enough, at the time, Allied medical personnel thought the epidemic might be "a biological warfare tool of the Germans," possibly from the use of mustard gas.[11]

While antiseptics then in use proved effective for superficial flesh wounds, they were only marginally successful for treating deep wounds. It would not be until the discovery of sulfonamide (sulfa) drugs in the mid-1930s, and the mass production of penicillin (discovered in 1928 by Alexander Fleming) in 1942, that medical personnel were able to substantially reduce or eliminate the chances of death from bacterial infection. The availability of germ-killing drugs in World War II saved countless lives that otherwise would have been lost to even the most minor of infected wounds.[12]

Finally, common causes of wound contamination leading to infection included bacteria or other pathogenic microorganisms that proliferated in the soil and mud, as well as in the ever-present pools of stagnant ooze and rainwater that collected in dugouts, foxholes, and bomb craters during the fall rainy season. There were also blast fragments, as well as other debris, including shreds of clothing from filthy, grimy, lice-infested uniforms. Investigations found that most infections initially began with clothing soiled by, for example, feces from rats and mice, from lice, fleas, and other parasites. Human waste due to poor hygiene and a lack of proper sanitation methods in the trenches was another prominent factor. A blast many times drives contaminants deep into a laceration.[13]

Dr. Harry L. Smith, Medical Detachment, 4th Division, provided a simple explanation of how the soil of the French countryside "was particularly ideal for the growth of organisms of all kinds." "Wounded men who lay on this soil," he explained, "would be likely to suffer infection very readily." "For centuries," Smith elaborated, "the peasants had heaped manure on their land and plowed it under, producing a medium in which germs throve in unimaginable profusion." These unusual circumstances caused battlefield wounds to become more readily contaminated, ultimately leading to irreversible complications. The presence of these microbes resulted directly in the deaths of an inordinate number of young men. The primary reason for this, Smith pointed out, was "the unfavorable conditions for prompt and effective medical and surgical care which arise in any war." Delay resulted in the rapid multiplication of pathogenic bacteria and other microorganisms, which was, because of the lack of germ fighting drugs, extremely difficult to reverse.[14]

In France, Thomas Hager noted in *Demon Under the Microscope*, "there was no such thing as a clean wound." Researchers found that most wounds "were dangerously septic from the very start" and "impossible … to clean effectively." As mentioned earlier, explosive shells "drove muddy, richly manured soil deep into ragged cavities in the flesh." The standard procedure for cleansing a wound was a method called "debridement," which involved washing with soap and water, and then carving away all dead and damaged flesh until the surgeon reached healthy tissue that was of "normal color." The next step was to apply a strong antiseptic solution, then close and cover.[15]

By the time the fallen battlefield soldier made it to the nearest field or evacuation hospital, his wounds were already festering with a host of potentially deadly microbes. In terms of the patient's chances of survival, it was already too late in the majority of cases. Once any type of bacterial infection started in the body, no drug existed at the time that could stop or reverse the extremely rapid rate of replication by bacteria. Binary fission, division yielding two daughter cells, can take place within five to twenty minutes. Doubling the population at this rate resulted in the multiplication of millions within in a brief span. The host of pathogenic microorganisms infecting the wound, "alone or in concert," caused "variations on the progress" of a particular disease, "any or all of which could kill [the] injured soldier."[16]

There were also a number of other factors contributing to secondary infections. Medical personnel often worked unmasked and bare-handed and without gowns, leading to the transfer and spread of potentially deadly microbes. Sterile latex gloves were available during the war, but medical personnel did not use them consistently. After World War I, the practice became routine. Battlefield conditions also resulted in the proliferation of annoying flies, fleas, lice, and mosquitoes, which also spread germs and infectious diseases. Keeping the swarms of these pesky insects away from open wounds during surgery was an annoying chore for both nurses and orderlies.[17]

* * *

Guerra passed away on October 7, 1918, from wounds received two days earlier. American Red Cross personnel buried his body at the nearby American

Bottom: Meuse Argonne American Cemetery, c. 1960s (copyright American Battle Monuments Commission).

Military Cemetery (Cimetière Militaire National), approximately two miles north of Lemmes and 6.5 miles southwest of the city of Verdun. The burial followed a brief graveside service by a chaplain and members of a Quartermaster Corps Graves Registration Service Company detail.

Shortly after Guerra's death, the Adjutant General's Office of the War Department in Washington, D.C., attempted to notify his sister Lena La Torre, listed as contact person on military documents, by Western Union Telegram and through the mail. Beginning again in 1921, the Quartermaster General's Office made several unsuccessful attempts to contact Guerra's next of kin to make formal arrangements for shipping the body back to the United States. Unfortunately, correspondence went unanswered because the La Torre family had moved from Bridgeport to Brooklyn without leaving a forwarding address. Later that year, the Quartermaster Corps relocated Guerra's remains to the Meuse-Argonne Cemetery near the village of Romagne-sous-Montfaucon, 26 miles (42km) northwest of Verdun.

Conclusion

When I learned of my great-uncle Matthew Guerra's existence and his tragic death in the Great War from my aunt Victoria, my initial reaction was one of complete surprise. Because of my longstanding interest in military history, his death in World War I intrigued me, so much so that for the next several days and weeks I could not stop thinking about him. My immediate thought was that I needed to locate as much information as I could find about the man and his brief life and times, as well as the specifics relating to the circumstances surrounding his demise on the battlefield in France. Guerra's was a life cut short, as happened to so many young men fighting in the Great War.

As my pursuit of relevant factual information continued, I began to become more acutely aware of the hardships and horrors Matthew and his fellow 58th Infantry Regiment, 4th Division soldiers faced in combat and in particular during the St. Mihiel (September 12–16, 1918) and Meuse-Argonne battles (September 26–November 11). The latter offensive, in which Guerra met his fate, ended the war. This, it turned out, was the deadliest battle in U.S. military history, involving 1.2 million men, and resulted in tens of thousands of wounded and more than 26,000 deaths out of the total 116,516 American lives lost during the war.

Initially, one major objective, decided upon shortly after embarking on the project, was to write a brief biography of Matthew Guerra for my family members, so that his memory would not fade away forever. After Victoria's passing, there would have been no one left in the family who would have had any knowledge at all of who Guerra was, that he ever existed, or that he paid the extreme sacrifice for his adopted country. In essence, the saga of the man's relatively brief time on the planet would have been lost to posterity. This history will now become part of the family lore, to be passed along from one generation to the next.

One thing I never expected was for the project to snowball as it did. Delving into Guerra's time in the U.S. Army resulted in the awareness that a large segment of America's immigrant population comprised the ranks of the military following the country's entry into the World War. One estimate places the number of soldiers born in foreign countries drafted into the military at "nearly half a million," estimated at more than "18 percent" of the total (Nancy Gentile Ford). At one point, I made the decision to expand the focus of my investigative endeavors toward learning all I could about these ethnic minorities, recent immigrants, who heeded the call to arms by the U.S. government in extraordinary numbers. Many had immigrated from or could trace their ancestry to one of the warring European nations.

I soon discovered, due in large part to the language barrier, that during the early stages of U.S. involvement in the conflict, military leaders were presented with a myriad of organizational and training problems as well as morale issues regarding non–English-speaking immigrant inductees. Presented here is an account of the contributions made by these newcomers as a group toward the Allied war effort and how their participation became a deciding factor in the overall outcome. The question arose, could America's involvement have ended the war when it did without their eventual participation?

Between 1850 and 1920, a flood of immigrants from foreign lands, estimated at more than 30 million (sources vary), poured into the country. The majority of the newcomers were from southern and eastern Europe. They were among the multitudes who immigrated to America, many with the fervent hope they would have a chance at a brighter and more prosperous life for themselves and their families. They came to escape a meager existence as peasants working farmland, vineyards, and raising livestock such as pigs, poultry, and sheep, in pastures on estates owned by wealthy noblemen and landlords. The promise of greater economic opportunities was the magnet that drew the masses, who viewed the United States as the "land of opportunity," across the oceans. Most came to find meaningful employment, something not always possible in their native land because of deteriorating economic and social conditions in Europe and elsewhere around the globe. There were others who came to escape religious, racial, and political persecution. As an interesting aside, I also learned that a substantial number of families with sons approaching draft-eligible age emigrated to escape military duty in their home country.

If the U.S. government's commitment to aid the Allies was to have a significant impact on the outcome of the conflict, leaders faced the task of increasing the size and strength of the armed services as rapidly as possible. As related earlier, officials looked upon the country's immigrant population as a valuable human resource, one that would provide a pool from which to draw much-needed manpower to help prosecute the war in Europe.

Draft legislation stipulated that only immigrants previously granted citizenship, or those who declared their intention to become citizens, were technically eligible for mandatory service. Non-declarant and enemy aliens were exempt. An unknown number of non-declarants, however, who did not take advantage of their exempt status, entered the service of their own free will and volition. Existing evidence indicates that Matthew Guerra, who had not filed his citizenship papers, was among the latter group. My contention is that he did so voluntarily, and that one might consider this a patriotic act on his part.

Upon reading more and more about the high percentage of immigrant soldiers in the military, their military education and training issues resulting primarily from the language barrier, and their eventual contribution to the war effort, I decided that I wanted to tell their story as well. That conclusion led to an expansion of my original research project culminating in this body of work. Along the way, my journey took many twists and turns—it has been an interesting and rewarding as well as a most exciting and fulfilling experience.

* * *

As the action of the various engagements involving Matthew Guerra's unit, Company C, 58th Infantry, 4th Division, unfolded before me, I felt as though I were following in his footsteps. This is especially true of his last days upon the planet. From existing testimony by survivors of the war who later provided detailed descriptive accounts and often moving narratives of their experiences, I tried to imagine myself in his place and predicament on the field of battle. In particular, I focused on the 4th Division operation to wrest the Bois de Fays from entrenched and determined German troops, described by one participant as "The Center of Hell." The vivid and detailed first-person eyewitness accounts enabled me to visualize in my mind what wartime conditions must have been like and the hardships and misery frontline combat troops had to tolerate and endure.

Essentially, I wanted to convey what these men had to suffer and bear for days and weeks at a time while bivouacked in those sodden trenches and holes infested by flies, lice, rats, and a host of other vermin. This was during the rainy season that characterizes the climate of northeastern France during that time of the year, and the landscape turned into a vast quagmire. The men cowered and trembled in utter fear, for to peer above the edge of the foxhole could very well mean a sniper's bullet between the eyes, without the man ever hearing the report of the rifle. The constant suffering these men had to undergo and live through at this time and place is literally unimaginable unless you are a war veteran and have experienced it firsthand. Those who have would never talk about the experience.

Medical treatment and procedures during the Great War were primitive at best by today's practices and standards. Unlike earlier wars, advances in the development of heavy mortars, artillery, and high-velocity weapons, as well as biological agents capable of inflicting terrible injuries, wreaked havoc with the human body. On the other hand, modern medicine was greatly influenced by the advances and breakthroughs made during World War I regarding the treatment of wounds and injuries, as well as the numerous practices and standards adopted and perfected by medical personnel.

As part of my study, I also sought to discover the plight of the wounded soldier—beginning with the process of evacuation from the battlefield, first to an aid station and then on to a more specialized medical facility farther to the rear. Subsequent research enabled me to outline some of the possible scenarios that unfolded leading up to and following Matthew's admittance to Evacuation Hospital #4. And later, what he had to endure while undergoing the various stages of hospitalization and treatment ending on the day he succumbed, we have to assume, as a direct result of complications due to his shrapnel wounds.

There is also a strong possibility that Guerra fell victim to the influenza virus during the 1918–1919 pandemic raging across Europe and around the world. Influenza killed more people in absolute numbers, an estimated 20 to 40 million, than any other disease outbreak in recorded history. An estimated half of the U.S. soldiers who died in Europe fell to the influenza virus alone.

* * *

At about age 20 or 21, Guerra relocated to the city of Bridgeport, Connecticut, to work at the Remington Arms Company, in full swing providing munitions to France and England before and following America's entry into the conflict. What were Guerra's interests before entering the military? During his time off at the plant in the evening and on weekends, he would likely have frequented some of the more popular gathering places with one or more co-workers in the city's "Central End Italian-American neighborhood," referred to as "Little Italy." The enclave, inhabited by a large population of Italian immigrants, is located in the city's North End on Madison Avenue near the Fairfield County Correctional Facility. Today, the area also has a significant Portuguese population. Guerra may also have spent some of his leisure time at one of the city's many other nightspots and dance halls that featured some of the area's popular vocalists and ethnic music of the period. These are places where he might have met young women his age.

I wondered whether he was a member of, or did he frequent any of the Italian-American or other social clubs in Bridgeport after work. There were several Italian clubs or organizations in the city—the Subalpino Social Club and the Province of Caserta Benevolent Society, both founded in 1910; and the Province of Benevento and Limitrofi Society, founded in 1912. I speculated whether he might possibly have been in the company of Frank Di Pesa of Bridgeport, a fellow soldier his age whom I believe was a close friend and the man he was with when wounded. Both men, drafted on the same day, ended up in the same division, regiment, and company.

Likewise, I could not help but wonder if there might have been a love interest in Guerra's life. Was she a woman of Italian extraction or a young American of Italian heritage? Possibly she would have been from his old Worcester neighborhood or someone he met later in the city of Bridgeport. Certainly, he must have encountered and interacted with many of the young women who worked at the Remington plant—was there an attractive co-worker? At this particular point in his life, he may have even become engaged to someone special. Had he met the young lady in the local community, at church or perhaps at a church gathering?

Was she at the train station to see Matthew off as he departed for Camp Upton to begin his stint in the U.S. Army? Had she corresponded with him while stationed at the camps and overseas? Did she promise to wait for his return? Upon learning of his death, did she weep for him?

Members of my immediate and extended family have always been churchgoers, a habit instilled in us from a young age. I telephoned the church closest to Guerra's home in Bridgeport, the Holy Rosary Italian Catholic Church, 365 E. Washington Avenue, opened in 1903. Back then it was Our Lady of Pompeii of the Holy Rosary. Guerra lived in a three-family home, commonly known as a "three decker," at 56 Crescent Avenue, approximately one-tenth of a mile from the church. I called the rectory to see if any evidence of his having been a parishioner still existed. The receptionist informed me that no records from the period have survived. On several occasions, I traveled to Bridgeport to explore Matthew's old neighborhood and to visit the city's World War I memorial that bears his name (see photographs).

* * *

As an afterthought, I also contemplated what Guerra might have done with his life had he survived the war. With the experience gained working at the Remington Arms Manufacturing Company, he might have found employment as a machine operator or a machinist in Bridgeport, or if he decided to return to his family in Worcester, at one of the city's many industries. The latter may have been a likelihood as his sister Lena and her husband Joseph La Torre, whom he lived with before the war, had relocated to Brooklyn shortly after he entered the army. In all probability, after his return he would have lived in Worcester and possibly taken a positon at

Conclusion 213

Guerra's cross at the Meuse-Argonne Cemetery. Name misspelled (copyright American Battle Monuments Commission).

the Harrington & Richardson Firearms Company, a manufacturer of revolvers and shotguns during peacetime and military weapons during both the World Wars. H&R produced "shoulder-type flare guns" for the military during World War I and mass-produced the U.S. M1 Garand rifle during the Second World War.

Had Guerra survived, he would most probably have married. As mentioned, his wife would possibly have been someone he had known before leaving to go overseas or would have met upon his return. My great-uncle would have been 46 or 47 when I was born in 1943. Considering the average life expectancy at the time, generally recognized to be between 60 and 70 years of age, I most assuredly would have, as a young man, gotten to know him in his later years. There would likely have been children and grandchildren whom I and other family members would have come to know and love.

* * *

Unfortunately, there is little possibility I will ever visit my great-uncle's final resting place in the Meuse-Argonne American Memorial Cemetery near Romagne-sous-Montfaucon, France, as I refuse to fly. Included in the book are a number of photographs of the cemetery and of his grave marker—the old cross with his name misspelled, and the new stone that eventually replaced it following a lengthy round of correspondence with American Battle Monuments Commission officials. I was curious as to the exact location of his gravesite within the cemetery and wrote to Mr. Dominique G. Didiot, Cemetery Associate, and he emailed a beautiful aerial photograph (in color) indicating the section and row (Plot C, Row 21, Grave 15).

I arrived at my final destination satisfied that I had done a thorough investigation and had accomplished all of my original goals and objectives. I seriously doubt there is any additional information out there pertaining to Guerra, although it is not completely out of the realm of possibility.

During my quest to find out about this chapter in my family's history, I feel that I have somehow made an intimate connection with the young man who was my great-uncle. Before going overseas, Matthew swore allegiance to the U.S. and became a citizen while undergoing recruit training at Camp Devens, an indication that he was proud to live in America, enough to answer the call to duty. He went willingly to serve, although he could have stayed home as an undeclared alien. Guerra did not seek the exemption he was entitled to that would allow him remain in the States, safe from harm.

Was Matthew Guerra a hero? In my eyes, all soldiers who served on the front lines or in a war zone—many of whom suffered physical injuries or psychological wounds (PTSD), some debilitating, and especially those who gave their lives for their country—are all heroes. This includes past wars as well as later military interventions such as those in Vietnam, Iraq, Afghanistan, and Syria, where there were no fixed or established front lines.

In closing, I was determined to keep the memory of Matthew Guerra

Cross—name corrected at the Meuse-Argonne Cemetery (copyright American Battle Monuments Commission).

alive. Through the pages of this book, my family, other relatives, and future generations will come to know about this nearly forgotten family member. Recorded here are the facts and details surrounding his journey into manhood, his service in the military, and his final days on the battlefields of France. I dedicate this work as a fitting and lasting tribute not only to my great-uncle, but to all the immigrant soldiers who participated in the Great War. As indicated earlier, this total included nearly half a million foreign-born soldiers, between 18 to 20 percent of the total, consisting of forty-six different nationalities. The exact number of foreign-born immigrants who fought and died for their adopted country is unknown, as the War Department made no distinction between native and foreign-born members of the military. This figure most probably mirrored the percentage comprising the total who lost their lives.

Chapter Notes

Chapter 1

1. Meuse-Argonne American Cemetery and Memorial (pamphlet), The American Battle Monuments Commission (ABMC), Court House Plaza II, 2300 Clarendon Boulevard, Arlington, VA, n.d., http://www.abmc.gov/.

2. Guerra's Service Record, "Service Records: Connecticut Men and Women in the Armed Forces of the United States During World War, 1917-1920, 3 vols." (Hartford, CT: Office of the Adjutant General, 1941), 235.

3. "Service Records: Connecticut Men and Women," 235.

4. "Burial File for Mattes Gerra, 370/65/19/07," Record Group: 092 War Department, Office of the Quartermaster General, National Archives and Records Administration (NARA), Old Military Records—RG 92, Washington, D.C.

5. Blue Star Mothers of America, Inc., New York, http://www.bluestarmothers.org/service-flag.

6. American Gold Star Mothers, Inc., Washington, D.C., 202-265, http://www.goldstarmoms.com/index.htm; Meuse-Argonne American Cemetery and Memorial (pamphlet).

7. The Canadian Anglo-Boer War Museum, http://angloboerwarmuseum.com/Boer70zz6_clarke_hoather.html; see also eBay and other websites.

8. Mauro Pucciarelli, *The Italian Army and Its Traditions: A Journey through the Military Historical Museums of Rome, Turin, and Pinerolo* (Rome: F. Motta, 1990); Richard Knotel, *Uniforms of the World: A Compendium of Army, Navy, and Air Force Uniforms, 1700-1937* (New York: Scribner's, 1980), 302-303, http://en.wikipedia.org/wiki/Bersaglieri.

Chapter 2

1. Ancestry.com, Operations, Inc., "Massachusetts Passenger and Crew Lists, 1820-1963," Provo, UT, 2006, http://search.ancestry.com/search/db.aspx?dbid=8745&geo_a=r&o_iid=41014&o_lid=41014&o_sch=Web+Property

2. Letter of Lucia Palumbo to the Adjutant General's Office, U.S. Army, Washington, D.C., September 1, 1932; Leonardo Tomaiolo, Lucia Palumbo, "Deposition taken before Field Examiner of Veterans Administration, VA," by W.H. Major, "Case of Matthew Guerra," January 17, 1938; Jerre Mangioni and Ben Morreale, *La Storia: Five Centuries of the Italian American Experience, 1492-1992* (New York: HarperCollins, 1992), 60, 68-72.

3. Deposition taken before Field Examiner W.H. Major, Veterans Administration (VA), "Case of Matthew Guerra," January 17, 1938; "Affidavit of Person Claiming to Have Stood in the Relation of Parent," September 3, 1932; Morris H. Cohen, *Worcester's Ethnic Groups: A Bicentennial Review* (Worcester, MA: Worcester Bicentennial Commission, 1976).

4. Roy Marcot, *Remington, "America's Oldest Gunmaker"* (Peoria, IL: Primedia, 1998), 157, 168-170; Alden Hatch, *Remington Arms in American History* (New York: Rinehart, 1956), 203-05; AncestryLibrary.com, "WWI

Draft Registration Cards, 1917–1918"; National Archives and Records Administration (NARA), Washington, D.C., Index to Petitions and Records of Naturalizations of the U.S. and District Courts for the District of Massachusetts, 1907–1966, Microfilm Publication, M1545, Record Group 21, June 25, 1918.

5. Marcot, 153–4, 170–171; Hatch, 224.
6. Marcot, 154, 171–175; Hatch, 224.

Chapter 3

1. Christian Albert Bach and Henry Noble Hall, *The Fourth Division: Its Services and Achievements in the World War* (Issued by the Division, 1920), 17; Hugh L. Scott, *Some Memories of a Soldier* (New York: Century, 1928), 552; The Great War Society, Doughboy Center; Michael J. McCarthy, *Planning the AEF: The Need for an Expeditionary Force*, A Selection from "Lafayette, We Are Here": The War College Division and American Military Planning for the AEF in World War I, http://www.worldwar1.com/dbc/plan1.htm.
2. Scott, 552; John B. Wilson, *Maneuver and Firepower: The Evolution of Divisions and Separate Brigades* (Washington, D.C.: Center of Military History—United States Army, 1998), 47.
3. Wilson, 49, 52; Wikipedia, RMS *Baltic* (1903), https://en.wikipedia.org/wiki/RMS_Baltic_(1903).
4. Wilson, 55–57.
5. Christopher M. Sterba, *Good Americans: Italian and Jewish Immigrants During the First World War* (New York: Oxford University Press, 2003), 32, 55; John Whiteclay Chambers II, "Selective Service," 540–541, in *The United States in the First World War: An Encyclopedia*, Anne Cipriano Venzon and Paul Miles, eds. (New York: Garland, 1995); Christopher Capozzola, *Uncle Sam Wants You: World War I and the Making of the Modern American Citizen* (New York: Oxford University Press, 2008), 25; David M. Kennedy, *Over Here: The First World War and American Society* (New York: Oxford University Press, 1980), 146–47; Jennifer D. Keene, *The United States and the First World War*, Seminar Studies in History (Harlow, England: Pearson Education, 2000), 40.
6. Capozzola, 25–26.
7. Capozzola, 26; Sterba, 55; John J. Newman, *Uncle, We Are Ready!: Registering America's Men, 1917–1918: A Guide to Researching World War I Draft Registration Cards* (North Salt Lake, UT: Heritage Quest, 2001), 4; John K. Ohl, *Crowder, Enoch Hebert (1859–1932)*, in Ann Cipriano Venzon and Paul L. Miles, eds., *The U.S. in the First World War—An Encyclopedia*, 182.
8. Nancy Gentile Ford, *Americans All! Foreign-born Soldiers in World War I* (College Station: Texas A&M University Press, 2001), 23; Historic Missourians: State Historical Society of Missouri, "George E. Creel (1876–1953)," http://shsmo.org/historicmissourians/name/c/creel/.
9. Chambers, 540–541; Sterba, 55; Ohl, 181; Wilson, 55, 57.
10. Chambers, 540–542; Sterba, 31–32, 55.
11. Newman, 57.
12. Wilson, 57.
13. Newman, 4–8; "World War I Draft Registrations," U.S. National Archives and Records Administration (NARA), New England; National Archives, Military Records, World War I Draft Registration Cards, https://www.archives.gov/research/military/ww1/draft-registration.
14. Capozzola, 22, 37; Kennedy, 152.
15. Capozzola, 22, 37; Kennedy, 152; Chambers, 541; Sterba, 55–56; Keene, 36.
16. Sterba, 55–56; Chambers, 540–542; Ford, 51–52.
17. Sterba, 57; Chambers, 541; Ford, 3, 51–52, 55–56; Kennedy, 156–58; Ohl, 182; Keene, 1; David J. Ulbrich and Matthew S. Muehlbauer, *Ways of War: American Military History from the Colonial Era to the Twenty-first Century* (New York: Routledge, 2014), 292.

Chapter 4

1. Sterba, 58, 67; Capozzola, 27–28; Keene, *United States*, 34–35; Kennedy, 150–51.
2. Sterba, 58, 67–68; Keene, 35.
3. Sterba, 67–68; Keene, 35; "Register Willingly, NO OUTBREAK IN CITY," *New York Times*, June 6, 1917, 2.
4. Jean Nudd, "World War I Draft Registration Cards, 1917–1918 [database on-line]," Ancestry.com, Provo, UT, USA: Ancestry.com Operations Inc, 2005, http://search.ancestrylibrary.com/search/db.aspx?dbid=6482; Ancestry.com, U.S., "World War I Draft Registration Cards, 1917–1918," http://www.

ancestry.fr/learn/library/article.aspx?article=1065.

5. Newman, 6, 16; "Registration Certificate, P.M.G.O., Section 276, Form No. 68"; "Worcester Enrolls 19,726 Young Men under the Selective Draft," *Worcester [MA] Telegram*, June 6, 1917, 1, 4; "Total Registration in Worcester 20,056; Only 6,709 Claim Exemption," *Worcester [MA] Evening Gazette*, June 6, 1917, 1.

6. Newman, 10, 25, 42; Sterba, 67–68; "Register Willingly," 2.

7. "Worcester Enrolls 19,726 Young Men under the Selective Draft," 4; Sterba, 58–59, 68–69; Newman, 42; "Register Willingly," 2.

8. "Answer for exemption not required," *Worcester Evening Gazette*, June 1, 1917, 1; *San Francisco Chronicle*, June 3, 1917, n.p.; Newman, 27.

9. "Worcester Enrolls 19,726," 4; "Total Registration in Worcester," 1.

10. "Worcester Enrolls 19,726," 4; Keene, 107.

11. Capozzola, 33, 45.

12. Sterba, 58–59; Newman, 42; "Register Willingly," 2.

13. Sterba, 67–68; "Register Willingly," 2.

14. "Great Response...," *Marlborough [MA] Enterprise*, June 6, 1917, 1; "Register Willingly," 1–2; Newman, 9; Keene, 35; "Worcester Enrolls 19,726," 1, 4; "Answer for exemption not required," 1; "Total Registration in Worcester," 1–2.

15. Keene, 33, 39–40; *Oxford Companion to American Military History*, John Whiteclay Chambers II, ed., "Conscription," 181; J.W. Gregory, *The United States Infantry: An Illustrated History, 1918* (London: Blandford Press, 1988), 157; "Crowder's Draft Report," *New York Times*, February 16, 1919, 41.

16. Matthew Guerra, WWI Draft Registration Cards, 1917–1918, AncestryLibrary.com.

17. Josiah Bartlett Lambert, *"If the Workers Took a Notion": The Right to Strike and American Political Development* (Ithaca, NY: Cornell University Press, 2005), 78.

Chapter 5

1. Chambers, "Selective Service," 540–541; Sterba, 55–56, 58–59, 71, 81; "NOTICE OF CLASSIFICATION, Form 1005—PPGC."

2. "The World War One Draft—Reporting of the First Draft Lottery—1917," *Washington Post*, July 21, 1917, 1–2; Glenvick Gjonvik Archives, "The World War One Draft," http://www.gjenvick.com/Military/WorldWarOne/TheDraft/SelectiveService System/1917-07-20-Draft-DrawingTheFirst Number.html#axzz4FzybdQtB.

3. "The World War One Draft," *Washington Post*, July 21, 1917, 1–2.

4. Sterba, 71; Capozzola, 28–29; Kennedy, 154; "The World War One Draft," *Washington Post*, July 21, 1917, 1–2.

5. Chambers, 541; Keene, *The United States*, 33.

6. Enoch H. Crowder, *Report of the provost marshal general to the secretary of war on the first draft under the Selective-service act, December 20, 1917* (Washington, D.C.: Government Printing Office, 1917), 23–24; Nudd, 1917–1918; Sterba, 68–69, 71, 81; Keene, 35–36; "The World War One Draft," *Washington Post*, July 21, 1917, 1–2.

7. Newman, 42.

8. "NOTICE OF CLASSIFICATION, Form 1005—PPGC."

9. Jean Nudd, Archivist, National Archives and Records Administration, in *Eastman's Online Genealogy Newsletter* 9, No. 3 (January 19, 2004): http://www.eogn.com/archives/news0403.htm; Nudd, 1917–1918; Keene, 35–36; Ford, *Americans All!*, 51–52, 55.

10. Ford, 48–49, 57–59.

11. Ford, 3, 52; Keene, 33, 106.

12. Ford, 67; "Crowder's Draft Report," *New York Times*, February 16, 1919, 41.

13. Kennedy, 157–58; Keene, 105–07.

14. "Crowder's Draft Report," 41; Ford, 67.

15. Newman, 42; Matthew Guerra, Draft Card, June 5, 1917, Ancestry.com.

16. Matthew Guerra, Draft Card, June 5, 1917, Ancestry.com.

Chapter 6

1. Capozzola, 23; Newman, 45.

2. Raymond H. Banks, "World War I Draft Registration: Draft Boards, exemptions, and Deferrals," 1997–98; Kennedy, 155.

3. Capozzola, 38.

4. Capozzola, 38; Sterba, 57, 68–69; Keene, *The United States*, 106–07; Ford, *Americans All!*, 53, 55, 66.

5. Keene, 36; Ford, 55–56; Banks; Enoch H. Crowder, *Second Report of the Provost Marshal to the Secretary of War* (Washington,

D.C.: Government Printing Office, Government Records Office, 1918), 94–96.
6. Keene, 36; Ford, 55–56; Banks; Theodore Kornweibel, Jr., *Investigate Everything: Federal Efforts to Compel Black Loyalty in World War I* (Indianapolis: University of Indiana Press, 2002), 76.
7. Sterba, 68; Ford, 55.
8. Sterba, 68–69; Kennedy, 155; Chambers, "Selective Service," 540.
9. Sterba, 69; Kennedy, 155; Keene, 36; Capozzola, 37.
10. Kennedy, 155; Keene, 36.
11. Ford, 36; Selective Service Regulations. Prescribed by the President under the authority vested in him by the terms of the Selective Service Law, United States War Department (Washington, D.C.: U.S. Government Publishing Office, 1918), Second edition (Form 999 A), 47.
12. Sterba, 68–69; Keene, 35–36; "Notice of Classification," Form 1005-PMGC (See Sec. 103, S.R.S.).
13. Sterba, 68–69; Selective Service Regulations, 47–48.
14. Selective Service Regulations, 48–49.
15. Ford, 66.
16. *Report Adjutant General State Minnesota, December 31, 1918, Brigadier General W.F. Rhinow, Adjutant General*, vol. 1 (Minneapolis, MN: Syndicate Printing, 1918), 17.
17. Ford, 55–56, 64, 66; Sterba, 57; Keene, 107.
18. Ford, 56–57; Sterba, 57; Keene, 107; Newman, 44; "British-American Draft Treaty and Its Enforcement Along the Canadian Border, 1917–1918," National Archives, Record Group 85: Records of the Immigration and Naturalization Service, 1787–2004, ARC Identifier 1115908/MLR Number A1, 323, A1, 9-A (...).
19. Ford, 63–64, 66; Sterba, 57; Keene, 106–07; Daniel Chauncey Brewer, *The Peril of the Republic: Are We Facing Revolution in the United States?* (New York: G.P. Putnam's Sons, 1922), 253; National Archives, Naturalization Records (New York), https://www.archives.gov/research/naturalization/naturalization.html.
20. Ford 63–64; Sterba, 57, 68–69; Keene, 107.
21. Ford 56–57. 63–64; Sterba, 57, 68–69; Keene, 106–107; "Crowder's Draft Report,"
New York Times, February 16, 1919, 41; Brewer, 253–54.
22. Ford, 56–57, 63; Brewer, 253.
23. Ford, 52–53; Sterba, 57; Keene, 38, 107.
24. Sterba, 57; Keene, 38, 107.
25. Capozzola, 38; John B. McMaster, *The United States in the World War (1918-1920)* (New York: D. Appleton, 1920), 44; "Net for Slackers to be Nation-wide," *New York Times*, September 2, 1918, 8.
26. Capozzola, 38; Sterba, 57; Keene, 38, 107; Ford, 52–54; "Net for Slackers to be Nation-wide," 8; U.S. House Military Affairs Committee, Drafting Aliens into Military Service, Hearings, 65 Congress, 1st Session, September 26, 1917, 22.
27. Sterba, 68–69; Keene, 38; Ford, 56, 63.

Chapter 7

1. "5,000 See Boys in Draft Leave for Camp Upton," *Bridgeport Post*, April 26, 1918, 1–2.
2. "5,000 See Boys in Draft Leave for Camp Upton," 1.
3. "5,000 See Boys in Draft Leave for Camp Upton," 1.
4. "5,000 See Boys in Draft Leave for Camp Upton," 1.
5. Frazier Hunt, *Blown In by the Draft: Camp Yarns* (Freeport, NY: Books for Libraries Press, 1918), 4–6; Alan D. Gaff, *Blood in the Argonne: The "Lost Battalion" of World War I* (Norman: University of Oklahoma Press, 2005), 15–17; Long Island Forum, Norval Dwyer, "The Camp Upton Story 1917–1921," February 1970, n.p., http://oldwww.longwood.k12.ny.us/history/upton/camp.htm.
6. Gaff, 18; Ford, *Americans All!*, 81, 105, 119–120.
7. Dwyer, n.p.
8. Dwyer, n.p.; Gaff, 15–17; Roger Batchelder, *Camp Devens, Described and Photographed* (Boston: Small, Maynard & Company, 1918), 13–14.
9. Gaff, 15–17.
10. Batchelder, *Camp Devens*, 14; William J. Robinson, *Forging the Sword: The Story of Camp Devens* (Concord, NH: Rumford Press, 1920), 19, 27–28.
11. Robinson, 19–20.
12. Robinson, 19–20; Batchelder, *Camp Devens*, 20.

13. Robinson, 27–28; Batchelder, *Camp Devens*, 20.
14. Robinson, 27–28; Batchelder, *Camp Devens*, 20.
15. Gaff, 17–18.
16. Robinson, 10–11; Batchelder, *Camp Devens*, 72–74; Roger Batchelder, *Camp Upton, Described and Photographed* (Boston: Small, Maynard & Company, 1918), 38.
17. Robinson, 10–11, 21; Batchelder, *Camp Devens*, 72.
18. Batchelder, *Camp Devens*, 72; Batchelder, *Camp Upton*, 36; J. Irving Crump, *Conscript 2989: Experience of a Drafted Man* (New York: Dodd, Mead and Company, 1918), 8.
19. Robinson, 22–23.
20. Crump, 7; Sterba, 108.
21. Gaff, 20.

Chapter 8

1. Gaff, 20.
2. Robinson, 20–21; Sterba, 108, 111.
3. Ancestry.com, Rootsweb, "Flag Allen Drewry," http://freepages.genealogy.rootsweb.ancestry.com/~kinfolke/WWI_Flag_Allen_DREWRY_1917_18.html.
4. Robinson, 20–21.
5. Sterba, 108; Crump, 12–15.
6. Ancestry.com, Rootsweb, "Grover A. Moran, Letters Home, Oct. 14, 1917," n.p., http://www.rootsweb.ancestry.com/~wvtucker/WWI.htm.
7. "World War I Letters, Feb. 24, 1918–April 19, 1919," Walter H. Lockard (Sgt.), March 6, 7, 10, http://www.wwiletters.com/.
8. "World War I Letters," Lockard, March 10, 1918, http://www.wwiletters.com/.
9. "World War I Letters," Lockard, March 10, 1918, http://www.wwiletters.com/.
10. ASVAB (The Armed Services Vocational Aptitude Battery), History of Military Testing: Learn how the military has used tests over the years to select and classify new recruits, http://official-asvab.com/Recruiters.htm.
11. ASVAB, History of Military Testing.
12. Robinson, 64–65.
13. Robinson, 20–21; Crump, 51–53; "World War I Letters," Lockard, March 6, 1918, http://www.wwiletters.com/.
14. Robinson, 21; American Life Histories, Manuscript Division Library of Congress, Manuscripts from the Federal Writers' Project, 1936–1940, Andrew Johnson, "I Did My Bit for Democracy," Levi C. Hubert, interviewer, Brooklyn, New York, November 20, 1938, n.p.; Gaff, 23.
15. Johnson, n.p.
16. Robinson, 20–21.
17. Johnson, n.p.; Crump, 25–26, 77.
18. Johnson, n.p.
19. Crump, 25, 77.
20. Robinson, 22; United States War Dept., *Infantry Drill Regulations, United States Army; 1911, With Corrections to November 1913* (Washington, D.C.: Govt. Printing Office, 1914).

Chapter 9

1. Sterba, 93.
2. Batchelder, *Camp Upton*, 22; Batchelder, *Camp Devens*, 64; Willis J. Abbot, *The United States in the Great War* (New York: Leslie Judge Company, 1919), 40; Ancestry.Com, Rootsweb, "Grover A. Moran, Letters Home, Oct. 14, 1917," n.p., http://www.rootsweb.ancestry.com/~wvtucker/WWI.htm.
3. Batchelder, *Camp Upton*, 3; Batchelder, *Camp Devens*, 64; Grover A. Moran, letter Oct. 17, 1917, http://www.rootsweb.ancestry.com/~wvtucker/WWI.htm.
4. Batchelder, *Camp Upton*, 3; Batchelder, *Camp Devens*, 58–59.
5. Batchelder, *Camp Upton*, 64; Robinson, 22, 30, 58–59.
6. Gaff, 25; "Marksmen Teach Soldiers: Pupils Even Learn to Make Repairs to Rifles While Blindfolded," *New York Times*, April 15, 1918, http://query.nytimes.com/gst/, 8; Robinson, 23.
7. Batchelder, *Camp Upton*, 64; Robinson, 61.
8. Abbot, 40.
9. Crump, 85–86, 88–89.
10. Robinson, 103–104, 106.
11. Robinson, 86–87; Batchelder, *Camp Devens*, 50–52, 58; see also, http://www.gjenvick.com/CampDevens/.
12. Robinson, 54, 61, 85–86.
13. Robinson, 88–89; *Holy Cross College Service Records, War of 1917* (Worcester, MA: Harrigan Press, 1920), 31.
14. Robinson, 88.
15. Robinson, 73, 78; Batchelder, *Camp Devens*, 54–55; Benedict Crowell, *America's*

Munitions 1917–1918 (Washington, D.C.: Government Printing Office, May 10, 1919), 204; Fredericks Memorial Military Museum, "U.S. Defense Grenades in World War I," Glen Hyatt, http://www.worldwar1.com/sfusdg.htm.
 16. Batchelder, *Camp Devens*, 54–55
 17. Robinson, 68–69; Gaff, 41, 83–85.
 18. Robinson, 68–69.
 19. Robinson, 69.
 20. Robinson, 103–104, 106.
 21. Robinson, 99.
 22. Robinson, 64.
 23. Robinson, 65.
 24. Robinson, 106.
 25. Robinson 108–09.
 26. Robinson, 110.
 27. Robinson, 109–10.

Chapter 10

 1. Batchelder, *Camp Devens*, 30, 32–33; Batchelder, *Camp Upton*, 24, 28; Robinson, 72–73, 77.
 2. Batchelder, *Camp Devens*, 32–33; Crump, 54–56.
 3. Batchelder, *Camp Devens*, 32; Batchelder, *Camp Upton*, 24.
 4. Roger Batchelder, *Camp Dix, Described and Photographed* (Boston: Small, Maynard & Company, 1918), 28–29; Batchelder, *Camp Devens*, 30, 32, 36; Batchelder, *Camp Upton*, 24.
 5. Robinson, 61, 73, 144–45.
 6. Batchelder, *Camp Devens*, 36–37; Batchelder, *Camp Upton*, 24; Batchelder, *Camp Dix*, 26, 30; Robinson, 61, 144; Ford, *Americans All!*, 106–07.
 7. Ford, 94–95.
 8. Robinson, 81.
 9. Robinson, 81.
 10. International Encyclopedia of the First World War, 1914–1918. "Raymond B. Fosdick, Joseph W. Ryan," http://encyclopedia.1914-1918-online.net/article/fosdick_raymond_b.
 11. Robinson, 75–76; Batchelder, *Camp Devens*, 28; John G. Buchanan (2nd Lt.), "War Legislation Against Alcoholic Liquor and Prostitution," *Journal of the American Institute or Criminal Law and Criminology* 9 (1919): 520–529, http://scholarlycommons.law.northwestern.edu/cgi/viewcontent.cgi?article=1668&context=jclc.
 12. Buchanan, 520; Ford, 90; George J. Anderson, "Making the Camps Safe for the Army," *Annals of the American Academy of Political and Social Science* 79 (1918): 144–45, 151.
 13. Robinson, 75–76; Anderson, 144–45.
 14. Robinson, 5, 19, 26, 74, 76.
 15. Robinson, 74–75.
 16. Robinson, 72, 75–76.
 17. Buchanan, 520; Robinson, 76.
 18. Buchanan, 520–521, 526.
 19. Buchanan, 525–26.
 20. Buchanan, 522–523, 526; Anderson, 145–146.
 21. Ford, 90, 98–99; Batchelder, *Camp Devens*, 78; Robinson, 59–60.
 22. Crump, 55–56; "Baseball Leads in Camps, Fosdick Commission Reports Athletic Activity Widespread," *New York Times*, May 27, 1918, 8.
 23. Abbot, 41; "World War I Letters, Feb. 24, 1918–April 19, 1918," Walter H. Lockard, March 21, 1918, http://www.wwiletters.com/bootcamp/1918Mar/1918_Mar21_Mother.htm.
 24. "World War I Letters, March 21, 1918"; Crump, 55–61; Robinson, 59 ("division athletic officer" appointed by Hodges), 61; Abbot, 41; Batchelder, *Camp Upton*, 40 (Camp Athletics); see Ford, 98–99; Robinson, 59, 61; Monte D. Cox, Cox's Corner Profiles, "Benny Leonard, The Ghetto Wizard ... 'The Brainiest of All Boxers,'" http://coxscorner.tripod.com/bleonard.html.
 25. Crump, 56–60; Abbot, 41; Batchelder, *Camp Upton*, 40 (Camp Athletics); "Baseball Leads in Camps, Fosdick Commission Reports Athletic Activity Widespread," *New York Times*, May 27, 1918, 8.
 26. Robinson, 60; Crump, 55–56, 106–107; "News and Notes of the Music World," *New York Times*, January 3, 1909, "Dramatic and Fashion Section," 6.
 27. Crump, 106–08; Robinson, 60.

Chapter 11

 1. Ford, *Americans All!*, 3, 67–68.
 2. Ford, *Americans All!*, 3, 67, 70, 81, 147, 157; Nancy Gentile Ford, *The Great War and America: Civil-military Relations During World War I* (Westport, CT: Greenwood, 2008), 33; Fred H. Rindge, Jr., "Uncle Sam's Adopted Nephews," *Harpers Monthly Magazine* 137 (June–November 1918): 281.
 3. Rindge, 281; "'Foreign Legion' Compa-

nies," *Infantry Journal* 15, no. 3 (September 1918): 252.
   4. Ford, *Americans All!*, 75, 85.
   5. Ford, *Americans All!*, 3, 67–68, 75; Rindge, 281; "'Foreign Legion' Companies," 252; Ford, *The Great War*, 43; Nancy Gentile Ford, "'Mindful of the Traditions of His Race': Dual Identity and Foreign-Born Soldiers in the First World War American Army," *Journal of American Ethnic History* 16, no. 2 (1997): 38; Capt. G.B. Perkins, "Camp Gordon Plan," *Journal of the U.S. Artillery* 49 (January–December 1918): 265; Capt. Edward E. Padgett, "Camp Gordon Plan," *Infantry Journal* 15, no. 5 (July 1918–June 1919): 334–35; "Making Americans of Alien Soldiers," *New York Times*, editorial, September 22, 1918, 40; Kennedy, 157; Keith Gandal, *The Gun and the Pen: Hemingway, Fitzgerald, Faulkner and the Fiction of Mobilization* (New York: Oxford University Press, 2008), 89.
   6. Ford, *Americans All!*, 74–75; Ford, *The Great War*, 43; Padgett, 335–36; Perkins, 266.
   7. "'Foreign Legion' Companies," 252.
   8. Gandal, 89; Ford, *Americans All!*, 86.
   9. Robinson, 35, 100, 167.
   10. "'Foreign Legion' Companies," 252.
   11. Ford, *Americans All!*, 85; Ford, *The Great War*, 44; Perkins, 265–66; Padgett, 335.
   12. Padgett, 335.
   13. Padgett, 335; Ford, *Americans All!*, 44, 52, 58–59, 83, 125; Ford, "Mindful," 36–37; Humanities and Social Sciences on Line, H-ETHNIC: Americanization of WW1 Soldiers, Nancy Gentile Ford, n.p.; Perkins, 265–66; Victor's Research & Writing, Blog at WordPress.com, http://h-net.msu.edu/cgi-bin/logbrowse.pl?trx=vx&list=h-ethnic&month=9909&week=a&msg=qHD6G2XLV/tC3LYkJhX93w&user=&pw= "The United States Military, A Melting Pot of Change," http://vicshistory.wordpress.com/category/history-534/.
   14. Padgett, 335; Ford, *Americans All!*, 55–56, 59–60; Ford, "Mindful," 36–37; Ford, Discussion Log, n.p.; Perkins, 266; David A. Laskin, *The Long Journey Home: An American Journey from Ellis Island to the Great War* (New York: HarperCollins, 2010), 140.
   15. Ford, *The Great War*, 33.
   16. Ford, *Americans All!*, 75; "'Foreign Legion' Companies," 252–53; Padgett, 335.
   17. Ford, *Americans All!*, 75; "'Foreign Legion' Companies," 252–53; Padgett, 335.

   18. Ford, *Americans All!*, 67–68; Ford, Discussion Log, n.p.; Padgett, 335; "'Foreign Legion' Companies," 252; Laskin, 140; Perkins, 265–66; "Making Americans of Alien Soldiers," *New York Times*, September 22, 1918, 40.
   19. "'Foreign Legion' Companies," 252; Gandal, 89.
   20. "'Foreign Legion' Companies," 252; Ford, *Americans All!*, 75–76, 127; Ford, "Mindful," 38; Ford, *The Great War*, 43; Kennedy, 157; Padgett, 334–35; "Making Americans of Alien Soldiers," *New York Times*, September 22, 1918, 40; Richard S. Faulkner, *School of Hard Knocks: Combat Leadership in the AEF* (College Station: Texas A&M University Press, 2012), 217.
   21. "'Foreign Legion' Companies," 252; Ford, *Americans All!*, 10, 127; "Making Americans of Alien Soldiers," *New York Times*, September 22, 1918, 40; Faulkner, 215, 217; Kennedy, 157.
   22. Ford, *Americans All!*, 127.
   23. Ford, *Americans All!*, 86; Perkins, 265–66; Gandal, 89.

Chapter 12

   1. Ford, *Americans All!*, 69–70, see Ch. 3, "The Camp Gordon Plan," note 8, 159; Padgett, 337; "'Foreign Legion' Companies," 252; Perkins, 268; Gandal, 89; Ancestry.com, U.S. Naturalization Records Index, 1794–1995.
   2. Stanislaw A. Gutowski, "Report on the Observations in Camp Devens, Massachusetts," December 28, 1917, Commission on Training Camp Activities (CTCA 15667), WDGSS.
   3. Ford, *Americans All!*, 68, 69–70, 81.
   4. Ford, *Americans All!*, 68–69, 70–71; 73–74; 80–81; Ford, "Mindful," 38–39; Ford, *The Great War*, 43–44; "Making Americans of Alien Soldiers, by Method Known as Camp Gordon Plan," *Trench and Camp* no. 16 (September 25, 1918); Padgett, 337; Perkins, 266.
   5. Gandal, 89–90, see Chapter 3, note 46; Gutowski, "Report on the Observations in Camp Devens, Massachusetts"; Stanislaw A. Gutowski, "Talk on Foreign Speaking Soldiers in Different Camps," September 7, 1918, 3, 10565110/27, MID-WDGS.
   6. Stanislaw A. Gutowski, "An Immigrant at the Crossroads," *Scribner's Magazine* 78, no. 2 (February 1925), http://www.unz.org/Pub/Scribners-1925feb-00185?View=PDF, 185–86.

7. Gutowski, "An Immigrant at the Crossroads," 185–86, 192; Lt. Stanislaw A. Gutowski, "Through the Mill of Americanization," *Scribner's Magazine* 78, no. 1 (July 25, 1925), 75.

8. Gutowski, "Through the Mill of Americanization," 75.

9. Laskin, 140; "Biographical Record, Alumni and Undergraduates," *Bostonia, Alumni Magazine of Boston University* 19, no.1 (June 1918); "Gutowski, Stanislaw A., Lieut., Harvard R.O.T.C.," *Boston University, World War Record*, Published by the Trustees of the University (Boston: Earnshaw), 324; Ford, *Americans All!*, 69–70, 80–81, 134–35, 158, 159, 161–62.

10. Ford, *Americans All!*, 68, 69–70, 81, see Ch. 3, "The Camp Gordon Plan," note 40, 161.

11. Ford, *Americans All!*, 68–70; Laskin, 140–41; Leon W. Rantlett and Leon L. Rantlett, see Draft Cards, Ancestry.com.

12. Ford, *Americans All!*, 69–70, see Camp Gordon Plan, note 9, 159; "'Foreign Legion' Companies," 252.

13. Ford, *Americans All!*, 69–70; "'Foreign Legion' Companies," 252.

14. Ford, *Americans All!*, 70.

15. Ford, *Americans All!*, 13–14, 70; Ford, "Mindful," 44; Laskin, 140.

16. Ford, *Americans All!*, 14, 70.

17. Ford, *Americans All!*, 13–14, 70, 105–06.

18. Ford, *Americans All!*, 128.

19. Ford, *Americans All!*, 128; Robinson, 106; Lockard, letter of March 22, 1918, to his Mother, http://www.wwiletters.com/bootcamp/1918Mar/1918_Mar22_Mother.htm; U.S. Department of Veterans Affairs, "History of U.S. Government Involvement in Insurance," July 1, 2008, http://www.benefits.va.gov/insurance/.

20. "History of U.S. Government Involvement in Insurance."

21. Ford, *Americans All!*, 128.

22. Ford, *Americans All!*, 128; Jennifer D. Keene, *World War I: Daily Life Through History Series* (Westport, CT: Greenwood, 2006), 45–46.

23. Ford, *Americans All!*, 128.

24. Ford, *Americans All!*, 128; Keene, 46.

25. Ford, *Americans All!*, 106, 127–28; Ford, "Mindful," 45–46; "'Foreign Legion' Companies," 253.

26. Wikipedia, *"The Polish-Soviet War,"* https://en.wikipedia.org/wiki/Polish%E2%80%93Soviet_War.

27. Casimir Pulaski Foundation, http://www.idealist.org/view/nonprofit/Dnp3kkffMxjd/; The Observer, Newspaper Archive (Rockford, Ill.), September 3, 1944, "Polish Group's Memorandum, On Eve of Dumbarton Talks, Supports Atlantic Charter," "Stanislaw A. Gutowki," "Secretary of the Polish American Congress," 4; Polish Groups, http://www.pac1944.org/history/history1.htm, contains photo of Gutowski (cannot be identified).

Chapter 13

1. Bruce W. Bidwell and Thomas F. Troy, *History of the Military Intelligence Division, Department of the Army General Staff: 1775–1941* (Frederick, MD: Publications of America, 1986), 185, 205; Ford, *Americans All!*, 9, 13–14, 68–83, 114–16.

2. Ford, *Americans All!*, 13, 69, 115.

3. Ford, *Americans All!*, 69–70.

4. Ford, *Americans All!*, 13–14, 113–14; Padgett, 340.

5. Ford, *Americans All!*, 68–69; Ford, "Mindful," 39.

6. Ford, *Americans All!*, 60–61, 114, 143; Ford, *The Great War*, 33, 55; John Patrick Finnegan, *Military Intelligence, Center of Military History, United States Army* (Army Lineage Series, 1998), 25; Laskin, 142; Sterba, 12.

7. Finnegan, 25, 107; Laskin, 142.

8. Finnegan, 25–26, 107; Laskin, 142; Ford, *American All!*, 68–69; Christopher H. Sterling, ed., *Military Communications: From Ancient Times to the 21st Century* (Santa Barbara, CA: ABC, CLIO, Inc. 2008), 491.

9. Bidwell, 124; Ford, *Americans All!*, 10, 114.

10. "Treatment of New Men," *Infantry Journal* 15, no. 4 (October 1918): 341–42; Ford, *Americans All!*, 113.

11. "Treatment of New Men," 341–42; Ford, *Americans All!*, 113.

12. Gandal, 91–92; Ford, *Americans All!*, 113.

13. Gandal, 91–92; National Archives and Records Administration (NARA), "Report of the Second Conference on Control of Morale," 15 May 1918, doc. 50109, box 150, entry 393, RG 165, "Extract from Confidential Bulletin No. 17," Part C, 2, 10565-414/1, MID-WDGS, July 17, 1918; Richard Slotkin, *Lost Battalions:*

The Great War and the Crisis of American Nationality (New York: Henry Holt, 2005), 92.

14. Gandal, 91; Ford, *Americans All!*, 123; National Archives and Records Administration (NARA), "Report of the Second Conference on Control of Morale," 15 May 1918, doc. 50109, box 150, entry 393, RG 165, "Extract from Confidential Bulletin No. 17," Part C, 2, 10565-414/1, MID-WDGS, July 17, 1918;

15. Faulkner, 214-15.

16. Faulkner, 215-16.

17. Faulkner, 215-16; Ford, *Americans All!*, 123.

18. Faulkner, 215-16; Ford, *Americans All!*, 123.

Chapter 14

1. Ford, *Americans All!*, 69-70; Ford, *The Great War*, 43.

2. Ford, *Americans All!*, 70-71 (report sent Mar. 4, 1918).

3. Ford, *Americans All!*, 71; "Honor Roll, Swietlik, Lt. F.X. (Instructor in Law School)," *Marquette Law Review* 2, no. 1 (1917): http://scholarship.law.marquette.edu/cgi/viewcontent.cgi?article=4807&context=mulr; See also, Marquette University Law School Faculty Blog, J. Gordon Hylton, "Francis X. Swietlik, Marquette Law School, and Polish War Relief," http://law.marquette.edu/facultyblog/2010/10/18/francis-swietlik-marquette-law-school-and-polish-war-relief/.

4. Ford, *Americans All!*, 70-71.

5. Ford, *Americans All!*, 71; Ancestry.com, Rootsweb, "Linn County War Registration, Linn County, Missouri," Henry Charles Steiman, draft registration, June 5, 1917; http://www.rootsweb.ancestry.com/~molinn/WWIDraftRegistration.htm.

6. Ford, *Americans All!*, 70-71.

7. Ford, *Americans All!*, 74.

8. Laskin, 141; "'Foreign Legion' Companies," 252-53; "Making Americans of Alien Soldiers," *New York Times*, 40.

9. Padgett, 334-35; "Making Americans of Alien Soldiers," *Trench and Camp*, 336; Ford, *Americans All!*, 79-80.

10. "Foreign Legion' Companies," 253; "Making Americans of Alien Soldiers," *New York Times*, 40; Ford, *Americans All!*, 76-77, 81-82.

11. Padgett, 334-35; Ford, *Americans All!*, 67-68, 70-71, 80; Ford, "Mindful," 35-37.

12. "'Foreign Legion' Companies," 70-71, 80.

13. Ford, *Americans All!*, 71-72.

14. Ford, *Americans All!*, 71-72; Ford, *The Great War*, 43; Victor's Research & Writing, Blog at WordPress.com, n.p., http://vicshistory.wordpress.com/2009/04/.

Chapter 15

1. Ford, *Americans All!*, 72-73.

2. Ford, *Americans All!*, 13, 72-73, 114.

3. Ford, *Americans All!*, 13, 72-73.

4. Sterling, 491.

5. Ford, *Americans All!*, 72-73, 81, 88, see Ch. 3, "The Camp Gordon Plan," note 18, 159.

6. Ford, *Americans All!*, 72, 88-89; Ford, *The Great War*, 39.

7. Raymond Blaine Fosdick, *Chronicle of a Generation: An Autobiography* (New York: Harper & Brothers, 1958), 186.

8. Ford, *Americans All!*, 10, 14, 68-69, 114-16.

9. Ford, *Americans All!*, 73

10. Ford, *Americans All!*, 74, 76, 79, 86, Ch. 3, "The Camp Gordon Plan," see note 22, 160; Ford, "Mindful," 35-57; Ford, *The Great War*, 43.

11. Ford, *Americans All!*, 74-76; "The Camp Gordon Plan," *Infantry Journal*, 436-37; see also Padgett, 334-340, and "Keep Up the Camp Gordon Plan," *Infantry Journal* 15, no. 5 (July 1918-June 1919), 603.

12. Peyton C. March, *The Nation at War* (Garden City, NY: Doubleday, Doran & Company, 1932), 365, 372-73.

13. "Newton D. Baker Dies in Cleveland," *New York Times*, December 26, 1937.

14. C.H. Cramer, *Newton D. Baker: A Biography* (Cleveland, OH: The World Publishing Company, 1961), 171.

15. Ford, *Americans All!*, 163.

16. Roy Talbert, Jr., *Negative Intelligence: The Army and the American Left, 1917-1941* (Jackson, MS: University Press of Mississippi, 1991), 27-28; John Patrick Finnegan, *Military Intelligence Story: A Photographic History* (Washington, D. C.: Center of Military History, United States Army, 1998), 31.

17. Talbert, 27-28.

18. Talbert, Jr., 27-28, Ford, *Americans All!*, 10, 73, 114.

19. Ford, *Americans All!*, 10, 13, 72-73, 114.

20. Ford, *Americans All!*, 73, 114.
21. Ford, *Americans All!*, 10–11, 114, 116.

Chapter 16

1. Ford, *Americans All!*, 67–68, 75; Padgett, 334, 336, 338; "'Foreign Legion' Companies," 252; "Making Americans of Alien Soldiers," *New York Times*, 40; James J. Cooke, *The All-Americans at War: The 82nd Division in the Great War, 1917–1918* (Westport, CT: Praeger, 1999), viii, 17.
2. Ford, *Americans All!*, 67–68, 75; Ford, *The Great War*, 43; "'Foreign Legion' Companies," 252.
3. Ford, *Americans All!*, 68, 76–77, 78, 82–83; "'Foreign Legion' Companies," 252; Laskin, 141; Victor's Research & Writing, Blog at WordPress.com, n.p., http://vicshistory.wordpress.com/2009/03/.
4. Ford, *Americans All!*, 77; Padgett, 336–37.
5. Ford, *Americans All!*, 78; Laskin, 141; "'Foreign Legion' Companies," 252–53.
6. Faulkner, 215–16.
7. Faulkner, 214–15.
8. Ford, *Americans All!*, 78.
9. Ford, *Americans All!*, 78, 125; Laskin, 141–42; "Making Americans of Alien Soldiers," *New York Times*, 40; "'Foreign Legion' Companies," 252–53.
10. Ford, *Americans All!*, 8, 77–78, 80; Padgett, 335, 339; see Perkins, 266; Gandal, 90.
11. Ford, *Americans All!*, 68, 76–77, 85, 86–87.
12. Ford, *Americans All!*, 68, 77–78, 85–86; Padgett, 340; "'Foreign Legion' Companies," 253; Victor's Research & Writing, Blog at WordPress.com, n.p.; Marlborough Churchill, memorandum for the Chief of Staff: "Extract from Confidential Bulletin No. 17," July 17, 1918, 10565–414/1.
13. "'Foreign Legion' Companies," 252–53.
14. "'Foreign Legion' Companies," 252; Padgett, 335–336; Perkins, 266.
15. "'Foreign Legion' Companies," 253; Ford, *Americans All!*, 67, 85; Padgett, 340; "Keep up the 'Camp Gordon Plan,'" 603.

Chapter 17

1. Padgett, 334–35; Batchelder, *Camp Dix*, 16.
2. Padgett, 334–35; Ford, *Americans All!*, 67–68, 74–75, 76, 85, 107–08, see Ch. 3, "The Camp Gordon Plan," note 23, 160.
3. Ford, 69, 73, 107–08.
4. Ford, 13, 69–70, 73.
5. Ford, 13, 69–70, 72–73, 85, see Ch. 3, "The Camp Gordon Plan," note 19, 159.
6. Ford, 73, 112, 114.
7. Gandal, 89–90.
8. Brig. Gen. Marlborough Churchill, Anne Venzon Cipriano and Paul Miles, eds., *The United States in the First World War: An Encyclopedia* (New York: Garland, 1995), 148.
9. Ford, *Americans All!*, 76–77, 79, 83, 107–08.
10. Ford, *Americans All!*, 6, 89, 106–07, 109–10, see Ch. 4, "Military Morale Uplifting," notes 63 and 64, 167.
11. Ford, *Americans All!*, 68–69, 112, see Ch. 3, "The Camp Gordon Plan," note 5 and 7, 159; Marlborough Churchill, Memorandum for the Chief of Staff, "Extract from Confidential Bulletin, No. 17," July 17, 1918, 10565-414/1, MID-WDGS.
12. Ford, *Americans All!*, 69, 73–75, 107–108; Laskin, 141.
13. Rindge, 282–84.
14. Rindge, 282–84; Ford, *Americans All!*, 110.
15. Perkins, 272; "Making Americans of Alien Soldiers," *New York Times*, 40; Ford, *Americans All!*, 109, see also photo section.
16. Christina Krysto, "Bringing the World to Our Foreign-Language Soldiers: How a Military Training Camp is Solving a Seemingly Unsurmountable Problem by Using the Geographic," *National Geographic Magazine* 34, no. 2 (August 1918): 81–90.
17. Ford, *Americans All!*, 108–09, see Ch. 4, "Military Morale Uplifting," note 61, 167.
18. Ford, *Americans All!*, 108–09, 110, see Ch. 4, "Military Morale Uplifting," notes 60 and 61, 167; Board of Instruction, Office of the Provost Marshall General, "Teaching English to Non-English Speaking Selectives," Bulletin 6 (Washington, D.C.: War Department, n.d.); Rindge, 282–84.
19. Rindge, 283–84; Perkins, 272.
20. Rindge, 283–84.
21. Rindge, 283–84.
22. Frank Parker Stockbridge, "Giving the Soldiers Books to Read," *The World's Work: A History of Our Time* 37 (November 1918–April

1919): 82–86; Ford, *Americans All!*, 106–08, 110.
23. Stockbridge, 83.
24. Stockbridge, 83; Laskin, 253; "'Foreign Legion' Companies," 253–54; Sanders Marble, ed., *Scraping the Barrel: The Military Use of Sub-Standard Manpower 1860–1960* (Bronx, NY: Fordham University Press, 2012), 135.

Chapter 18

1. Ford, *Americans All!*, 79–80, see Ch. 3, "The Camp Gordon Plan," notes 35, 161; Ford, "Mindful," 35.
2. Ford, *Americans All!*, 78–79, see Ch. 3, note 43, 162; Ford, "Mindful," 38–39.
3. Ford, *Americans All!*, 78, 80–81, see Ch. 3, note 33, 160–61.
4. Ford, *Americans All!*, 72, 77–79, 80–81, see Ch. 3, note 37, 161.
5. Ford, *Americans All!*, 79–80, see Ch. 3, note 35, 161.
6. Ford, *Americans All!*, 80.
7. Ford, *Americans All!*, 8, 69, 90, 122, 134, see Ch. 5, "Mindful of the Traditions of his Race," note 24, 170–71; Laskin, 141; "The Camp Gordon Plan," 436–437; Slotkin, 92–93.
8. Ford, *Americans All!*, 78, 81–82, see Ch. 3, note 40.
9. Ford, *Americans All!*, 81, 134, see Ch. 3, notes 28 and 41, 160–1; "The Camp Gordon Plan," 437.
10. Ford, *Americans All!*, 81–83, 86, see Ch. 3, note 41, 161; Slotkin, 92; "'Foreign Legion' Companies," *Infantry Journal*, vol. 15, July 15, 1918, 252–53.
11. Ford, *Americans All!*, 82, see Ch. 3, note 43, 162.
12. Rindge, 281.
13. Russell Contreras, "How World War I Planted the Seeds for the Mexican American Civil Rights Movement," Albuquerque, NM, 2011, http://russcontreras.tumblr.com/post/46107497910/how-world-war-i-planted-the-seeds-for-the-mexican; See Jose A. Ramirez, *To the Line of Fire!: Mexican Texans and World War I* (College Station: Texas A&M University Press, 2009), 36–38; Ford, *Americans All!*, 82–83, see Ch. 3, "The Camp Gordon Plan," note 45, 162.

Chapter 19

1. Robinson, 111–113; *Order of Battle of the United States Land Forces in the World War, American Expeditionary Forces: Divisions*, vol. 2, Center of Military History United States Army, Washington, D.C., 1988, 290–293; Harry F. Hodges, Brig. Gen., U.S. Army, Commanding, 76th Division, "Brief History of the 76th Division," Records of the American Expeditionary Forces (Record Group 120), National Archives and Records Administration, Modern Military Records (NWCTM), Textual Archives Services Division, College Park, MD, 2 pages, n.d.; *History of the 304th Infantry Regiment* (76th Div.), published by the War Department (Ansbach, Germany: C. Brügel & Sohn, 1945), 218–219.
2. Robinson, 106; 111–113; *Order of Battle*, 290–293; *Massachusetts in the World War—Report of the Commission on Massachusetts' Part in the Great War*, compiled and edited by Lt. Col. Eben Putnam, U.S. Army, vol. 1 (Boston: Commonwealth of Massachusetts, 1931), 245–246; Port of Debarkation, Boston, "Movement of troops overseas from Port of Boston"; *History of the 304th Infantry Regiment*, 218–219.
3. Robinson,106; 111–114; *Order of Battle*, 291–293; Hodges, *Brief History of the 76th Division* (see above).
4. Robinson,110; *Memorial and Peace Day, Circular No. 226*, compiled by L.L. Blair, Illinois Historical Survey (Springfield, IL: May 30, 1928), 40.
5. John J. Pershing, *Final Report of Gen. John J. Pershing* (Washington D.C.: Government Printing Office, 1919), 39–40; Edward G. Lengel, *To Conquer Hell: The Meuse-Argonne, 1918* (New York: Henry Holt, 2008), 60–61.
6. Lengel. 60–61; John J. Pershing, *Report on the Battle of St Mihiel, November, 1919*, Source Records of the Great War, vol. 6, Charles F. Horne, ed., *National Alumni 1923*, firstworldwar.com: http://www.firstworldwar.com/source/stmihiel_pershing.htm.
7. Pershing, *Final Report*, 40–41; John J. Pershing, *My Experiences in the World War* (New York: Frederick A. Stokes, 1931), 253–55, 263; Lengel, 61.
8. George L. Morrow, *The Fifty-Eighth Infantry in the World War, 1917–1919* (58th Infantry History Association, 1919), 85–87.

9. Pershing, *Final Report*, 40–1, 51–52; Pershing, *My Experiences*, 253–55, 261, 263, 270; Enoch Barton Garey, Olin Oglesby Ellis, and Ralph Van Deman Magoffin, *American Guide Book to France and Its Battlefields* (New York: Macmillan, 1920), 153; Lengel, 52–53, 61; Christian Albert Bach and Henry Noble Hall, *The Fourth Division: Its Services and Achievements in the World War* (Issued by the Division, 1920), 142–43, 148.

10. Morrow, 85–87; *History of the 1st Battalion, 58th Infantry Regiment*, Box 48,290/83/24/06, 16 pages, 12.

11. Morrow, 85–87; Bach and Hall, 144.

12. Morrow, 84–85; Bach and Hall, 146–47.

13. Morrow, 84–85, 87; Bach and Hall, 146–47.

14. *4th Division, Summary of Operations in the World War*, prepared by the American Battle Monuments Commission (Washington D.C.: U.S. Government Printing Office, 1944), 44–45.

15. *4th Division*, 6; Pershing, *Final Report*, 590.

16. *4th Division*, 6; Pershing, *Final Report*, 44.

17. Pershing, *Final Report*, 43; Pershing, *My Experiences*, 290; Bach and Hall, 153–54; Paul F. Braim, *The Test of Battle: The American Expeditionary Forces in the Meuse-Argonne Campaign* (Newark, DE: University of Delaware Press, 1987), 382.

18. Pershing, *My Experiences*, 285; Frank Freidel, *Over There: An American Experience in World War I—The Story of America's First Great Crusade Overseas* (Short Hills, NJ: Burford Books, 1964), 177.

19. Pershing, *My Experiences*, 285–86; Freidel, 177–78; Pershing, *Final Report*, 45; Bach and Hall, 156; Braim, 382.

20. Freidel, 177.

21. Bach and Hall, 149, 150–51.

22. Bach and Hall, 156, 157–58.

23. Bach and Hall, 156; Pershing, *My Experiences*, 284, 286–87; Freidel, 177–78, 179.

24. Bach and Hall, 168–69.

25. Bach and Hall, 156; Freidel, 177–78; Braim, 381; *4th Division*, 6.

Chapter 20

1. Lengel, 62–63, 64; Braim, 380–81; "Meuse-Argonne Campaign," in Anne Cipriano Venzon and Paul L. Miles, *The United States in the First World War: An Encyclopedia*; John S.D. Eisenhower, with Joanne T. Eisenhower, *Yanks: The Epic Story of the American Army in World War I* (New York: Simon & Schuster, 2001), 212–13, 215–17.

2. Lengel, 64.

3. Braim, 382; Bach and Hall, 156.

4. Braim, 382; Lengel, 62; Pershing, *My Experiences*, 290–91.

5. Braim, 382; Lengel, 33–34; Pershing, *My Experiences*, 290–91; Bach and Hall, 157; Eisenhower, 210–12; see map, "Plan of Attack of First Army, September 26, 1918," *American Armies and Battlefields of Europe*, American Battle Monuments Commission, vol. 3 (Washington, D.C.: Government Printing Office, 1938).

6. Bach and Hall, 144–45, 153–54; Lengel, 58; Robert Laplander, *Finding the Lost Battalions: Beyond the Rumors, Myths and Legends of America's Famous WWI Epic* (Raleigh, NC: Lulu Press, 2007), 72; Pershing, *Final Report*, 43–44; Freidel, 184–85.

7. Pershing, *Final Report*, 43–44; Pershing, *My Experiences*, 283; Bach and Hall, 153–54; Freidel, 184–85; William T. Walker, *Betrayal at Little Gibraltar: A German Fortress, a Treacherous American General, and the Battle to End World War I* (New York: Simon & Schuster, 2016), xxi, 1, 6.

8. Laplander, 72; Lengel, 290.

9. Laplander, 72–74; Pershing, *Final Report*, 43; Pershing, *My Experiences*, 170, 283; Bach and Hall, 153–54; Freidel, 184–85; Douglas Wilson Johnson, *Battlefields of the World War, Western and Southern Fronts: A Study in Military Geography* (New York: Oxford University Press, 1921), 406.

10. Lengel, 59–60.

11. Bach and Hall, 59, 74, 154–55; Lengel, 59–60, 64; Eisenhower, 203; Pershing, *Final Report*, 45.

12. Bach and Hall, 157; Lengel, 59–60, 64; Eisenhower, 203, 223; Braim, 382.

13. Eisenhower, 210–12.

14. Eisenhower, 210–12.

15. Eisenhower, 204, 218–19.

16. Eisenhower, 187, 203, 212; Pershing, *Final Report*, 40–41.

17. Eisenhower, 210–12.

18. Fleming, n.p.

19. Fleming, n.p.; Bach and Hall, 157;

Hunter Liggett, *AEF: Ten Years in France* (New York: Dodd, Mead, and Company, 1928), 167–68.
20. Bach and Hall, 157.
21. Fleming, n.p.; Lengel, 33; see Pershing, *My Experiences*, 297.
22. Fleming, n.p.; Pershing, *Final report*, 44, 47;
23. Lengel, 64–65; Pershing, *Final Report*, 45; *4th Division*, 6; Kennedy, 197.
24. Bach and Hall, 155.
25. Bach and Hall, 155; Lengel, 60.
26. Bach and Hall, 158, 162–163; Braim, 382; Eisenhower, 213; Venzon, 382.
27. Braim, 382–83.
28. Braim, 382.

Chapter 21

1. Bach and Hall, 182; U.S. Army Medical Department, Office of Medical History, Chapter 2, "World War I, The Ambulance Service," 43, http://history.amedd.army.mil/booksdocs/HistoryofUSArmyMSC/chapter2.html.
2. Bach and Hall, 181–82; Morrow, 104; Wikipedia, "Military Police Corps (United States), World War I," http://en.wikipedia.org/wiki/Military_Police_Corps_(United_States).
3. Faulkner, 310–11.
4. Bach and Hall, 181, Morrow, 104.
5. Bach and Hall, 157, 182; Morrow, 103–04; David C. Homsher, *American Armies and Battlefields in Europe* (Washington, D.C.: American Battle Monuments Commission (ABMC), 1927), 172–177.
6. Bach and Hall, 182–83; Morrow, 106–07; Lengel, 199–200.
7. Bach and Hall, 183, 185–86; Frederic Louis Huidekoper, *The History of the 33rd Division, A.E.F.* (Springfield: Illinois State Historical Library, 1921), 92.
8. Bach and Hall, 182–83; Morrow, 104, 106–8.
9. Bach and Hall, 183; U.S. Army Medical Department, Office of Medical History, Chapter 27, "Second Phase—Operations of the Third Corps, Meuse-Argonne operation, November 25, 1918," 291, http://history.amedd.army.mil/booksdocs/wwi/fieldoperations/chapter27.html.
10. Bach and Hall, 183; Morrow, 107–09.
11. Bach and Hall, 183–84.
12. Bach and Hall, 183–84.
13. Bach and Hall, 183–84, 187.
14. Julius Ochs Adler (Maj.), ed., *History of the Seventy-Seventh Division, August 1917–November 1918* (1919), 43.
15. Adler, 42–43; The Great War Society, "Legends and Traditions of the Great War, Words, Expressions & Terms popularized 1914-1918," http://www.worldwar1.com/heritage/wordswar.htm; "The First World War Poetry Digital Archives, Trench Songs," University of Oxford, www.oucs.ox.ac.uk/wwllit.
16. Adler, 43; Herbert Jager, *German Artillery of World War One* (UK: Crowood Press, 2001), 71.
17. Adler, 43–44.
18. Adler, 43; Ronald Haycock and Keith Neilson, *Men, Machines & War* (Waterloo, ON: Wilfrid Laurier University Press, 2012), 148.
19. The First World War Poetry Digital Archive, University of Oxford, "Trench Songs," www.oucs.ox.ac.uk/wwllit.
20. Adler, 43; Bach and hall, 74.
21. Adler, 42–43; Griffith University, Paul Hinckley, "Battlefield Colloquialisms of the Great War (WW1)," http://www.ict.griffith.edu.au/~davidt/z_ww1_slang/index_bak.htm; Firstworldwar.com: a multimedia history of world war one, "Dug-out," http://www.firstworldwar.com/atoz/dugout.htm.
22. Bach and Hall, 182–83; Lengel, 200.
23. Frederic May Wise and Meigs O. Frost, *A Marine Tells It to You* (New York: J.H. Sears, 1929), 273–74.
24. Wise, 273–74.
25. Wise, 274–75.
26. Edwin L. James, "Furious Fighting Along Our Front," *New York Times*, October 6, 1918, 1, 4.
27. James, 1, 4; Bach and Hall, 203, 206.
28. James, 4.
29. James, 1, 4; MilitaryHistoryOnline.com, Del Kostka, "Air Reconnaissance in World War One,"
http://www.militaryhistoryonline.com/wwi/articles/airreconinwwi.aspxmilitaryHistoryOnline.com.
30. James, 4.
31. Bach and Hall, 182, 184; Morrow, 111.
32. Bach and Hall, 182, 184, see photo facing 197 (shows the Bois de Fays); Morrow, 111.
33. Item Number, REP0006C, Record Group 120, 4th Division Historical Files, Box

49, "Field Messages," 58th Infantry, October 1–8, 1918, 290/83/24/06.

Chapter 22

1. Lengel, 325–26; Forum Eerste Wereldoorlog (War Forum), WWI Ultimate Forum for the Netherlands and Flanders, Map of "Bois du [de] Fays," http://www.forumeerstewereldoorlog.nl/viewtopic.php?p=432457&sid=83414454234948c3bf6eb943795faf27.

2. Lengel, 325–26; Item Number, REP-0006C, Record Group 120, 4th Division Historical Files, Box 49, "Field Messages," 58th Infantry, October 1–8, 1918, 290/83/24/06; Wise and Frost, 278; Bach and Hall, 187–88; Morrow, 113–14; September 5, 1918—Col. Frederick M. Wise USMC commanded the Army's 59th Regiment of the 8th Infantry Brigade, 4th Division, until January 4, 1919; September 12, 1918—Col. Hiram I. Bearss USMC commanded the U.S. Army's 102nd Regiment of the 51st Infantry Brigade, 26th Division, in the St. Mihiel offensive.

3. Wise, 275; Bach and Hall, 185–86; Morrow, 111–12.

4. Wise, 175.

5. Wise, 175; Bach and Hall, 185–86, 187; Morrow, 111–12; U.S. Army Medical Department, Office of Medical History, Chapter 2, World War I, "The Ambulance Service," 692, 709, http://history.amedd.army.mil/booksdocs/HistoryofUSArmyMSC/chapter2.html.

6. Wise, 275–76.

7. Ernest John (Major), "History of the First Battalion, Fifty-Eighth Infantry, Fourth Division (Regular)" (Washington, D.C.: National Archives and Records Administration (NARA), 13.

8. Bach and Hall, 187–88.

9. Lengel, 78, 473.

10. Ashby Williams, *Experiences of the Great War; Artois, St. Mihiel, Meuse-Argonne* (Roanoke, VA: Stone, 1919), 79.

11. Adler, 43.

12. RECORD GROUP 120, ENTRY 267, OPERATIONS REPORTS, 4TH DIVISION, MAP #1, BOX 3306, 290/81/18/02; "Field Messages," 58th Infantry, October 1–8, 1918, Item Number, REP0006C, Record Group 120, 4th Division Historical Files, Box 49, 290/83/24/06.

13. United States Department of the Army, "Full Text Citations for Award of the Distinguished Cross, World War I, to members of the U.S. Army," http://www.homeofheroes.com/members/02_DSC/citatons/01_wwi_dsc/dsc_05wwi_Army_B.html.

14. James W. Block, WWIS, "Typescript, 'History of the 59th U.S. Infantry, 4th Division, Regular Army,'" on file among the "WWI Veterans Survey Collection," U.S. Army Military History Institute (USMHI), Carlisle, Pennsylvania.

15. Bach and Hall, 187; Harry L. Smith, M.D., in collaboration with James R. Eckman, *Memoirs of an Ambulance Company Officer* (Rochester, MN: Doomsday Press, 1940), n.p., see "Chapter 10. War's End."

16. Robert Lee Bullard (Maj. Gen., U.S.A. Retired), *Personalities and Reminiscences of the War* (Garden City, NY: Doubleday, 1925), 273.

17. Bullard, 278; Wise, 277–78.

18. Wise, 281.

19. Bullard, 273–74.

20. Bullard, 274; Bach and Hall, 188–89, 302; Wise, 279.

21. Bullard, 274.

22. Bullard, 274; Wise, 279; Block.

23. Bach and Hall, 188–89,

24. Bach and Hall, 204; Smith, Chapter 9; see also "Meuse-Argonne American Cemetery (WWI)," Jeffrey Aarnio, Assistant Superintendent, http://www.worldwar1.com/dbc/ma_cemetery.pdf, and http://www.worldwar1.com/dbc/ma_cemetery.pdf.

25. "Meuse-Argonne American Cemetery (WWI)," Aarnio.

Chapter 23

1. Robert B. Cole (Maj.) and Bernard Eberlin (Capt.), eds., (1919), 48.

2. Smith, Chapter 4, n.p., available online at http://net.lib.byu.edu/~rdh7/wwi/memoir/Ambco/officerTC.html.

3. Smith; Bach and Hall, 181–82.

4. Paul Stanley Bond, Lt. Col., and C.F. Martin, Lt. Col., U.S. Army, *Medical Service in Modern War, An Exposition of the Tactical Functions of the Medical Department in Campaign* (Menasha, WI: The Collegiate Press, George Banta Publishing Company, 1920); see "Evacuation Hospitals," 52–53; War Department, Annual Report of the Surgeon General,

1919, U.S. Army (Washington, D.C., Government Printing Office, 1920), vol. 1, 1465–66; Chapter 5, Evacuation Hospitals, 3181–82; U.S. Army Medical Department, Office of Medical History, Chapter 5, Evacuation Hospitals, 172, http://history.amedd.army.mil/booksdocs/wwi/fieldoperations/chapter5.html.

5. For photographs showing the extent of the road congestion, see enclosed; see also Bach and Hall, opposite p. 165, "View at Esnes showing traffic on road from Montzèville at a time when it was not as heavy as usual. September 29, 1918," opposite p. 173, "Scene on the road from Esnes to Malancourt," September 27, 1918, and opposite p. 188, "View from Cuisy, looking north, showing long line of 4th Division supply trucks... Taken October 6, 1918." See also, "Traffic jam at Esnes on the Meuse-Argonne front, Sept. 1918," opposite 165; Bach and Hall, 180–81.

6. U.S. Army Heritage and Education Center, Carlisle Barracks, Carlisle, PA, WWI Veterans' Survey Project, U.S. Army Military History Institute, USAMHI (Typescript Memoires), Loren D. (Larry) Duren, Jr., Co. K, 58th Reg., 4th Div., "An Experience, and a Few Other Things I Have Liked, August 13, 1925" 41–42, www.carlisle.army.mil/ahec/VeteranSurveys.cfm.

7. Smith, Chapter 4, n.p.

8. Alfred W. Crosby, *America's Forgotten Pandemic: The Influenza of 1918* (New York: Cambridge University Press, 2003), 163.

9. Crosby, 160–61, 163, 205–06; Gina (Bari) Kolata, *Flu: The Story of the Great Influenza of 1918 and the Search for the Virus That Caused It* (New York: Farrar, Straus and Giroux, 1999), 6–7, 44; Jennifer Hsiao, "The Great Influenza Epidemic of 1918," *The Concord Review*, 8, 80, 83.

10. Crosby, 158, 160–61, 205; Kolkata, 5, 159; Hsiao, 81–82; *Office of the Surgeon General, Medical Department of the U.S. Army in the World War* (Washington, D.C.: Government Printing Office, 1921–1929), 809.

11. Crosby, 160–61, 163; Spartacus International, established by John Simkin in September 1997, Hsiao, 80; Molly Billings, "The Influenza Pandemic of 1918," June 1997, modified RDS February 2005, 07 November 2011, n.p., http://virus.stanford.edu/uda/.

12. Thomas Hager, *The Demon Under the Microscope: From Battlefield Hospitals to Nazi Labs, One Doctor's Heroic Search for the World's First Miracle Drug* (New York: Three Rivers Press, 2006), 5, 8; Eric Lax, *The Mold in Dr. Florey's Coat: The Story of the Penicillin Miracle* (New York: Holt, Henry & Company, Inc., 2005), 15.

13. Hager, 17, 26.

14. Smith, Chapter 2, n.p.

15. Hager, 9, 26.

16. Hager, 20, 26, 28.

17. Hager, 17.

Bibliography

Abbot, Willis J. *The United States in the Great War.* New York: Leslie Judge, 1919.
Bach, Christian Albert, and Henry Noble Hall. *The Fourth Division: Its Services and Achievements in the World War.* Issued by the Division, 1920.
Batchelder, Roger. *Camp Devens, Described and Photographed.* Boston: Small, Maynard & Company, 1918.
_____. *Camp Dix, Described and Photographed.* Boston: Small, Maynard & Company, 1918.
_____. *Camp Upton, Described and Photographed.* Boston: Small, Maynard & Company, 1918.
Bidwell, Bruce W., and Thomas F. Troy. *History of the Military Intelligence Division, Department of the Army General Staff: 1775–1941.* Frederick, MD: Publications of America, 1986.
Block, James W. WWIS, "Typescript, 'History of the 59th U.S. Infantry, 4th Division, Regular Army,'" on file among the "WWI Veterans Survey Collection," USMHI, Carlisle, PA.
Bond, Paul Stanley, and C.F. Martin. *Medical Service in Modern War: An Exposition of the Tactical Functions of the Medical Department in Campaign.* Menasha, WI: Collegiate Press, George Banta Publishing, 1920.
Braim, Paul F. *The Test of Battle: The American Expeditionary Forces in the Meuse-Argonne Campaign.* Newark: University of Delaware Press, 1987.
Brewer, Daniel Chauncey. *The Peril of the Republic: Are We Facing Revolution in the United States?* New York: G.P. Putnam's Sons, 1922.
Bullard, Robert Lee. *Personalities and Reminiscences of the War.* Garden City, NY: Doubleday, Page & Co., 1925.
"The Camp Gordon Plan." Infantry Journal 15, No. 5 (November 1918): 437. U.S. Infantry Association. Washington, D.C.
Capozzola, Christopher. *Uncle Sam Wants You: World War I and the Making of the Modern American Citizen.* New York: Oxford University Press, 2008.
Cooke, James J. *The All-Americans at War: The 82nd Division in the Great War, 1917–1918.* Westport, CT: Praeger, 1999.
Crosby, Alfred W. *America's Forgotten Pandemic: The Influenza of 1918.* New York: Cambridge University Press, 2003.
Crowder, Enoch H. *Final Report of the U.S. Provost Marshall to the Secretary of War on Operations of the Selective Service System to July 15, 1920.* Washington, D.C.: Government Printing Office, 1920.
_____. *Report of the Provost Marshal General to the Secretary of War on the First Draft*

Under the Selective Service Act, Dec. 20, 1917. Washington, D.C.: Government Printing Office, 1917.

_____. *Second Report of the U.S. Provost Marshall to the Secretary of War on Operations of the Selective Service System to Dec. 20, 1918.* Washington, D.C.: Government Printing Office, 1919.

Crump, J. Irving. *Conscript 2989: Experience of a Drafted Man.* New York: Dodd, Mead and Company, 1918.

Dwyer, Norval. "The Camp Upton Story, 1917–1921," *Long Island Forum*, January 1970, 6–10; Part 2, February 1970, 31–34; Part 3, March 1970, 54–57.

Eisenhower, John S.D., with Joanne T. Eisenhower. *Yanks: The Epic Story of the American Army in World War I.* New York: Simon & Schuster, 2001.

Faulkner, Richard S. *School of Hard Knocks: Combat Leadership in the AEF.* College Station: Texas A&M University Press, 2012.

Finnegan, John Patrick. *Military Intelligence, Center of Military History, United States Army.* Washington, D.C.: Army Lineage Series, 1998.

Fleming, Thomas. "Meuse-Argonne Offensive of World War I: Goal with Price to Be Paid." *Military History Magazine* 10, No. 4 (October 1993): 46–53.

Ford, Nancy Gentile. *Americans All! Foreign-born Soldiers in World War I.* College Station: Texas A&M University Press, 2001.

_____. *The Great War and America: Civil-Military Relations During World War I.* Westport, CT: Greenwood, 2008.

_____. "'Mindful of the Traditions of His Race': Dual Identity and Foreign-Born Soldiers in the First World War American Army." *Journal of American Ethnic History* 16, No. 2 (Winter 1997): 35–57. University of Illinois Press on behalf of the Immigration & Ethnic History Society.

"'Foreign Legion' Companies." *Infantry Journal* 15, No. 3 (1918): 252–254. The U.S. Infantry Association. Washington, D.C.

Freidel, Frank. *Over There: An American Experience in World War I—The Story of America's First Great Crusade Overseas.* Ithaca, NY: Burford Books, 1964.

Gaff, Alan D. *Blood in the Argonne: The "Lost Battalion" of World War I.* Norman: University of Oklahoma Press, 2005.

Gandal, Keith. *The Gun and the Pen: Hemingway, Fitzgerald, Faulkner and the Fiction of Mobilization.* New York: Oxford University Press, 2008.

Gutowski, Stanislaw A. "Report on the Observations in Camp Devens, Massachusetts," December 28, 1917, CTCA 15667, WDGSS, 1.

Hager, Thomas. *The Demon Under the Microscope: From Battlefield Hospitals to Nazi Labs, One Doctor's Heroic Search for the World's First Miracle Drug.* New York: Three Rivers Press, 2006.

Homsher, David C. *American Armies and Battlefields in Europe.* Washington, D.C.: American Battle Monuments Commission (ABMC), 1927.

Hsiao, Jennifer. "The Great Influenza Epidemic of 1918." *The Concord Review.*

Hunt, Frazier. *Blown In by the Draft: Camp Yarns.* Freeport, NY: Books for Libraries Press, 1918.

John, Ernest. "History of the First Battalion, Fifty-Eighth Infantry, Fourth Division (Regular)." National Archives and Records Administration (NARA).

Johnson, Douglas Wilson. *Battlefields of the World War, Western and Southern Fronts: A Study in Military Geography.* New York: Oxford University Press, 1921.

Keene, Jennifer D. *The United States and the First World War: Seminar Studies in History.* Harlow, England: Pearson Education, 2000.

_____. *World War I: Daily Life Through History Series.* Westport, CT: Greenwood, 2006.

Bibliography 235

"Keep Up the 'Camp Gordon Plan.'" *Infantry Journal* 15, No. 7–12 (July 1918–June 1919): 603. The U.S. Infantry Association. Washington, D.C.

Kennedy, David M. *Over Here: The First World War and American Society.* New York: Oxford University Press, 1980.

Kolata, Gina (Bari). *Flu: The Story of the Great Influenza of 1918 and the Search for the Virus That Caused It.* New York: Farrar, Straus and Giroux, 1999.

Laplander, Robert. *Finding the Lost Battalions: Beyond the Rumors, Myths and Legends of America's Famous WWI Epic.* Raleigh, NC: Lulu Press, 2007.

Laskin, David A. *The Long Journey Home: An American Journey from Ellis Island to the Great War.* New York: HarperCollins, 2010.

Lax, Eric. *The Mold in Dr. Florey's Coat: The Story of the Penicillin Miracle.* New York: Holt, Henry & Company, 2005.

Lengel, Edward G. *To Conquer Hell: The Meuse-Argonne, 1918.* New York: Henry Holt & Company, 2008.

Liggett, Hunter. *AEF: Ten Years in France.* New York: Dodd, Mead, and Company, 1928.

McMaster, John B. *The United States in the World War (1918-1920).* New York: D. Appleton, 1920.

Mangioni, Jerre, and Ben Morreale. *La Storia: Five Centuries of the Italian American Experience, 1492-1992.* New York: HarperCollins, 1992.

March, Peyton C. *The Nation at War.* Garden City, NY: Doubleday, Doran & Company, 1932.

Morrow, George L. *The Fifty-Eighth Infantry in the World War, 1917-1918-1919.* 58th Infantry History Association, 1919.

Newman, John J. *Uncle, We Are Ready!: Registering America's Men, 1917-1918: A Guide to Researching World War I Draft Registration Cards.* North Salt Lake, UT: Heritage Quest, 2001.

Nudd, Jean, archivist. World War I Draft Registration Cards, 1917-1918. U.S. National Archives and Records Administration, Northeast Region, Pittsfield, MA.

Order of Battle of the United States Land Forces in the World War, American Expeditionary Forces: Divisions, vol. 2. U.S. Army Center of Military History, Washington, D.C., 1988.

Padgett, Edward E. "Camp Gordon Plan." *Infantry Journal* 15 (October 1918): 334–40. The U.S. Infantry Association, Washington, D.C.

Perkins, G.B. "Camp Gordon Plan." *Journal of the U.S. Artillery* 49 (January–December 1918): 266. Ft. Monroe, VA: Coast Artillery School Press.

Pershing, John J. *Final Report of Gen. John J. Pershing.* Washington, D.C.: Government Printing Office, 1919.

———. *My Experiences in the World War.* New York: Frederick A. Stokes Company, 1931.

———. *Report on the Battle of St. Mihiel, November 1919.* Source Records of the Great War, vol. 6, ed. Charles F. Horne, National Alumni, 1923.

Rindge, Fred H., Jr. "Uncle Sam's Adopted Nephews." *Harpers Monthly Magazine* 137 (June–November 1918).

Robinson, William J. *Forging the Sword: The Story of Camp Devens.* Concord, NH: Rumford Press, 1920.

Slotkin, Richard. *Lost Battalions: The Great War and the Crisis of American Nationality.* New York: Henry Holt & Co., 2005.

Smith, Harry L., M.D., in collaboration with James R. Eckman. *Memoirs of an Ambulance Company Officer.* Rochester, MN: Doomsday Press, 1940.

Sterba, Christopher M. *Good Americans: Italian and Jewish Immigrants During the First World War.* New York: Oxford University Press, 2003.

Talbert, Roy, Jr. *Negative Intelligence: The Army and the American Left, 1917-1941.* Jackson: University Press of Mississippi, 1991.

"Treatment of New Men." *Infantry Journal* 15, No. 4 (October 1918): 341–42. The U.S. Infantry Association. Washington, D.C.

Ulbrich, David J., and Matthew S. Muehlbauer. *Ways of War: American Military History from the Colonial Era to the Twenty-First Century*. New York: Routledge, 2014.

Venzon, Anne Cipriano, and Paul Miles, eds. *The United States in the First World War: An Encyclopedia*. New York: Garland, 1995.

Williams, Ashby. *Experiences of the Great War: Artois, St. Mihiel, Meuse-Argonne*. Roanoke, VA: Stone, 1919.

Wilson, John B. *Maneuver and Firepower: The Evolution of Divisions and Separate Brigades*. Washington, D.C.: Center of Military History—United States Army, Army Lineage Series, 1998.

Wise, Frederic May, and Meigs O. Frost. *A Marine Tells It to You*. New York: J.H. Sears, 1929.

Index

Adler, Maj. Julius Ochs: *History of the 77th Division* 180–82, 193
African Americans 34, 36, 66, 98, 114, 181
alcohol or alcoholic beverages 33, 54, 86–87, 89
aliens conscripted against their will 50
Alpha and Beta testing 64–65
American Battle Monuments Commission (ABMC)/headquarters 9–11, 13, 207, 213–14
American Civil Liberties Union (ACLU) 48
American deaths 8, 51, 204–6
American Expeditionary Force (AEF) 25–27, 58, 132, 153, 174, 197
American Gold Star Mothers 15–17
American Library Association (ALA) 85, 90, 144
American Psychological Association (testing) 64–65
American Union Against Militarism (AUAM; predecessor of the American Civil Liberties Union [ACLU]) 48
American Red Cross 53, 206–7
America's Foreign Legion/Foreign Legion Companies 4–5, 49, 101, 131, 139, 145, 148
Anti-aircraft: American 179, 186; German 179
Argonne Forest 153–55, 160, 164–65, 168–71, 176
Austrian 88-German heavy field guns 180, 191
Ayer, MA (location of Camp Devens) 20, 57–58, 68, 70, 72, 76, 82, 88–89, 101, 104, 150

Bach, Col. Christian A. 161–62, 165, 168, 179–80, 185–86, 190–91, 196, 198, 202
bacteria (microbes) 71, 205–6
Baker, Secretary of War Newton D. 27–30, 33, 38–39, 43, 69, 86–87, 109, 116, 123, 125–28, 145–47
Banks, Raymond H. (historian) 43
basic training 18, 62, 66, 69–83
Batchelder, Roger (historian) 56–57, 70, 73, 75, 78, 84–86, 90

battle stragglers (aka "shell holers") 175
Blacks 16, 31–32, 36, 66, 97–99, 102, 114, 202
Bliss, Maj. Gen. Tasker H. Bliss (Chief of Staff of the U.S. Army) 30
Block, Sgt. Maj. James W. 195–96
Blue Star Flag/Blue Star Mothers of America 16–17
Bois de Cunel 189; map 200
Bois-de-Fays (Bois-du-Fays; "Woods of the Fairies") 7, 166–68, 176–79, 184–200, 210; map 200
Bois de Forêt 167, 176, 178, 189; map 200
Bois de la Côte 189; map 200
Bois de Malaumont 178, 186, 188; map 200
Bois-des-Ogons 176–77, 179, 186, 190; map 200
Boston, MA, 22, 57, 81–82, 100, 102, 109, 150
Braim, Dr. Paul (historian) 160, 163, 173
Brewer, D. Chauncy (chief of the Foreign-Speaking Soldier Sub-section [FSS]) 100–1, 109–10, 117, 119–20, 127–129, 137–38
Bridgeport, CT 2, 10, 12–14, 19, 23, 25–26, 37, 41, 52–53, 207, 211–212; WWI Memorial 12–14
Bridgeport Post 53
Bryan, Capt. Emery L. (intelligence and morale officer at Camp Upton) 142
Bryan, Capt. Eugene C. (intelligence and morale officer at Camp Gordon) 130, 132–33, 134, 136
Buchanan, 2nd Lt. John G. (U.S. Army Sanitation Corps) 62, 87–89
"Buffalo Soldiers" (92nd Division) 15, 66
Bullard, Maj. Gen. Robert (III Corps) 27, 165, 196–98
Bureau of War Risk Insurance (BWRI) 5, 15, 17, 23, 105–107
Burris, Vic K. 187, 195

Cabanatuan (Japanese) Prison Camp Raid 13
Cameron, Maj. Gen. George (Fifth Corps commander) 165, 169
Camp Devens 18, 20, 50, 56–58, 68–86, 80,

237

238 Index

88, 90–91, 95, 98, 101, 103–104, 109–114, 120, 132, 147–48, 150–153, 214–15
Camp Funston 30
Camp Gordon 55, 62, 98, 121, 126–27, 130–35, 145–49
Camp Gordon Plan 130–135, 147–49
Camp Lee 63, 114, 148
Camp Upton 52–60, 64, 68–69, 73, 91–92, 142, 147–8, 212
SS *Canopic* 22
Capozzola, Dr. Christopher (MIT professor) 28, 31, 43, 50
casualty clearing station, 7–8
categories of immigrants 31–32, 40
Central Powers 32, 40, 95, 110, 124–27, 136
Chambers, John Whiteclay II (historian) 31
Chauchet 183–84
chemical shells 180
Churchill, Brig. Gen. Marlborough 99, 101–3, 113–14, 128, 138–39, 146–48
citizenship offered to aliens 48
classifications for the grouping of non-English-speaking recruits, 118
Co. C, 58th Infantry Regiment (4th "Ivy" Division) 12, 13, 153
Commission on Training Camp Activities (CTCA) 86–91, 104–5, 122–24
Committee on Public Information 28–29
conscription 23, 28–29, 32, 35, 44, 47–49
Conscription Act (May 18, 1917) 44
Contreras, Russell (Associated Press writer) 149
Côtes de Meuse/Meuse Heights 171
Crosby, Alfred W. (historian) 204–5
Crowder, Provost Marshal Gen. Enoch H. 5, 28–31, 38–39, 41, 44, 47–49
Crump, Author J. Irving: *Conscript 2989: Experience of a Drafted Man* 44, 60, 63–66, 67, 74, 84, 91–92

declarant aliens 5, 32, 40, 48–50
Declaration of War Against Germany 3, 27, 86–87, 149
deferments and exemptions 37, 43–51
Draft Act 26–32, 89
draft classifications 40
draft dodgers 4, 37, 42
draft registration boards 30–31, 56
draft registration card 25, 28–9, 33–35, 42, 50, 97, 138, 147
Drewry, Flag Allen 62
Duren, Pvt. Loren "Larry" 202–3
Dwyer, Norval (historian) 55

Eisenhower, Joanne T. (historian): *Yanks* 169–70, 173
Eisenhower, John S.D. (historian): *Yanks* 169–70, 173
enemy aliens 32, 40, 45, 48–50, 95–96, 124, 210

Etzel-Giselher Stellung 166–67; map 175
Evacuation Hospital No. 4. 8, 14, 201–202
exemptions *see* deferments

Factor, Benjamin 42
58th Infantry (Guerra's Regiment) 6, 13, 152,157, 159, 176, 178–79, 184, 186–88, 190–91, 193–94, 197–99, 201–3, 208, 210
First Expeditionary Force 26–27, 154
Foch, Field Marshal Ferdinand 152–6, 161–63, 166
Fond de Ville au Bois 186, 190
Ford, Nancy Gentile 5, 28–29, 32, 41, 44–45, 47–50, 93, 94, 96, 109–110, 112–13, 117, 121–22, 124–25, 128–29, 133–34, 137–39, 146, 178, 209
Foreign Legion companies 4–5, 49, 101, 131, 139, 148, 252–255
Foreign-Speaking Soldier Sub-section (FSS) 100, 109–115, 129
Form 1009 39
Fort Riley, Kansas 30
Fosdick, Raymond B. 87, 104, 122–25, 128
Fourth "Ivy" Division 3, 6, 10, 13, 152–155, 157–59, 161–62, 165, 170–71, 174–75, 177–78, 185–88, 190, 192–99, 201–6, 208, 210
foxholes 156–57, 182, 191–93, 196, 199, 295
Freedom of Information Act (FOIA) 10
French Chauchet 183–84
Freya Stellung 175
funk-holes (cubbyholes) 182

Gaff, Alan D. (author) 55–56, 58, 60–61, 72–73
Gallwitz, Gen. Max von 154–55, 168, 172–73
German Army Air Service 167–68, 179, 185–86, 199
German Artillery 153, 166, 169, 181, 191, 199
German defense lines ("Stellungen") 166–67; map 175
German 15 cm heavy field Howitzer 181
German submarines 3, 105, 150
German Twelfth Army (Group von Gallwitz) 168
Germany, Declaration of War 26
"Gold Star Mother" status 15–18, 53
Gold Star Pilgrims 15–17
Grandpre 167, 170–171
Graves Registration Service 207
Gregory, Adj. Gen. John H. 55
Gregory, J.W. Urwin 36
Guerra, Matteo (Matthew) 1–25, 37, 41–42, 49–50, 52, 58, 97, 106, 114, 129, 150, 153, 157, 165, 168, 171, 178, 186, 188, 192–93, 195, 198–200, 201–4, 208–15
Gutowski, Lt. Stanislaw 100–108, 109–111, 116–120, 121, 125, 129, 131–148

Hager, Thomas (author) 206
Haig, Sir Douglas (commander-in-chief, British Expeditionary Force [BEF]) 152-3

Hall, Henry Noble 161–62, 165, 168, 179–80, 185–86, 190–91, 196, 198, 202
Harding, Pres. Warren G. 28
Hindenburg Line (Siegfried Stellung) 167, 170; map 175, 176, 189
Horgan, 1st Lt. Herbert A. (chief of the Foreign-Speaking Soldier Sub-section [FSS]) 54, 128–29, 133, 137–39, 145–48
Hunt, Col. Elvid 133
Hunt, Frazier (amateur war correspondent) 53–54

"I Want to Go Home" (WWI trench song) 181
immigrants, categories 31–32
immunizations/inoculations 63–64
Imperial German Army Air Service (Luftstreitkräfte) 185–86
Individual Deceased Personnel File (IDPF) 14–15
infection of wounds, 63, 87, 89, 203, 205–6
infectious diseases, 22, 57, 87 (VD), 204–6
influenza 138, 204–205, 207, 211

James, Edwin L. (war correspondent) 185–86
John, Maj. Ernest 191
Johnson, Pvt. Andrew 15, 66–67
Johnson "Jack" (John Arthur) 181

Kaiser's Imperial Flying Corps (Deutsche Luftstreitkräfte) 185–86
Keene, Jennifer D. 31, 34, 36, 39–41, 44–46, 48, 50–51
Kennedy, David M. (historian) 41–43, 45
Keppel, Frederick P. 123–25, 139, 141
Knights of Columbus 85, 90–91, 104
Kondratiuk, Leonid E. 5
Kriemhilde Line/Stellung (Etzel-Giselher Stellung) 166–67, 170; map 175, 176, 178
Kuhn, Maj. Gen. Joseph 169

Laskin, David A. (historian) 97, 104, 112, 147
Lengel, Edward D. (historian) 164–68, 184, 188–89, 192
Leonard, Benny (Benjamin Leiner) 91
liberalized naturalization process 49
Liggett, Maj. Gen. Hunter (I Corps commander) 165, 170
local draft boards 4, 30, 38–9, 43, 46, 55–58, 97
Lost Battalion/77th Division 171

MacArthur, Gen. Douglas 13, 127, 138
Marshall, Col. George C., Jr. 160–63
medical checks 56–57, 62–64, 193, 202–5
Metz, Germany 153, 161, 172
Meuse-Argonne American Cemetery and Memorial 9–11, 14, 188, 198, 206–7, 213–14
Meuse-Argonne Offensive/Campaign: Phase One 6, 121, 129, 153, 159–60, 164–173, 198, 207; Second Phase 174–187, 189, 204

Meuse Heights (Cotes de Meuse) 171
Meuse River 153, 159–60, 164, 169, 171, 176–78, 198
microbes/pathogens/bacteria 71, 206
Military Intelligence Section (Military Intelligence Division [MID]) 95, 98, 100, 107, 109, 112, 116, 122–23, 137–39
Military Morale Section (MMS) 112–13, 122–23, 128–29, 132, 137–38, 144, 147
military police 174–75
Military Records Request Form (SF-180) 9–10
Minenwerfer or "Minnie Werfer" (mine launcher or thrower) 180–81
Mitchell, U.S. Col. William "Billy" 155–56
Monte Sant Angelo, Italy 3, 22–23
Montfaucon ("Mount of the Falcon") 165–66, 168–70; map 175, 176, 185
Moran, Grover A. 63, 70–1
Morrow, Capt. George L. 155–57, 176–178
Morton, Honorable James H. 82
Mucci, Lt. Col. Henry A. 12–13
Muehlbauer, Matthew S.: *Ways of War* 32

national order of selection 32–43
National Personnel Records Center (NPRC) 14; fire 9
Naturalization Law 32, 49
New York Times 35–36, 41, 50, 130, 133, 185
Newman, John J. (historian) 35, 39
No Man's Land 77, 80, 162, 167, 173, 176
non-declarant exemption 32, 40, 44–45, 47–48, 50
non-declarant resident aliens 4–5, 32–40, 42–45, 47–50, 97, 210
Notice of Classification 45–46
Nudd, Jean (archivist) 34

Oath of Allegiance 48–49
O'Hallorhan, Inspector Edward P. 88
Ohl, John K. (historian) 28
order of call/selection 38–39

Padgett, Capt. Edward R. 94, 96–97, 119, 130–31, 133, 136
Palumbo family 1–3, 13, 15–24, 153
paratyphoid fever/typhoid fever 63–64
Patton, Lt. Col. George S., Jr. (commander of the U.S. Tank Department) 155, 164
penicillin 205
Perkins, Capt. George B. (chief of the Military Morale Section [MMS]) 96, 107, 112, 128–29, 132–34, 147
Pershing, Gen. John J. "Blackjack" 26–27, 30, 66, 69, 127, 138, 153–159, 160–61, 164–66, 168–173, 176, 183, 189, 198
Pétain, Gen. Henri Philippe 152, 154, 160, 166, 169
physical/medical examinations 62–64
Pilgrimage of Remembrance 17
Polewaczyk, Gina Palumbo 18

Post-Traumatic Stress Disorder (PTSD) 7, 112, 214
Powell, Capt. Cassius M. 29
Przybyszewski, Lt. Walter S. 146–48
psychological testing (of recruits) 7, 64–65, 112, 191, 204

recruit processing 6, 58, 61–68, 95
registrant's questionnaire (form 101) 40, 45–47
registration card 25, 42, 52
registration dates 34, 36, 41
registration day 33–37
religious groups 55
Remington Arms 2, 8, 23, 25, 37, 53, 211–12
Rickenbacker, Lt. Eddie 186
Robinson, William J. (*Boston Globe* staff reporter) 57, 62, 65–66, 75–76, 78–82, 86, 88–89, 91, 105, 150, 152

St. Mihiel Offensive 6, 129–73, 208
Scott, Maj. Gen. Hugh L. (U.S. Army Chief of Staff) 26
Section 95, Selective Service Regulations 46–47
Selection of Candidates 29, 31–32, 38–42
Selective Service Act 28–29, 31–32, 34, 39–40, 43, 45–46, 89
Selective Service System/Administration/Act 5, 27–51
Sell, Martha (FOIA) 10
shell shock 191–93
shell types 181
Siegfried Stellung (Hindenburg Line) 167; map 175
Slackers 44, 50
Smith, Dr. Harry L. 205–6
soldier portraits 18–21
Spanish influenza (epidemic) 138, 204–5, 211
Standard Military Records Form (SF180) 9
Stellungen (fortified defense lines) Giselher, Kreimhilde, and Freya, 166–67, 170, 173, 176, 178, 193
Sterba, Historian Christopher M., 33–5, 44–46, 49–50, 60, 62, 69
Sughrue, Officer/Police Matron. Mary A., 88–89
Sullivan brothers 16
Swietlik, Lt. Francis X. 116–18, 134

Tablets of the Missing 9–10
tanks 155–64, 170, 178, 185

U-boats, German 3–4, 150
Ulbrich, David J.: *Ways of War* 32
Union Metallic Cartridge Company (UMC) 2, 23, 25, 37, 53, 211–212
U.S. Army Air Force 155, 168, 179, 185–86
U.S. Army Graves Registration Service Department 10, 14, 207
U.S. Army Infantry Journal 4–5, 94, 100, 125, 130–34, 144, 147
U.S Army Personnel Command (PERSCOM 14
U.S. Army Quartermaster Corps 14, 17, 30, 65–66, 120, 207
U.S. Army Sanitary Corps 87–89
U.S. Declaration of War 4
U.S. Enfield 25
U.S. Tank Department 155, 164, 170, 178, 185

Van Deman, Col. Ralph 109–112,116, 119, 122–129, 138
venereal disease (VD) 22, 87–90, 118
Volker Stellung 175
Von Gallwitz, Gen. Max 154–55, 168, 172–73
Von Marwitz, Gen. Georg 172–73

War Department 4, 69, 95, 100, 104, 106, 109, 120, 124, 128, 131, 135, 137
"War Legislation Against Alcoholic Liquor and Prostitution" 89
Washington, DC 36, 38, 111, 133, 207
Weisz, Lt. Eugene C. 131, 145, 148
Whizzbangs 180–81
Wiesenschlenken Stellung 175
Williams, Lt. Col. Ashby 192–93
Wilson, John B. (military historian) 30
Wilson, Pres. Woodrow 3, 13, 26–8, 30, 33–37, 48–49, 52, 126–27, 142, 184
Wise, Marine Col. Frederic M. (commander, 59th Infantry Regiment) 184–85, 189–91, 196–97
Wood, Capt., Ernest (Camp Devens intelligence and morale officer) 114
Worcester, MA 2, 13, 17, 21–22, 24, 35, 76, 83, 153, 212
Work or Fight Order 29
World War I Memorial 12, 13,

Yerkes, Robert M. (president of the American Psychological Association [APA]) 64–65
Young Men's Christian Association (YMCA) 64, 82, 84–85, 92–93, 104–5, 140–44

www.ingramcontent.com/pod-product-compliance
Lightning Source LLC
Chambersburg PA
CBHW051218300426
44116CB00006B/620